Praise for This Book

A handful of boilerplate and about five lines of custom code, and suddenly, exploding arrows! All of a sudden, doing something cool in the context of a fully realized 3D game engine is very easy. And that's how programming has to be learned...in easy, bite-sized chunks.

➤ **Carl Cravens**
   Linux system architect and Minecraft dad

Learn to Program with Minecraft Plugins explains things very well—no programming experience required. It's very helpful for new programmers. And so far, it's been an excellent vehicle for some quality father-son bonding.

➤ **Mel Riffe, Minecraft dad, and Noah Riffe, age 12**

Phenomenal. Approachable and simple, without talking down to the audience. I could see anyone at any age reading this.

➤ **David Bock, age 44**

I really liked making the server plugins. My favorite was the cow shooter.

➤ **Jonathan Knowles, age 13**

Go, you—this book is awesome!

➤ **Stina Qvarnström**
   Developer, Bool Noridc AB, Sweden

Ssssssssssss

➤ **A creeper**

Learn to Program with Minecraft Plugins

Create Flying Creepers and Flaming Cows in Java

Andy Hunt

The Pragmatic Bookshelf

Dallas, Texas • Raleigh, North Carolina

Many of the designations used by manufacturers and sellers to distinguish their products are claimed as trademarks. Where those designations appear in this book, and The Pragmatic Programmers, LLC was aware of a trademark claim, the designations have been printed in initial capital letters or in all capitals. The Pragmatic Starter Kit, The Pragmatic Programmer, Pragmatic Programming, Pragmatic Bookshelf, PragProg and the linking *g* device are trademarks of The Pragmatic Programmers, LLC.

Every precaution was taken in the preparation of this book. However, the publisher assumes no responsibility for errors or omissions, or for damages that may result from the use of information (including program listings) contained herein.

Our Pragmatic courses, workshops, and other products can help you and your team create better software and have more fun. For more information, as well as the latest Pragmatic titles, please visit us at *http://pragprog.com*.

Minecraft is ®, ™, and © 2009–2014 Mojang/Notch.

The team that produced this book includes:

Brian Hogan (editor)
Potomac Indexing, LLC (indexer)
Candace Cunningham (copyeditor)
David J Kelly (typesetter)
Janet Furlow (producer)
Ellie Callahan (support)

For international rights, please contact *rights@pragprog.com*.

Printed in the United States of America.
ISBN-13: 978-1-937785-78-9
Printed on acid-free paper.
Book version: P1.0—May 2014

Contents

Acknowledgments ix

Start Here xi

1. **Command Your Computer** 1
   Use the Command Line 2
   Move around in File Directories 5
   Start at the Desktop 11
   Common Commands 12
   Next Up 13

2. **Add an Editor and Java** 15
   Install an Editor to Write Code 16
   Install the Java Programming Language 18
   If the Java Command Is Not Found 20
   Other Reasons It Might Not Work 22
   Install the Minecraft Client and Server 23
   Next Up 29

3. **Build and Install a Plugin** 31
   Plugin: HelloWorld 34
   Configure with plugin.yml 35
   Build and Install with build.sh 36
   Next Up 39

4. **Plugins Have Variables, Functions, and Keywords** . . . 41
   Keep Track of Data with Variables 42
   Plugin: BuildAHouse 45
   Plugin: Simple 50
   Organize Instructions into Functions 52
   Use a for Loop to Repeat Code 58
   Use an if Statement to Make Decisions 59

Compare Stuff with Boolean Conditions   60
Use a while Loop to Repeat Based on a Condition   62
Next Up   63

5.   **Plugins Have Objects** **65**
Everything in Minecraft Is an Object   65
Why Bother Using Objects?   67
Combine Data and Instructions into Objects   69
Plugin: PlayerStuff   73
Next Up   76

6.   **Add a Chat Command, Locations, and Targets** **77**
How Does Minecraft Know About Your Plugin?   77
Plugin: SkyCmd   78
Handle Chat Commands   79
Use Minecraft Coordinates   80
Find Nearby Blocks or Entities   83
Plugin: LavaVision   84
Next Up   86

7.   **Use Piles of Variables: Arrays** **87**
Variables and Objects Live in Blocks   87
Plugin: CakeTower   90
Use a Java Array   92
Plugin: ArrayOfBlocks   95
Use a Java ArrayList   97
Plugin: ArrayAddMoreBlocks   99
Next Up   100

8.   **Use Piles of Variables: HashMap** **101**
Use a Java HashMap   101
Keep Things Private or Make Them Public   104
Plugin: NamedSigns   106
Next Up   111

9.   **Modify, Spawn, and Listen in Minecraft** **113**
Modify Blocks   114
Plugin: Stuck   114
Modify Entities   119
Spawn Entities   120
Plugin: FlyingCreeper   121
Listen for Events   122

Plugin: BackCmd   125
Check Permissions   129
Next Up   131

10. **Schedule Tasks for Later**   133
What Happens When?   133
Put Code in a Class by Itself   135
Make a Runnable Task   138
Schedule to Run Later   139
Schedule to Keep Running   139
Plugin: CowShooter   140
Next Up   143

11. **Use Configuration Files and Store Game Data**   145
Use a Configuration File   147
Plugin: SquidBombConfig   150
Store Game Data in Local Files   151
Use PermaMap   153
Plugin: LocationSnapshot   154
Plugin: BackCmd with Save   157
PermaMap: Save and Load a Java HashMap   162
Next Up   167

12. **Keep Your Code Safe**   169
Install Git   170
Remember Changes   170
An Easy Undo   174
Visit Multiple Realities   177
Back Up to the Cloud   181
Share Code   183
Next Up   185

13. **Design Your Own Plugin**   187
Have an Idea   188
Gather Your Materials   188
Lay Them Out   190
Try Each Part   193
Knit It All Together   202
Just the Beginning   209

A1. **How to Read Error Messages** 211
    Java-Compiler Error Messages 211
    Bukkit Server Error Messages 215

A2. **How to Read the Bukkit Documentation** 217
    Bukkit JavaDoc Documentation 217
    Oracle JavaDoc Documentation 219
    The Wiki and Tutorials 219

A3. **How to Install a Desktop Server** 221
    The Easy Way: LogMeIn 222
    The Harder Way: By Hand 223

A4. **How to Install a Cloud Server** 229
    What Is the Cloud? 229
    Remote Operating Systems 230
    Remote Access 232
    Installing Packages 237
    Installing Java 238
    Running Remotely 238
    Domain Name 240
    What's Next 240

A5. **Cheat Sheets** 241
    Java Language 241
    YAML Files 245

A6. **Glossary** 247

A7. **Common Imports** 253

Bibliography 255

Index 257

Acknowledgments

A very special thanks to my son Stuart for suggesting this book and answering a lot of my dumb questions about Minecraft, and to the rest of my family for putting up with me as I disappeared under headphones and typed away in an imaginary world.

Thanks to my editor Brian Hogan, managing editor Susannah Pfalzer, production manager Janet Furlow, and that wizard of layout and XSLT, David Kelly.

Thanks to my early reviewers: David Bock, Jerrel Blankenship, Jedidja Bourgeois, Aditya Gupta, Daniel Hampikian, Chris Johnson, Jonathan Knowles, and Brian VanLoo; and my tech reviewers, Ana Blaser, A. Mitch Bullard, Scott Davis, Ian Dees, Jeff Holland, Nicholas LaMuro, Tim Langr, Jeremy Sydik, Andrew Walley, and Bruce Williams; and a very special thanks to the ever-eagle eye of Dr. Venkat Subramaniam.

Also a special thanks to the beta readers, especially Carl Cravens, Scott Lyden, and Erich Pfisterer.

Bukkit (including CraftBukkit and the Bukkit API) is free, open source software that provides the means to extend the popular Minecraft multiplayer server. It is located at http://www.bukkit.org.

Start Here

Welcome!

Thanks for taking the time to pick up this book. I hope you'll find it a quick read and have a lot of fun along the way. If you've never written a program before, don't worry. We'll take it slow and start at the very beginning. No experience required.

Everyone loves Minecraft. I think a big reason for its success is that you get to participate in making the game. You get a chance to build; to create. Whether it's a quick shelter in survival mode or a huge Redstone simulation or your very own castle, you get to create.

But sometimes the Minecraft game's built-in capabilities aren't enough. You want to do something more. You want to shoot flaming cows or encase an opponent in a cage of solid rock. For these and many other extra abilities, you need to add features to the game itself.

Applications on your computer or phone are written in a special kind of text we call *programming languages*. They're not as huge or hard to learn as natural languages, such as English or Spanish or Chinese, but they are different from the language you use to write and talk in every day.

There are many, many programming languages in use today. Some are very popular and not very powerful. Some are used only by a handful of people but are incredibly powerful and difficult to master.

Minecraft is written in the Java programming language. Java is moderately powerful, but it also has some hard and confusing parts. We'll focus on the basics and sidestep the difficult stuff.

This is a fast-and-loose book to get you programming in Java quickly. You'll learn enough of the Java programming language to create your own Minecraft plugins and accomplish common tasks in Java.

We'll take a look at setting up your own Minecraft server and sharing and keeping cloud-based backups of the code you write, and we'll take a peek at a few advanced coding techniques.

Who This Book Is For

This book is aimed at readers who have no experience programming, but who do have some experience playing Minecraft. If you aren't familiar with Minecraft, there are plenty of videos and books to help you get started. But I'm guessing you're already pretty adept at and enthusiastic about Minecraft, and you want to learn the programming end.

Readers younger than 8 or 9, or readers of any age who are having trouble understanding programming in Java, might want to take a short detour and experiment with a friendlier programming language first. Scratch and the newer version, Snap!,[1] are great little languages that help you learn the basic concepts of programming. They show how programming elements fit together visually. Once you get the hang of that, then coming back to a text-based language like Java can make a lot more sense.

Otherwise, you just need a modern computer running Windows, Mac OS X, or Linux, and we'll go from there.

Getting Started

Minecraft is designed as a "client-server" application. That means it's split into two parts.

First, there's the client, which is the application you run on your desktop or laptop computer. The client renders images of the Minecraft world and accepts your commands to move and act in the game.

Second, there's the server, which keeps track of everything in the game, including all the players who are connected, their inventories, what they've built, where they are, and so on. Most of the time the server is running on some faraway machine in another part of the country. But it could be running on your laptop or desktop computer as well.

The client and the server talk to each over the network, the same way you use a web browser to connect to servers and play games or see pictures of cats.

To add or change functionality in the Minecraft game, you have to add to or change the Java program on the server. That's what you'll learn to do in this

---

1.   http://scratch.mit.edu, http://snap.berkeley.edu

short book: program in Java by writing Java instructions (which we call "source code," or just "code" or the "program") to create *plugins* for the Minecraft server. A plugin is just a piece of code that you add to an existing program.[2]

Before we get started with plugins, you need to set up a local Minecraft server for testing, and install the Java programming language and a couple of other applications. We'll go over all of that in the first few chapters. Installing stuff isn't very much fun by itself. In fact, it's boring as dirt. But we'll try to get through the dirt pile as fast as we can.

In fact, to help you keep track of your progress, a "Your Growing Toolbox" sidebar at the end of each chapter shows a progress bar. You'll start from just plain dirt:

And finish up with 100% grass:

Some chapters will go faster than others and some will add more than others, but you *will* keep making progress.

Swimming in the Deep End

Because we've got a lot to cover in a small space, I'm going to try to show you things first, maybe even use them first, and then explain them in detail a little later. Sometimes that can feel like you've been thrown into the deep end of the pool. When you see something that doesn't make sense yet, don't worry about it. Just let it wash over you; the explanation will be along shortly.

In many cases, you can use something successfully even if you don't really understand how it all works. I can turn a desk lamp on and use it without understanding how electricity is generated. I could even build my own desk lamp without understanding how to build a big power-station generator. I just need to know how my part fits in.

We'll focus on how your part fits in as much as possible.

---

2. Some folks also write Minecraft *mods*, which take place in the graphical client, but we won't cover those here. Mods are mostly concerned with loading new skins; the plugin development we'll do is closer to what professional programmers do and actually changes the game mechanics, not just the look.

Getting Help

There's a forum on the book's website for questions, updates, and tips. Just point your browser to http://pragprog.com/book/ahmine and click on the Discuss tab.

On that same home page, there's a link for Source Code where you can download all the source code from this book.[3]

Please download that to your Desktop now—you'll use your computer's Desktop for most of our work, but more on that in a bit. Meanwhile, start downloading.

I'll wait.

The download is an archive file created using zip, so you need to unzip it on your Desktop. You can use unzip from the command line (for Mac OS X or Linux), or for Windows you can use WinZip or the free 7-Zip.[4]

Got it installed and unpacked? Great!

As we go along, you'll learn how to use new tools and learn new ways to use those tools. We'll keep track of the new stuff you learn with that "toolbox" at the end of each chapter. By the end of the book you'll have enough in your toolbox that you'll be able to design and code your own plugins from scratch!

Conventions

Code or commands that I'm showing you as examples look like this:

```
$ I've typed all of this as an example for you.
```

For code or commands that you're supposed to type in, I'll show it with a shaded background like this:

```
$ you type this part here (but not the dollar-sign prompt)
```

Things in *italics* are placeholders; you don't type them in directly, so something like this:

```
me.sendMessage( string msg );
```

means you would replace the italic part, like this:

```
me.sendMessage("Creepers are coming.");
```

Now let's see how to work this thing.

---

3. The exact link is http://media.pragprog.com/titles/ahmine/code/ahmine-code.zip.
4. Available from http://www.winzip.com or http://www.7-zip.org

## CHAPTER 1

Command Your Computer

Your Toolbox

In this chapter you'll learn about the shell, where you can type commands to your computer. You'll add these topics to your mental toolbox:

- How to open a command shell and type commands
- How files and directories make up the file system
- How to navigate around directories in the file system

One of the earliest and greatest computer games that created a world for you to explore was Colossal Cave Adventure,[1] way back in 1976. It was a purely text-based adventure—there were no images or graphics. You typed instructions to the game using simple sentences, commanding it to "go north" or "take axe" or "kill troll" as needed. And it did as you asked, even killing the troll with your bare hands.

Today, text commands are still in games—even Minecraft has text commands. You've probably typed commands in Minecraft's chat window using a "/" character.

You're going to issue commands to your computer to build plugins and work with files in very much the same way, using the *command line*.

The command line is a powerful tool that lets you work on your local computer as well as on distant computers in the cloud. In fact, we'll cover how to do exactly that later on in the book, in Appendix 4, *How to Install a Cloud Server*, on page 229.

---

1. http://en.wikipedia.org/wiki/Colossal_Cave_Adventure

You can even use the command-line processor to write programs; it contains a full programming language by itself, separate from Java. I've done a little of that for you, with a couple of scripts that help you build and install plugins. We'll use those as we go along.

If you're already familiar with using the command line, feel free to skip to the end of this chapter on page 12.

Use the Command Line

The command line looks something like this on my computer. Yours may use different colors and fonts, and you can usually set these to your liking. I apparently prefer black letters on a tan background:

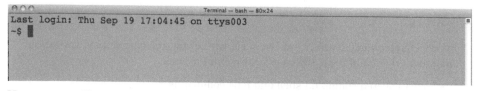

You access the command line a little differently depending on the kind of operating system you're running, which will be one of these:

Windows

> Windows comes with a very bare-bones command line. You get to it by running cmd.exe. If your version of Windows has a "Start" command, then you might be able to select Start-Run and enter cmd.exe or just use the search box that comes up to find and run cmd.exe. But I don't recommend using cmd.exe by itself; see the instructions in the box on page 3.

Mac OS X

> Open the application via Applications -> Utilities -> Terminal.

Linux

> If you're running Linux, you likely already know how to get to a command-line shell. But for the sake of completeness, and because it's called different things, try any of these: open a shell, start a Konsole, or right-click on the Desktop to open a Terminal.

(Fortunately, all of these pesky differences between Windows, Mac, and Linux disappear once you're writing Java code: Java runs the same on each platform.)

Once you have your command-line application up and running, you're ready to type commands into the command-line processor, or *shell*, as I'll call it. You'll be using a few simple commands that I'll show you as we go along.

Install BusyBox on Windows

The Mac OS X and Linux environments are based on Unix, which has a very rich command-line environment, including a full-featured shell. There's a published standard for that environment, called POSIX, which includes commands and language features. The POSIX standard shell is really an entire programming language by itself, and you can write shell scripts to do basic tasks on the computer for you.

Windows, however, isn't as sophisticated. The default command processor doesn't do much at all, the commands have different names, and directory and file names are specified differently.

So in order to keep things consistent for everybody, I recommend that Windows users download BusyBox. It installs a more professional, POSIX-compliant standard shell and common commands—the same ones that Mac OS X, Linux, and the rest of the world uses.

To install the command shell and basic commands for Windows, download this file to your Desktop: ftp://ftp.tigress.co.uk/public/gpl/6.0.0/busybox/busybox.exe

Once it's downloaded to your Desktop, rename the file from busybox.exe to sh.exe. Then open a cmd.exe window and type this:

```
C:\> cd Desktop
C:\> C:\Windows\system32\cmd.exe /c sh.exe -l
```

Now you'll see a new shell with a dollar-sign prompt. That's where we'll run commands and do our work. Notice an important detail: this is running sh.exe with a -l flag (which you would pronounce as "minus ell"), which tells it to act like a "login shell" where you can type commands.

For convenience's sake, you can make a batch file on your Desktop to launch this command shell for you. To do that, create a text file and save it to your Desktop. Name the file shell.bat and type this line of text in the file:

```
C:\Windows\system32\cmd.exe /c sh.exe -l
```

Save the file, and now you can double-click on shell.bat, and you'll have a POSIX-compatible shell. With that done, you can access the commands we'll use (things like ls, mv, cp, and pwd), and you'll specify directory names with "/" instead of the Windows "\" character, so everything will work the same on Windows as on Mac and Linux.

You'll also be able to employ the command scripts that we'll use to build and install plugins.

For more information on BusyBox for Windows, see its home page.[a]

---

a.   http://intgat.tigress.co.uk/rmy/busybox/index.html

Each shell prints out a short message indicating it's ready for you to type something in. But instead of a straightforward prompt like "Ready for you to type, master," most command prompts are a little more cryptic.

Windows will show something like C:\>. Linux and Mac systems might show $ or %. Any of these prompts might include additional information, like your name, the computer's name, or a directory name. Since that will be different for everyone, I'm going to choose the simplest one for the examples in this book and show the command prompt as a $. Whatever your prompt looks like, that's where you type in commands.

DO NOT TYPE IN THE DOLLAR SIGN ($). I'll show it to indicate where you type, but you *don't* type the $:

```
$ you type this part here, but not the dollar sign
```

When you're done typing in a command and want the computer to run it, press the `Enter` (or `Return`) key on your keyboard. That's the easy part. Next you just need to learn a few basic commands to type in!

You can list the files and directories with the *directory listing* command:

```
$ ls
```

To change your current directory, you use the *change directory* command. For example, to change the directory to the Desktop, you'd type

```
$ cd Desktop
```

and be transported to the Desktop (or any other directory whose name you enter).

For instance, when your shell first opens up, you'll be in some sort of default directory or folder (sometimes called a *home* directory). You can see what files are there by typing the command ls (short for "list files") and pressing `Return`.[2]

You'll see a listing of a bunch of files. Type cd Desktop, and you'll be in your Desktop directory. Type the command ls, and you'll see a list of all the files on the Desktop. Now you're working at the command line! Let's delve into that a little bit more.

---

2. On stock Windows using cmd.exe, you'd have to type dir (short for "directory listing") instead. Also, while the rest of the world uses a "/" in directory names, Windows uses a "\." These and other tiresome differences are why I recommend using the POSIX-standard bash shell for Windows as described in the box on page 3.

Move around in File Directories

Normally when you want to look at files on your computer's hard drive, you use graphical programs like Explorer on Windows or the Finder on Mac. Either way, the idea is to show you the files, folders/directories, and applications/programs on the computer so you can navigate around and run things.

We're doing the same thing here, but in a more powerful way and without graphics. If you're already familiar with doing this, please feel free to skip to the end of this chapter for a small treat. Otherwise, read on.

The collection of files and folders on your computer is called the *file system.* At any point in time a Finder (or Explorer) window on your Desktop or in your command shell is sitting in some current directory. On your Desktop you might have several folder windows open, each looking at a different folder (directory) on your disk.

Each command-line shell window you have open works the same way: for each window, there is a *current directory.* Some systems are set up to show the current directory in your prompt. But you can always find out where you are by typing the command pwd (which stands for "print working directory"):

```
$ pwd
/Users/andy/Desktop
```

Try this now: open a fresh shell, and before doing anything else, type pwd at the prompt (shown here as a $—yours may be different):

```
$ pwd
```

That will print out your *home directory*, which every one of your shells will start from.

In each shell, all the commands you run will run with this particular idea of a current directory (or current working directory). Many programs you use will look here, in the current directory, to run, open, and save files.

If you haven't yet, download to the Desktop the files that came with this book,[3] and unzip the archive there.[4] That will unpack to a directory named code, which contains all the examples from this book.

Under code there are a bunch of plugin directories, one for each plugin in this book. We'll start off looking at the HelloWorld plugin files. Under that directory are a few other files and subdirectories.

---

3. http://media.pragprog.com/titles/ahmine/code/ahmine-code.zip
4. Use unzip at the command line, or on Windows use WinZip or 7-Zip.

Start with this:

```
$ cd Desktop
```

And you'll be here:

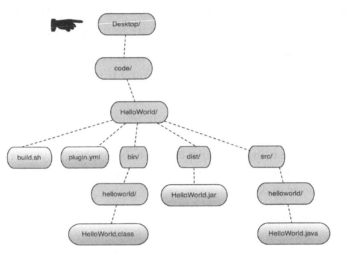

(If that didn't work, try cd ~/Desktop, or check the end of this chapter for hints.)

Next go down into the code directory by typing this:

```
$ cd code
```

Now you're here:

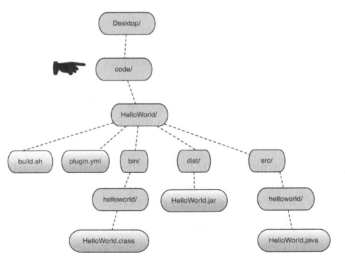

Go down into HelloWorld:

```
$ cd HelloWorld
```

And now you're here:

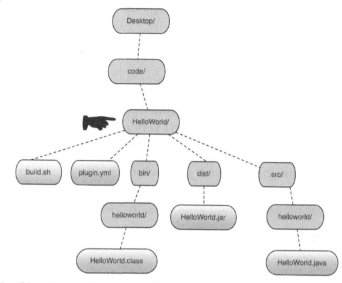

Now list the files there. You'll see this:

```
$ ls
bin/        build.sh   dist/      plugin.yml   src/
```

My system (Mac OS X) is configured to show directories with a slash at the end. (If yours isn't, try typing ls -F.) So here I have two files and three directories in my current directory. File types are often represented by the last part of the file name—its suffix. Here I have a shell script with an .sh suffix, and a Yaml file with a .yml suffix. Down in the src/ directory there's a helloworld subdirectory; there I have a Java source file with a .java suffix (more about these kinds of files as we go along).

To go down into the src directory, type cd src, and you're there.

```
$ cd src
$ ls
helloworld
```

Then down one more into helloworld:

```
$ cd helloworld
$ ls
HelloWorld.java
```

In the src/helloworld directory, there's the HelloWorld.java file—the "guts" of our first plugin.

But now you're down in HelloWorld/src/helloworld. How do you get back up to HelloWorld? To go up just one level, you'd type this:

```
$ cd ..
```

Or to go up two levels, type this:

```
$ cd ../..
```

That's two periods (or dots), which is pronounced "up one." One dot by itself means the current directory, which isn't very useful with cd, but we will use "." with other commands—especially when copying files.

But now suppose you need to visit a directory that isn't just in the current directory or up one. How do you get there? Suppose I'm somewhere completely different, like /home/minecraft, and I want to go to /Users/andy/Desktop/code/HelloWorld.

I'd do something like this:

```
$ cd /Users/andy/Desktop/code/HelloWorld
```

The leading slash makes the difference. Earlier, when you typed cd src, the cd command looked for src right under the current directory. But if instead you typed cd /src it would look for a directory named src under a directory named "/"—which we call the *root*.

Root is the topmost directory on your system. It's above your code, above your Desktop, above everything. Somewhere under root are your home directory and Desktop. In my case, that's /Users/andy/Desktop. I could get there the slow way by typing this sequence of commands:

```
$ cd /
$ cd Users
$ cd andy
$ cd Desktop
```

But we'll see a much easier way in just a moment. And speaking of shortcuts, you don't even need to spell out each directory name fully, like D-e-s-k-t-o-p.

On most systems, there's a nice keyboard shortcut to save you from typing out long names—the Tab key. If you type in the first few letters of a long name then press the Tab key, it will autocomplete to the long name. Suppose I'm in my code directory:

```
$ ls
BackCmd          EarthMover    PermaMap
SquidBomb        FlashMob      PlayerStuff
SquidBombConfig  FlingCmd      SaveAHash
CowShooter       HelloWorld    SkyCmd
DataDemo         ListDemo      Stuck
```

If I type cd H Tab it will autocomplete to

```
$ cd HelloWorld/
```

and I can just press Return. For short names it might not look like much, but if you have a long directory name like RumpelstiltskinReincarnationSpellPlugin, typing Ru Tab begins to look mighty appealing.

Copy and Paste

Sometimes you might want to copy a bit of text and paste it at the command line. For instance, you might want to copy a line from this book and paste it in.

Copy and paste at the command line can be a little different from copying in an application like Mail or a web browser. You still click and drag the mouse to select text to begin with.

On Linux, you can use Ctrl-C to copy and Ctrl-V to paste.

On Mac you use ⌘C and ⌘V to copy and paste.

On Windows the commands are slightly different. After selecting text, you need to press Enter to copy, then right-click or Ctrl-V to paste.

If this doesn't work for you, you might need to enable this feature. Right-click the top bar of the window and select Properties. On the Options tab, in the Edit Options section, check QuickEdit Mode to turn it on.

Try This Yourself

Let's make some directories and files using the command line. You're going to make your own copy of a plugin, with directories and all.

Start off in your Desktop directory (make sure you're there by typing pwd) and make a new directory called myplugins using the mkdir command.

```
$ cd Desktop
$ pwd
/Users/andy/Desktop
$ mkdir myplugins
```

List out the files on your Desktop (using ls), and you'll see all the files you have there as well as the new directory, myplugins. Let's go down into myplugins and do some work.

```
$ cd myplugins
```

Do a pwd to confirm you're in the myplugins directory.

If you do an ls here you won't see anything—we haven't made any files there yet. Let's fix that by making the directory structure, which will be the same as for the HelloWorld plugin. Start by making a directory named for the plugin itself:

```
$ mkdir HelloWorld
```

And (you guessed it!) cd down into HelloWorld.

```
$ cd HelloWorld
```

Now you can make a few directories that you'll need: src, src/helloworld, bin, and dist. Go ahead make those directories here now:

```
$ mkdir src
$ mkdir src/helloworld
$ mkdir bin
$ mkdir dist
```

Use ls to make sure they are there.

```
$ ls
src/ bin/ dist/

$ ls src
helloworld/
```

Now you need two files here, which you can copy from the book's example code. You can drag and drop using your regular graphical windows, or use the copy command, cp:

```
$ cp ~/Desktop/code/HelloWorld/build.sh .
```

The tilde character (~) is shorthand for "my home directory." And hey—we got to use the single dot! The whole command line means "copy this file to the current directory."

You'll need another file too, so copy that over while you're here.

```
$ cp ~/Desktop/code/HelloWorld/plugin.yml .
```

Now you've created the directories and supporting files that you'll need for a plugin.

If It Doesn't Work

One area where you might run into problems is if your home directory contains spaces. For instance, if you're on Windows and your name is "John Smith," typing in a command using the tilde, like this:

```
$ cp ~/Desktop/code/HelloWorld/build.sh .
```

> ## Files on Your Desktop
>
> We'll do all of our work on the Desktop because that's the easiest place for you to find files, and it's the same across Windows, Mac, and Linux.
>
> Out in the real world you probably wouldn't want to clutter up your Desktop with each new project you work on. But until you get more comfortable moving things around and setting things up, stick to the Desktop.

makes it look like you typed this:

```
$ cp C:/Users/John Smith/Desktop/code/HelloWorld/build.sh .
```

The computer interprets that as saying "copy C:/Users/John to Smith/Desktop/code/HelloWorld/build.sh" and an extra dot. You'll get the error that there is "no such file or directory."

You have two workarounds: you can use a relative path, by typing ".." for parent directories, so you go "up two" and down into code:

```
$ cp ../../code/HelloWorld/build.sh .
```

Or just type it in by hand, using quotation marks around the part that contains the offensive space:

```
$ cp C:/Users/"John Smith"/Desktop/code/HelloWorld/build.sh .
```

Another problem you might run into is not being in the directory that you think you are. When in doubt, you can always do a pwd command to print your current working directory:

```
$ pwd
/Users/andy/Desktop
```

Here I'm in my Desktop directory, which is where we'll be starting off for most of our work.

Start at the Desktop

On most systems, you should be able to type cd Desktop to get to your Desktop. If that doesn't work, you may need to type cd ~/Desktop—using the tilde shortcut—or you might need to spell the whole thing out, as in cd /Users/andy/Desktop.

However you accomplish it, when I say "start at your Desktop" or just cd Desktop, that's what you'll always need to do, whether it's from anywhere, like this:

```
$ cd Desktop
```

from your home directory first:

```
$ cd
$ cd Desktop
```

using a tilde for the home directory:

```
$ cd ~/Desktop
```

explicitly typing the name of your home directory:

```
$ cd /Users/andy/Desktop
```

or doing that with quotes because you have spaces in the name:

```
$ cd /Users/"John Smith"/Desktop
```

No matter what, it will always be shown here as just

```
$ cd Desktop
```

And Now for Some Fun

In this book's downloaded code, in your Desktop/code directory, there's a special subdirectory named Adventure. Using the command line, cd there and have a look at those files and directories.

You can use ls to list the directories as we've done here. To take a quick look at text files (named .txt), you can use the cat command.

Start at your Desktop (however that works for you, as described in the last section).

```
$ cd Desktop
$ cd code
$ cd Adventure
$ cat README.txt
These are some files to make exploring the file system a little more fun.
```

Do an ls and see what else is there and explore a bit in the subdirectories. See what treasures—and what dangers—you find.

Common Commands

Here are some of the most common commands you'll use at the shell:

java	Run Java classes and Java archives (JARs) as a program
javac	Compile Java source code to class files
cd	Change the directory
pwd	Print the working (current) directory
ls	List files in the current directory

cat	Display the contents of a file
echo	Display text; also display environment variables using the $ prefix
mkdir	Make a new directory
cp	Copy a file
mv	Move a file
rm	Remove (delete) a file permanently (Use this with extreme caution; this is not the same as the Trash, and there is no "undo.")
chmod	Change file permissions (including read, write, and execute)
.	(single dot) Means the current directory
..	(two dots) Means the parent directory
~	(tilde) Means your home directory

Next Up

Next you need a way to type in the Java source code. You'll need Java itself, and an application to put it all together for you. We'll install all of that in the next chapter, and then get to building plugins.

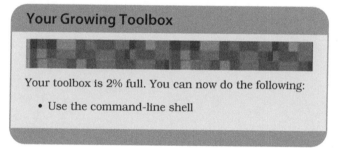

Your Growing Toolbox

Your toolbox is 2% full. You can now do the following:

• Use the command-line shell

## CHAPTER 2

Add an Editor and Java

Your Toolbox

In this chapter you'll install several new applications on your computer, and add these tools to your toolbox:

- The Java language compiler, javac, and the runtime application, java
- The Minecraft graphical client
- The Minecraft server that we'll be modifying

To write programs in Java, you need something to write with: some way of editing Java text files. While you could use a bare-bones text editor like Notepad or TextEdit, that's a really painful way to do it.

And you can't use Microsoft Word or another office-style word processor. Those applications aren't designed for programming, and they don't store files in a format that Java can use—Word files are filled with fonts, colors, sizes, and all sorts of formatting information.

What you need is a text editor that's designed for programming. I've got a good one for you, which we'll see next. You'll also need to install Java to build and run plugins, and you'll need Minecraft, of course. With all that installed, you'll be set to build a plugin in the next chapter.

This chapter may contain some new (and possibly cryptic) commands and potentially confusing concepts. It's okay if you don't know what these mean and don't understand fully right now; these aren't things you'll run into day-to-day when writing plugins; they're just a few necessary evils you need to get everything installed.

Let's start with the editor.

Install an Editor to Write Code

You write plugins and programs by typing in kinda-English words and some funny punctuation. Most things you write will be longer than a text message but shorter than an essay in English class. You need a proper editor to type in your programs.

My suggestion is an editor called *Sublime Text* (see the screenshot in Figure 1, *Text editor with syntax highlighting*, on page 16). It's available as a download and runs on Windows, Mac, and Linux.[1]

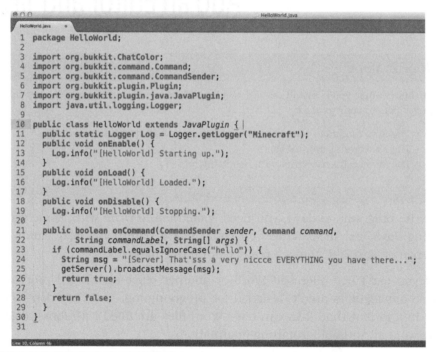

Figure 1—Text editor with syntax highlighting

You can try the free evaluation (there's no time limit, but it will nag you every so often) or cough up some bucks and purchase it. If you have a different editor that you read about or prefer, that's fine—you can use that. On Windows, for example, you might want to look at the free editor Notepad++.[2] The choice of an editor is very much a personal one. There is no "right" answer, size, shape, or color. But you do need an editor that has the right features.

---

1. http://www.sublimetext.com
2. http://notepad-plus-plus.org/download/v6.4.2.html

One great advantage of an editor built for programmers is a feature called *syntax highlighting*. The editor knows about different parts of the Java language and will make language elements like functions, variables, strings, and keywords show up in different colors and fonts (see the example in the following figure). That kind of visual support can be really helpful when you're first learning what all those different things mean. We'll get to exploring all of that in a chapter or two, but first, choose your soon-to-be-favorite editor and install it.[3]

So fire up Sublime Text (or some other suitable code editor) and give it a whirl. If you've used anything similar to Word, this will seem at least a little familiar: there's a menu bar at the top, and under the File menu you'll see useful choices like New, Open, and Save.

Go ahead and type in some text. Maybe write a two-line short horror story or something ("the reflection in the mirror blinked"). Click and drag to select text, and press Delete to remove it. For now it's just a plain old text editor, so we don't need to try anything too fancy.

Try This Yourself

Let's make sure you can create a file, edit it, and save it. We're not quite ready for a full plugin yet, so let's start with a simple test file.

In the editor's menu, start with File -> New File to create an empty buffer that you can type into.

Before you start typing, save the file by name. Select the menu item File -> Save As and save the file as CreeperTest.java on your Desktop. Just like that—with a capital C and T, and lowercase other letters. Now that you've saved the file, your editor will know you're going to type in Java code.

Type in the following text, just like I did:

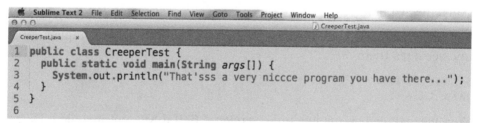

```
public class CreeperTest {
  public static void main(String args[]) {
    System.out.println("That'sss a very niccce program you have there...");
  }
}
```

---

3. You might also look into using IntelliJ IDEA or Eclipse. These are full development environments that include an editor and build support, but they can be complicated and hard to manage for beginners.

Be sure to copy the text *exactly*, starting with "public class" through to the last "}"—including all punctuation, spelling, capitalization, and spacing. Use the Delete key (sometimes labeled "backspace") to erase any mistakes.

Now select File -> Save to save the file with your text.

Ta-da! Now you have a file with Java source code.

And the computer has no idea what to do with it. It's just a file of text; as far as your computer knows, it could be a recipe for snacks or an essay or a list of game cheats. We need to fix that next.

What you need now is Java itself.

Windows Paths

Just a reminder that when we're using the bash shell from BusyBox, all directories use a forward slash ("/"). But the rest of the Windows system will still use backslashes ("\").

So what Windows and the installation programs call this:

```
C:\Users\yourname\Desktop\server
```

we'll call this:

```
C:/Users/yourname/Desktop/server
```

Install the Java Programming Language

"Java" isn't just one application—it's actually several. There's the Java compiler, javac, the Java program runner, java, and the archiver utility, jar. javac takes your text file and creates a magical pile of gunk it calls a *class file*. You run the java command and tell it to use that pile of gunk, and your program springs to life. We'll look at that process in more detail as we go along, but that's the gist of it.

You might have Java installed already. Try running the Java compiler, javac, and see if it's there:

```
$ javac -version
javac 1.6.0_65
```

Yup, it's installed on my machine, version 1.6. If it was not installed, I'd get a message like this:

```
$ javac -version
bash: javac: command not found
```

You might also want to check that your java is indeed the same version as your javac (it should be, but things happen):

```
$ java -version
java version "1.6.0_65"
Java(TM) SE Runtime Environment (build 1.6.0_65-b14-462-11M4609)
Java HotSpot(TM) 64-Bit Server VM (build 20.65-b04-462, mixed mode)
```

If you need to install Java, you'll want the Java Development Kit Standard Edition (JDK SE) version 6 or later, which you can download for different operating systems.[4] Depending on your operating system and vendor, you may or may not have Java installed yet, you might only have java and not javac, or you might have a slightly different version. Again, you'll need Java JDK 1.6 or later to work with the examples in this book.

No matter which operating system's installer you use, I heartily recommend you accept all the default answers to any installer questions, especially for the install location. Java and its associated programs can get more than a little quirky and fussy if things aren't where they expect.

So go download the Java Development Kit (JDK) installer and follow its instructions.

Depending on your platform, you might need to add the JDK's bin directory to your "path." We'll look at what that means and how you do it in the next section.

But first let's try a little exercise and see if it works.

Try This Yourself

With the JDK installed, you can now run that test program you typed in.

Again, this is just a simple program to make sure Java is happy. It's not a Minecraft plugin yet, but it's a start. As soon as you get this working, you'll be ready to start building Minecraft plugins.

cd to your Desktop and make sure the CreeperTest.java file is there:

```
$ cd Desktop
$ ls
CreeperTest.java
```

Now run the Java compiler on CreeperTest.java by executing the javac (Java compiler) command.

---

4.   http://www.oracle.com/technetwork/java/javase/downloads/index.html

```
$ javac CreeperTest.java
$ ls
CreeperTest.class CreeperTest.java
```

The javac program first checks to make sure it understands everything you typed in the CreeperTest.java file. If there are no mistakes, then it creates the binary class file.

But the odds are that most of the time *there will be mistakes.* Don't worry if you get a ton of error messages: you didn't break your computer. Programming languages like Java are notoriously picky about capitalization, punctuation, and all the other things we type in that file.

Remain calm. (That, by the way, is generally good advice when working with computers.)

Try to decipher the message the computer gives you, and double-check all the code against our example from a moment ago. We'll walk through several likely problems next. There's also some advice in Appendix 1, *How to Read Error Messages*, on page 211. If all else fails, don't forget this book has a website where other folks are wrestling with this stuff too!

Once javac happily finishes its work without errors, you're ready to run.

You can call Java to run your program, giving it the name part only (not the .class suffix):

```
$ java CreeperTest
That'sss a very niccce program you have there...
```

Hey, it worked! Congratulations—you've compiled and run your first piece of code. Skip ahead to the Minecraft installation section that starts on page 23.

Otherwise, let's see what might have gone wrong.

If the Java Command Is Not Found

The most likely error you'll see is "javac not found" or "java not found," which means that even though you installed Java, your shell couldn't find the java.exe or javac.exe applications. Here's what's going on:

The commands you've used so far are either built in or were installed by the BusyBox installer. But when you install Java, the computer may not know where you put it.

When you go to type in the command javac, the computer needs to find an executable named "javac" (on Windows it's javac.exe, on Mac/Linux, just javac). There are a couple of standard places that it knows to look. On Windows, that might include a directory like C:\windows\System32, and on Mac/Linux there could be several directories, like /usr/bin, /usr/local/bin, and so on.

Because the system has its own commands that you shouldn't mess with, and because you want to add your own commands to run, it turns out there are a lot of places the computer needs to look! You can tell it exactly where to look with a list of directory names. We call that your *search path*, or *path* for short.

You can see what's in the path for your shell window by typing this:

```
$ echo $PATH
```

For the shell/command-line processor to find a command to execute, it must be in a directory that's in your search path. So you'll need to add Java's bin directory to your path.

That directory's location depends on your operating system and what installer you used. A typical location for Windows would be C:\Program Files\Java\jdk1.7.0_45\bin (your version numbers may be a little different).

On Mac, it's probably installed in /usr/bin or /usr/local/bin, both of which are already in your path. But it might be installed someplace else completely, like in /opt/local/java.

In any case, once you've located the install directory for Java, you'll see a bin directory in there. In that bin directory you'll see java, javac, jar, and a whole bunch of other things. You'll need to add the full path for that bin directory to your shell's PATH.

The PATH is a list of directories, separated by a colon (semicolon on Windows). To change your PATH for the bash shell that we're using, follow these steps:[5]

1. In the shell, navigate to your home directory by typing cd, by itself. Confirm the full path of your home directory by typing pwd.

2. Using your text editor, create or edit the bash startup file in your home directory. Normally this will be a file named .profile or .bash_profile in your home directory (note the leading dot). On Windows using BusyBox, you have to use .profile. Otherwise you should use .bash_profile. ls won't normally show files with a leading dot, but ls -a will show it if the file already exists. You may need to create it from scratch, and that's okay.

3. Add a line to the file to modify the PATH setting, adding Java's bin directory, separated by a colon (:)—or a semicolon (;) on Windows.

---

5. If you run into trouble with this method, especially with Windows, take a look at http://www.java.com/en/download/help/path.xml.

For example, on Linux or Mac, if my JDK was installed in /opt/local/java, I'd add a line to .bash_profile that said

```
export PATH="$PATH:/opt/local/java/bin:"
```

On Windows, you need to change the backslashes to slashes and use semi-colons instead of colons, so if Java's installed in C:\Program Files\Java\jdk1.7.0_45\bin you add a line to .profile that says this:

```
export PATH="$PATH;C:/Program Files/Java/jdk1.7.0_45/bin;"
```

Save and close the file, then close and reopen your command-line windows to pick up the new settings.

Seriously—you have to close all your open command-line windows and reopen them for this to take effect.

To check your path and see if your new setting worked, type this:

```
$ echo $PATH
```

You should see your new entry that includes Java's bin.

Other Reasons It Might Not Work

Here are some other things that might go wrong even if the PATH is set correctly:

Make sure you are in the right directory; type ls and check that the file CreeperTest.java is right there.

Make sure you're typing javac CreeperTest.java (with the .java part). Otherwise you might see a truly confusing error message like this one:

```
error: Class names, 'CreeperTest', are only accepted if
annotation processing is explicitly requested
```

If the javac command reports some kind of "syntax" or "not found" or "not defined" error, that means it doesn't understand the text in the CreeperTest.java file, so you may have mistyped something. These kinds of errors might look something like this:

```
CreeperTest.java:1: class, interface, or enum expected
```

Or you might see some other error message. The number in between the colons (:1:) is the line number where the typo is located.

If you can't find the typo, grab a fresh copy of the file from this book's downloaded source code, at code/install/CreeperTest.java, and try that.

If the java command can't find CreeperTest.class, make sure the javac command ran okay and that it produced a .class file successfully. You should be in that same directory when running java.

If you see this error

```
Exception in thread "main" java.lang.NoClassDefFoundError: CreeperTest/class
```

you may have accidentally typed java CreeperTest.class instead of java CreeperTest. To recap, these are the commands to compile and then run:

```
$ javac CreeperTest.java
$ java CreeperTest
```

That is, you must specify the .java suffix when compiling, but do not type in the .class part when running with java.

Also, check to see if there's a setting for CLASSPATH:

```
$ echo $CLASSPATH

$
```

It should be blank. If it's not, make sure it at least includes a single dot (".") to include the current directory.

If all else fails, don't be afraid to ask around for help. Programming is most often a team effort.

Phew! That was the hardest part.

Once you have Java working, you need to install the Minecraft parts.

Install the Minecraft Client and Server

Minecraft is a client-server system, so you'll need both parts: the desktop graphical client that you use to play the game, and the server process that you connect to, where we'll add plugins.

Install the Minecraft Graphical Client

You probably have this part already, but if not, download the Minecraft installer for your computer from http://minecraft.net. Follow the installer instructions.

When you play Minecraft, this "client" is the application that you run. It connects to your paid account at http://minecraft.net. Once you launch the client, you'll see a screen like this:

There are also clients for Apple's iOS and Android devices, including smart-phones, but they are a dead end. As I'm writing this, they don't connect to normal Minecraft servers, so they can't use our custom plugins.

The client handles the graphics and sound, and lets you type chat commands in the game. But right now it has no local game to connect to—guess we better go grab and download that server code.

Install the Bukkit Server

Now for the fun part. You'll be adding plugins to your own server, so you'll need CraftBukkit, a special Minecraft server from the fine folks at Bukkit that's designed to use plugins.

Make a directory named server on your Desktop (that means it would be located in a directory named something like /Users/yourname/Desktop/server):

```
$ cd Desktop
$ mkdir server
```

We'll call this your server directory, and that's where you'll install the server parts.

The Bukkit project comes in two different JAR files: craftBukkit.jar, which is used to run the game server, and bukkit.jar, which is what we use to develop new plugins.

Hop on the Web and visit the Bukkit project's main page at http://wiki.bukkit.org/ Main_Page. Under the Downloads section, you'll see two items:

- CraftBukkit - Recommended Build *(for running the Minecraft server)*
- Bukkit API - Recommended Build *(used to develop new plugins)*

You need both. Each JAR will be named with extra version numbers (something like craftbukkit-1.6.4-R1.0.jar; your numbers will probably be larger). Download both files to your Desktop/server directory, and rename them to just craftbukkit.jar and bukkit.jar.

You can do that from the shell with the mv (move file) command and the wildcard character (*), which matches all the numbers so you don't have to type them out:

```
$ cd server
$ pwd
/Users/andy/Desktop/server
$ ls
bukkit-1.6.4-R2.0.jar craftbukkit-1.6.4-R1.0.jar
$ mv craftbukkit*.jar craftbukkit.jar
$ mv bukkit*.jar bukkit.jar
$ ls
bukkit.jar craftbukkit.jar
```

The example code for this book contains a subdirectory named runtime. In the runtime directory you'll see a startup script named start_minecraft. Copy it to your server directory using the copy command, cp. You're still in that directory, so you can just copy using ".." to refer to the Desktop, and "." to refer to your current directory, server:

```
$ cp ../code/runtime/start_minecraft .
```

We'll use that start_minecraft script to start up and run the server. It's going to run the Java command, passing in an option to make sure we have enough memory to run (the magical-looking -Xmx1024M), and then passing in the JAR file to run, craftbukkit.jar:

```
java -Xmx1024M -jar craftbukkit.jar
```

The first time the Minecraft server runs, it creates a whole bunch of files, including the default World. Go ahead and run it (still in the server directory):

```
$ ./start_minecraft
```

Note I used "./" as part of the command name. That will run the command from the current directory. If the current directory (".") is in your path, you won't need to use the "./" sequence.

If you get an error that reads ./start_minecraft: Permission denied, then you'll need to type in the following line to make the file executable:

```
$ chmod +x start_minecraft
```

Once the server launches, Minecraft will spew a bunch of text out to your terminal. Here's what that looks like on my machine; your directory names, timestamps, and version numbers will be different, but should look something like this:

```
$ cd Desktop
$ cd server
$ ./start_minecraft
229 recipes
27 achievements
14:20:45 [INFO] Starting minecraft server version 1.6.4
14:20:45 [INFO] Loading properties
14:20:45 [INFO] Default game type: SURVIVAL
14:20:45 [INFO] Generating keypair
14:20:46 [INFO] Starting Minecraft server on *:25565
14:20:47 [INFO] This server is running CraftBukkit
version git-Bukkit-1.6.4
(Implementing API version 1.6.4)
...
14:20:51 [INFO] Done (3.644s)! For help, type "help" or "?"
>
```

And it's now waiting for you to type a command at the > prompt.

There's a lot of spew in the middle there that I left out, but you get the idea.

When you're ready, you can stop your Minecraft server any time by typing the command stop, like this:

```
>stop
14:29:05 [INFO] CONSOLE: Stopping the server..
14:29:05 [INFO] Stopping server
...
14:29:05 [INFO] Saving players
14:29:05 [WARNING] DSCT: Socket closed
14:29:05 [INFO] Saving worlds
14:29:05 [INFO] Saving chunks for level 'world'/Overworld
14:29:05 [INFO] Closing listening thread
14:29:06 [INFO] Saving chunks for level 'world_nether'/Nether
14:29:06 [INFO] Saving chunks for level 'world_the_end'/The End
14:29:06 [INFO] Stopping server

$
```

And you'll be back to the command-line prompt again.

Start it back up (if you shut it down), and with your server running, you can now connect from a local Minecraft client. As usual, log in to your Minecraft account and get ready to connect to a multiplayer server:

Notice the version number in the lower left-hand corner. You may need that in a minute.

Now you need to add your local server. Click on Add Server and type in a name for your server. Use localhost for the server address, as shown here:

Your server will show up on the pick list (along with any other servers you regularly connect to), as shown in the following image:

Minecraft Versions

When you start up the Minecraft game, you can tell what version to use. Normally you can use whatever the latest version is. However, as I write this the latest version of the Bukkit server is 1.6.4, but the client that you just installed defaults to the new Minecraft 1.7, which Bukkit doesn't support yet. That won't work.

You'll need to tell the Minecraft client to use the correct version.

In the Minecraft startup program, click the Edit Profile button in the lower left.

Click that, and in the dialog box that pops up, look for the Use Version setting. Change the option to use release 1.6, or whatever is the current version of your Minecraft server, and click Save Profile.

By the time you read this, the version numbers might be completely different. Whatever the versions are, you'll need to check the version in the client and make sure it matches the server's version.

Select your server from the list, then click the Join Server button. Welcome to the world!

If you get disconnected right away, you may have a version mismatch; see *Minecraft Versions*, on page 28 for help.

Once connected, you're in the Minecraft world on your own local Minecraft server. Congratulations!

You can take this time to do a little setup in the Minecraft world. Maybe build yourself a nice house before the creepers come....

Next Up

That's a great start, and now you have a full-fledged Minecraft server running on your own computer.

In the next chapter we'll roll up our sleeves and compile and install our first real plugin.

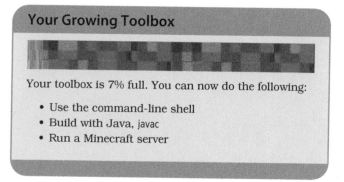

Your Growing Toolbox

Your toolbox is 7% full. You can now do the following:

- Use the command-line shell
- Build with Java, javac
- Run a Minecraft server

## CHAPTER 3

Build and Install a Plugin

Your Toolbox

After completing this chapter you'll know how to

- Compile Java source code to .class files, pack them in a JAR, and install them on a Minecraft server
- Run your local server with a new plugin
- Connect to your local server

Now that you have the tools installed, we'll build a simple, basic plugin. It won't do much as plugins go, but it will make sure you can build and run your own plugins, and it will act as starting point (or skeleton) for all the plugins we'll write in this book.

So how do your typed-in instructions end up running on a Minecraft server? Here's how the whole process works.

You type Java language instructions (we call that "source code") and save them into a text file, and then the Java compiler, javac, reads your text file and converts it into something the computer can run.

You went through this process already with the simple CreeperTest.java program you typed in previously.

For the source code you type into a file named CreeperTest.java you'll get a *binary* (not text) file named CreeperTest.class. A binary file is just a file of numbers —it makes sense to the computer, but not to humans.

Because a typical program might use lots and lots of class files, you usually archive a bunch of class files into a JAR file, and Java runs the code from the JAR.

Java (the java program itself) will read class files and JAR files to create a running process on the computer. With Minecraft, this will be the server process that your Minecraft clients connect to. For now, the only client will be you.

The following figure shows how these parts all fit together.

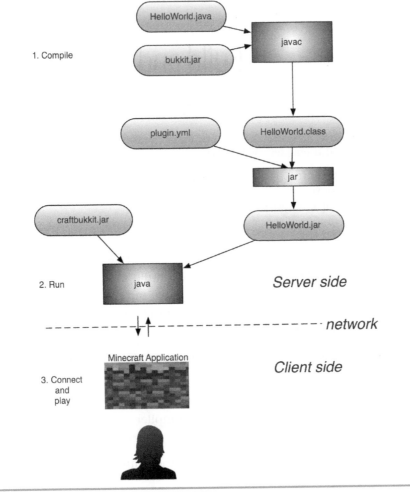

Figure 2—Compile a plugin and run it on the server.

In the Java world, you have to place all these files in specific places for this all to work. We made a directory structure like that earlier, all ready for your version of the HelloWorld plugin. I've also got a complete plugin all set up for you in the HelloWorld directory in the code for this book, which you downloaded to Desktop/code/HelloWorld.

So in Desktop/code/HelloWorld, you'll find a directory tree for the source code, under src. You'll also see a bin directory where the compiled class files are created, and a dist directory where the class file and configuration files are packed together into a jar file. When you're ready to share your plugin with others, you'll give them the JAR.

HelloWorld is one development directory. You'll probably have one of these for each plugin you develop, each with its own src, bin, dist, and so on.

Then over in your server directory at Desktop/server, you have the Minecraft server files, including the craftbukkit.jar, which contains all the bits you need to run the game, as well as the bukkit.jar we're using to develop code in the Minecraft worlds. Also in server, there's a directory for plugins that the Minecraft server will use when it runs.

When working on code in the development directory, the last step when you're ready to test it out in a server is to copy the jar file up to the server's plugin directory (see the following figure). We'll see how to do that automatically in just a second.

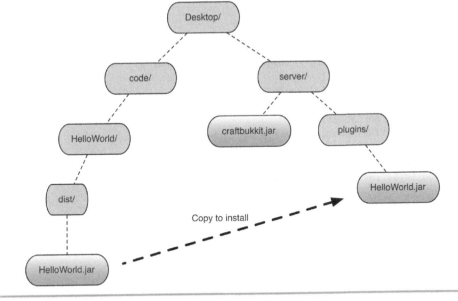

Figure 3—Installing a plugin

Java tends to use paths and configuration files to specify where all these files and directories live. It can get a little tricky at times, as there are a lot of moving parts, and it's frustrating when Java can't find some critical file that is sitting right there in front of you. Just because *you* know where a file is doesn't mean Java knows.

Now let's look at the source code, then cover how to build and install it.

Plugin: HelloWorld

It's a long-held tradition in the programming world to start off with a simple test program that prints out the message "Hello, World." So we'll start off by building and running an existing plugin that does that in Minecraft—except we'll send out a slightly more interesting message.

Here is the Java source code for our HelloWorld plugin, which is already typed in for you in the file ~/Desktop/code/HelloWorld/src/helloworld/HelloWorld.java.[1] There's a lot of weird stuff in here.

HelloWorld/src/helloworld/HelloWorld.java
```
❶ package helloworld;
❷ import java.util.logging.Logger;
  import org.bukkit.ChatColor;
  import org.bukkit.command.Command;
  import org.bukkit.command.CommandSender;
  import org.bukkit.plugin.Plugin;
  import org.bukkit.plugin.java.JavaPlugin;
❸ public class HelloWorld extends JavaPlugin {
    public static Logger log = Logger.getLogger("Minecraft");
    public void onLoad() {
      log.info("[HelloWorld] Loaded.");
    }
    public void onEnable() {
      log.info("[HelloWorld] Starting up.");
    }
    public void onDisable() {
      log.info("[HelloWorld] Stopping.");
    }
    public boolean onCommand(CommandSender sender, Command command,
                      String commandLabel, String[] args) {
      if (commandLabel.equalsIgnoreCase("hello")) {
        String msg = "[Server] That'sss a very niccce EVERYTHING you have there...";
        getServer().broadcastMessage(msg);
        return true;
      }
      return false;
    }
  }
```

---

1. If you haven't downloaded the code for this book to your Desktop yet, grab it now from http://media.pragprog.com/titles/ahmine/code/ahmine-code.zip. You can use unzip from the command line to unpack the archive and create all the files.

Don't be discouraged if this looks like space-alien speech or Elvish right now. We'll make sense out of it over the next several chapters. Instead focus on what *is* familiar: there are some English words in there, like "import" and "public" and "return," and what might be sentences or statements of some kind, which all end with semicolons (";"). There are also some strange characters like "{" and "}" that seem to be important.

What does it all mean? Well, this plugin implements a user command, /hello, which will broadcast the traditional creeper greeting, "That'sss a very niccce EVERYTHING you have there..." to all online players in Minecraft.

Notice that the name of this plugin is declared as public class HelloWorld on the line at ❸. That's the same name as the file name that contains this code: HelloWorld.java. This piece of code is also set up to be in a *package*—that is, a group of related files—using the same name on the line at ❶. The package name is all lowercase, and it's also the directory name where our Java source code file lives, under src/ in helloworld/HelloWorld.java. It's important that the names in all of these places match; a typo on one of them can lead to strange errors.

You use import statements (you'll see these beginning on the line at ❷) to get access to other things that you need in your plugin, like parts of the Bukkit library and other Java libraries. If you forget to include an import for something you need, you'll get an error that says "cannot find symbol" because Java doesn't know what you mean. For your convenience, I've included a list of all the imports we're using in Appendix 7, *Common Imports*, on page 253.

Configure with plugin.yml

But this source code alone isn't enough; you also need a configuration file so that Minecraft can find and launch your plugin. The configuration file is named plugin.yml and looks like this:

```
HelloWorld/plugin.yml
name: HelloWorld

author: AndyHunt, Learn to Program with Minecraft Plugins
website: http://pragprog.com/book/ahmine
main: helloworld.HelloWorld

commands:
    hello:
        description: Say Hello to everyone!
        usage: /hello [optional message]

version: 0.1
```

Here's a description of what this file needs. Don't worry much about the details yet—it will make more sense as we get farther into the book.

name
    Name of the plugin—in this case, HelloWorld.

author
    Name of the author (that's you).

main
    Name of the package and class that Java will run to start this plugin (*package.classname*).

version
    Version number of your plugin. Start low, and increment the number each time you release a new version to the world.

commands
    A list of the user commands this plugin supports.

For each command, you have to specify three things:

- *command*: The command a user can type in

- *description*: A simple description of what the command does

- *usage*: A description of the command usage and any options

The format is important: the white space that's used to indent some lines needs to be there, using spaces, not tab characters. It all needs to line up, and the tags (names followed by a colon—":") need to be spelled just as shown here. You can find more details on the YAML format in Appendix 5, *Cheat Sheets*, on page 241.

Build and Install with build.sh

The commands you've been typing in your terminal window can also be saved into a file; that way you can run them over and over again without having to retype them each time. We call this a *shell script*, and it's another way to program the computer.

Building a plugin is only a little more complicated than compiling a single Java file as we did last chapter, but even so, it involves a lot of commands we don't want to have to type out every time.

To make it easier, I've made a shell script for you named build.sh that will do the three main steps:[2]

1. Use javac to compile the .java source to .class files.

2. Use jar to archive the class files and configuration file.

3. Copy the JAR file to the server.

After that, you'll need to stop and restart the server so it can pick up the changes.

The build script needs to know where your server directory is located. At the very top of the script, it says this:

```
MCSERVER=$HOME/Desktop/server
```

For most people that should just work if your server directory is located on your Desktop. If that doesn't work, you'll need to edit the build.sh file and change that directory so that the MCSERVER= points to your local Minecraft server directory. That MCSERVER= setting is how the script knows where to find the server.

Let's try it out and see what happens.

At your command line, change your current directory to the HelloWorld directory. From there, run the build.sh script. So for me, I can start anywhere and go to my home directory, then I can cd down into Desktop, then code, then HelloWorld:

```
$ cd
$ cd Desktop
$ cd code/HelloWorld
$ ./build.sh
```

(Remember, no matter how you actually get to your Desktop, I'll just show it as cd Desktop from now on for reference. You may need to do a cd ~/Desktop or start at your home directory and go down, depending on your particular system.)

You should see results that look a lot like this:

```
Compiling with javac...
Creating jar file...
Deploying jar to /Users/andy/Desktop/server/plugins...
Completed Successfully.
```

Check to see that the file really was installed in the server directory:

---

2. For larger projects, folks use tools like Ant, Maven, or Gradle when the build becomes more complex and has to manage dependencies among many parts. But that's overkill for our needs here.

```
$ cd Desktop
$ cd server/plugins
$ ls
HelloWorld.jar
```

Yup, the JAR file is in the server directory. Success!

If you get errors, here are a few things to check:

- If you see warning: [options] bootstrap class path not set in conjunction with -source 1.6, ignore it. It's just Java being picky. We'll cover how to take care of that later in the book.

- If you get the error ./build.sh: Permission denied you might need to type chmod +x build.sh to give the script executable permission.

- If you get the error package org.bukkit does not exist followed by a ton of other errors, it's not finding the server directory (see below).

- If you're seeing syntax errors, make sure you are using a fresh copy of the files downloaded from this book's website, with no local modifications.

- If everything compiles okay but you get an error trying to copy the JAR file, make sure the server directory is correct.

If the script is having trouble finding the server directory, edit build.sh and change the MCSERVER= directory name to the correct location of your Minecraft server.[3]

Once it compiles and installs, you are excellent! Now you have a compiled plugin, ready for the Minecraft server to use.

If your server is still running, it won't know about this new plugin. You have to either stop it and then restart it, like this:

```
$ cd ~/Desktop/server
$ ./start_minecraft
```

or use the reload command at the server console if it's already running:

```
>reload
08:47:32 [INFO] [HelloWorld] Loading HelloWorld v0.1
08:47:32 [INFO] [HelloWorld] Loaded.
08:47:32 [INFO] [HelloWorld] Enabling HelloWorld v0.1
08:47:32 [INFO] [HelloWorld] Starting up.
08:47:32 [INFO] Server permissions file permissions.yml is empty, ignoring it
08:47:32 [INFO] CONSOLE: Reload complete.
>
```

---

3. Make sure it's spelled correctly and starts with a "/" character so that you have the full path to your server starting at the root directory.

And there's the startup message from our new HelloWorld plugin. If you don't see any message from HelloWorld starting up, then your minecraft server can't find it. Make sure the HelloWorld.jar file is in the server's plugins directory, stop the server, and try starting it up again.

Once you're connected and in the Minecraft world, you can test out your fine new command from the client chat window. In the Minecraft game, just start typing /hello and see what happens. As soon as you type the "/" character, you'll see that you're typing in a chat window at the bottom of the screen. Press `Return` and...

...you should see our message appear in the server log console and in the game window. This is what it looks like in the server console:

```
14:47:58 [INFO] AndyHunt issued sever command: /hello
14:47:58 [INFO] [Server] That'sss a very niccce EVERYTHING you have there...
```

Getting around in Minecraft

In case you aren't familiar with the Minecraft graphical user interface (GUI), here are a couple of quick tips. You can check out some of the many YouTube tutorials or official docs for more.

The keys `W`, `A`, `S`, and `D` move you forward, backward, left, and right, respectively. Use the `Spacebar` to jump.

Use the mouse to control the direction you are facing.

You "hit" things with your left mouse button—for example, to strike with a sword or dig with a pickaxe or shovel.

You "use" items with your right mouse button—for example, placing an item or opening a door.

You type commands to Minecraft with a leading "/" character. You can change the game to creative mode with /gamemode c, and back to survival mode with /gamemode s.

Next Up

Congratulations! You just compiled and installed a plugin from source code, installed it on your local server, connected, and tested it out!

With that out of the way, we'll spend the next few chapters taking a deeper look at all the source code that makes a plugin, and see what makes Java tick so you can make your own plugins.

Your Growing Toolbox

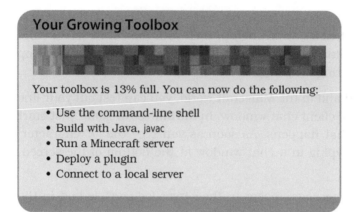

Your toolbox is 13% full. You can now do the following:

- Use the command-line shell
- Build with Java, javac
- Run a Minecraft server
- Deploy a plugin
- Connect to a local server

## CHAPTER 4

Plugins Have Variables, Functions, and Keywords

Your Toolbox

In this chapter we'll take care of a lot of the basics of writing Java code. With the new tools in your toolbox, you'll know the following:

- What the funny characters mean in Java
- How to use *variables* to hold number and character string values
- How to declare and use *functions*: lists of Java instructions
- How to control code with if, for, and while statements

As you may have noticed, there is a lot of text in the plugin source code that I haven't explained yet. Let's dig deeper into Java and take a look at what all that text means—it's the raw material of programming plugins.

As you saw in Chapter 3, *Build and Install a Plugin*, on page 31, a program in Java is just a text file. Look at the text in HelloWorld.java: there's a lot of sort-of English words, and some strange-looking punctuation. All of it means something, and the Java compiler is mighty picky when it's reading your text. First of all, spelling counts. Entity is not the same as Entitee. Player is not the same as player, so uppercase and lowercase matter, too. There are times when you use uppercase, and times you need to use lowercase.

Each of those odd characters you see has a special meaning, and they're used for different things. Here are some examples (don't worry much about the details yet):

//

Comment, used to leave a note for yourself or others. Java will ignore anything you type from after the double slash to the end of the line.

/* longer comment */

Used for longer comments, either on one line or spanning multiple lines.

( )

Parentheses, used when calling a function and passing data to it, like this: System.out.println("Hello, Creeper");.

[ ]

Brackets, used for choosing one item from a list of items, like this: second = myArray[3];.

{ }

Braces, used to mark the beginning and end of a section of code.

.

Dot, used to select a part of something. Most often you use this to select a function that's part of an object, like System.out.println() or player.getLocation().

;

Semicolon, used to mark the end of a code statement. Leaving the semi-colon off at the end of a line of code is a surefire way to make Java angry and have it spew hundreds of error messages at you.

Some words you type are special, and you have to use them the way Java says to. Other words you can make up yourself, and could be anything from ImmortalPlayer to rathead. So how does this all fit together?

To create a program or a plugin in Java, you use all these bits of text to create two different kinds of things: data and instructions. That's all there is to any computer program or to a Minecraft plugin. It's all just data and instructions. Here's how we work with them.

First I'll show you how you declare and use these things, and then you'll need to try it yourself in your very first plugin.

Keep Track of Data with Variables

Data are facts—things like your age or the color of your bicycle. To work with these facts in Java, you hold them in *variables*. A variable is a holder of data. Think of it like a small box you can put things in.

In Minecraft, we use variables to keep track of things like players in the game, a player's current health and location, and all the other data we need to know.

(In fact, you're going to add some variables to a piece of code in just a minute—a plugin that will build you a house.)

A variable is the box that holds that data. You can put a label on the box, but that's just a label for your convenience—it doesn't affect what's in the box.

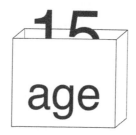

Here's how to use variables. For this example, we'll make a variable called age, and tell Java to set the value of that variable to 15, either in two steps or all in one step:

```
int age;
age = 15;
```

or

```
int age = 15;
```

The important part here is that you're telling Java the *type* of the variable you want to make—in this case, an integer whole number (no fractional part or decimal point), which is abbreviated as int.

There are lots of types in addition to int, including float and double, which hold fractional numbers (with decimal points); String, which holds a sequence of characters such as "Hello, World!"; types you can create yourself, such as NunChuck or CowBell; and types that Minecraft defines, such as Player and Location. Any time you declare a variable in Java, you need to specify the type for that variable. Java can't guess; you need to tell it.

You can create the variable and assign its value in one step, or create the variable first and then assign it later. In either case you can put a new value in that variable any time you want.

This is okay:

```
int age = 15;
age = 39;
age = 21;
```

However, you can't declare it a second time. This won't work:

```
int age = 15;
int age = 21;
// Error!
```

Instead, only declare it as int age once, then use age = to change the value if needed.

Now, just because you "labeled the box" *age* doesn't mean it really has to hold an age. There's nothing to stop you from putting some other number in that box:

```
int age = 2048;
```

That's perfectly legal Java code, as 2048 is a perfectly reasonable number. It might be okay for the age of a historical relic, but it's not a realistic age for a person. Setting that age for a person would be stupid, but there are no laws against stupidity. That means it's up to you to give variables names that make sense. Renaming this variable to something like ageInYears might make more sense, to avoid problems like the famous crash of the Mars climate orbiter.[1]

Java does try to keep you from mixing apples and oranges. Although it doesn't know that you're using an int as a "human age," it does know the difference between things like an int, a float, a String, and so on. And it won't let you mix up those types. If you've declared that a variable should hold an integer, you can't try to store a String in it. This will throw an error:

```
int age = "Old enough to know better";   // Error!
```

We tried to store a string of characters in an int. That won't work, and Java will complain. You can't go the other way either. Here we're trying to store an integer value (42) into a variable declared to hold a string of characters (a String):

```
String answer = 42;    // Error!
```

But for common types such as numbers and strings, there are ways you *can* convert things back and forth as needed, if it makes sense. For instance, suppose you read a numeric value from something the user typed, and it was given to you as a String named str. You can make it an int like this:

```
String str = "1066";
int value = Integer.parseInt(str);
// value is now set to 1066 as a number
```

---

1. One set of programmers used metric units and the other used Imperial units. Oops: http://mars.jpl.nasa.gov/msp98/news/mco990930.html

So you can convert, but you have to do it yourself; Java won't guess for you. There's a list of common type conversions, including ones we haven't covered here, in Appendix 5, *Cheat Sheets*, on page 241.

Let's try that out.

Plugin: BuildAHouse

I've got a plugin already set up for you; all you need to do is declare some variables and you can give the /buildahouse command.

First make your way to the downloaded code, into the BuildAHouse plugin:

```
$ cd Desktop
$ cd code/BuildAHouse/src/buildahouse
$ ls
BuildAHouse.java MyHouse.java
```

You're going to edit the file MyHouse.java, which is one small part of this whole plugin. Right now it looks like this:

```
BuildAHouse/src/buildahouse/MyHouse.java
package buildahouse;
public class MyHouse {
  public static void build_me() {
    // Declare width
    // Set width to the number of blocks
    // Declare height
    // Set height to the number of blocks
    BuildAHouse.buildMyHouse(width, height);
  }
}
```

If you try to compile and install that with ./build.sh like we did with HelloWorld, you'll get two errors:

```
$ cd Desktop
$ cd code/src/BuildAHouse
$ ./build.sh
Compiling with javac...
src/buildahouse/MyHouse.java:10: cannot find symbol
symbol  : variable width
location: class buildahouse.MyHouse
    BuildAHouse.buildMyHouse(width, height);
                             ^
src/buildahouse/MyHouse.java:10: cannot find symbol
symbol  : variable height
location: class buildahouse.MyHouse
    BuildAHouse.buildMyHouse(width, height);
                                    ^
2 errors
```

And that's your first mission: declare and set an int variable named width and an int variable named height, and set them to something reasonable for a house, perhaps no smaller than 5 blocks high and 5 blocks wide. Or maybe 10×10 if you're feeling spacious.

Delete those comment lines and replace them with your two variables for width and height. Save the file, and then go ahead and run build.sh again:

```
$ ./build.sh
Compiling with javac...
Creating jar file...
Deploying jar to /Users/andy/Desktop/server/plugins...
Completed Successfully.
```

Stop and restart your server, then connect (or reconnect) your Minecraft client.

Pick a nice-looking spot in the Minecraft landscape, and type the command /buildahouse. Bam! You are now inside your brand-new, creeper-proof house, which was built to the exact dimensions you specified with your width and height variables. A right-click will open the door, by the way.

Different Kinds of Numbers

Java makes a distinction between *integer* whole numbers (with no decimal point, like 8) and *floating-point* numbers with a fractional part (with a decimal point), like 10.125.

For plain old whole numbers, you use an int, like we've seen.

Floating-point numbers can be float or double. A double is larger and can store numbers much more precisely, but at the cost of needing more space and power to manage. But computers are fast and have plenty of storage these days, so almost everyone just uses double any time they need a double-precision, floating-point, fractional number.

When you type a number with a decimal point in Java, it assumes you've typed a double:

```
3.1415 // assumed to be a double
```

But if you really need the number to be a float, you have to stick the letter f on the number:

```
3.1415f // now it's a float, not a double.
```

We'll need to use floats in just a minute to play a sound effect, because that's what Bukkit requires to set the volume and pitch of the sound. And in general you might need a floating-point number more often than you think.

For example, let's look at a simple division problem. In Java, you write division using the "/" character (instead of ÷), so to divide the number 5 in half you'd write 5 / 2. Depending on how you do the division, though, the answer might surprise you.

- 5 / 2 is 2 (just 2, nothing more)
- But 5 / 2.0 is 2.5, as you would expect
- 5.0 / 2.0 is also 2.5

Why is 5 divided by 2 equal to only 2? On a math quiz, that would be wrong. But we're not dividing real numbers here; we're dividing int numbers, so the result is another whole number; another int. There are no fractions at all.

If you want the answer to include fractions, then at least one of the numbers involved has to have a fractional part. That's why 5 divided by 2.0 (note the extra .0) gives us the real answer of 2.5 (two and a half). This time, we're using an int (5) and a double (2.0).

Sometimes you won't care about fractional parts or remainders (leftovers). If you're calculating something that doesn't *have* fractional parts, then all-int math is just fine. Half of a Player or a Cow doesn't make sense (unless you're making hamburger). But if you need fractional answers, then at least one of the numbers involved has to be a double or a float.

Here's a handy list of several of the common math operators you might need:

Addition:	+
Subtraction:	-
Multiplication:	*
Division:	/

They work just as you'd expect, but there are some handy shortcuts.

```
int health = 50;
health = health + 10;
```

is the same as

```
int health = 50;
health += 10; // Same thing
```

Both result in health being set to 60.

You can use expressions like += and -= to change the value of a variable without having to repeat its name. Hey, less typing. I like it.[2]

If you're just adding 1 or subtracting 1, then there's an even easier way of typing it:

```
int health = 50;

health--; // Subtracts 1 from health
health++; // Adds 1 to health
```

In case you want to get really fancy and use more-advanced math, including trig functions like sine and cosine, constants like pi, and that sort of thing, Java has libraries with all of that ready for you to use.

Strings of Characters

There's more to the world than numbers, though. While your government or school may know you as a string of numbers like #132-54-7843, your friends call you by a name that's a string of characters, like "Jack" or "Jill" or "Notch."

In Java, you use a String type to handle strings of characters. We'll use strings in Minecraft a lot, for names of players, names of files, messages—any kind of text data that can change value, like a number does.

To specify a string in code literally, you put it inside double quotes, which looks "like this". We'll use strings in our plugins and look more at what you can do with strings as we go along.

---

2. The best programming languages make you type the fewest characters to get something done while still making sense.

You can add strings together using a plus sign:

```
String first = "Jack";
String middle = "D.";
String last = "Ripper";

String name = first + " " + middle + " " + last;
// Now name will be "Jack D. Ripper"
```

Note that strings are your *data*, which is different from the characters we use to give Java instructions (our program *code*).

Try This Yourself

It's time to try out some of these ideas: we'll make a simple plugin from scratch.

In the BuildAHouse plugin, I had a bunch of code that you didn't see that actually did the house-building, and all you had to do was declare a few variables. But now you're going to make *an entire plugin from scratch*, all by yourself.

To keep things a little on the simple side, at first you're just going to print out some values. In fact, let's call this plugin Simple.

First you need to make a Simple directory for the new plugin, with a src/ subdirectory, a src/simple subdirectory, and with a plugin.yml and build.sh, just like we had in HelloWorld. Since you might be doing this a lot, I've made a shell script named mkplugin.sh that will get you started.

Run it with the name of the plugin you want to create, and it will make the directories underneath your current directory and start you off with barebones Java code:

```
$ cd Desktop
$ code/mkplugin.sh Simple
$ cd Simple
$ ls
bin/        build.sh  dist/        plugin.yml src/
$ cd src
$ ls
simple/
$ cd simple
$ ls
Simple.java
```

The file Simple.java lives up to its name; it's doesn't actually *do* anything.

You'll be adding some code in between where it says Put your code after this line
and ...and finish your code before this line, as shown at the bottom of the following
listing.

Open this file (Desktop/Simple/src/simple/Simple.java) in your text editor and get ready
to type.

Plugin: Simple

```
Simple/src/simple/Simple.java
package simple;

import java.util.logging.Logger;
import org.bukkit.command.Command;
import org.bukkit.command.CommandSender;
import org.bukkit.entity.Player;
import org.bukkit.plugin.Plugin;
❶ import org.bukkit.plugin.java.JavaPlugin;

public class Simple extends JavaPlugin {
  public static Logger log = Logger.getLogger("Minecraft");
  public void onEnable() {
    log.info("[Simple] Start up.");
  }
  public void onReload() {
    log.info("[Simple] Server reloaded.");
  }
  public void onDisable() {
    log.info("[Simple] Server stopping.");
  }
  public boolean onCommand(CommandSender sender, Command command,
                           String commandLabel, String[] args) {
    if (commandLabel.equalsIgnoreCase("simple")) {
      if (sender instanceof Player) {
        Player me = (Player)sender;
        // Put your code after this line:
❷
        // ...and finish your code before this line.
        return true;
        }
    }
    return false;
  }
}
```

Don't worry about all that extra program text yet. We'll talk about that more
as we go along. For now just put new code on the lines as shown, and it will
work fine. Here's what you're going to do:

First, add an import statement at the top of the file, after the other import lines at ❶. Type in the following:

```
import org.bukkit.Sound;
```

Next, after where it says // Put your code after this line: at ❷, do this:

1. Create an integer variable named myAge and set it to whatever your age is.

2. Make another integer variable named twiceMyAge and set it equal to myAge multiplied by 2.

3. Create a float variable named volume and set it equal to 0.1.

4. Create a float variable named pitch and set it equal to 1.0.

5. Create a double (floating-point) variable named dayOnIo and set it equal to 152853.5047. That's how many seconds a day lasts on Jupiter's moon, Io.[3]

6. Create a string named myName and set it to your name.

7. Display each of these values by sending a chat message to the player, using me.sendMessage(*string msg*). For example, to display your name, type this:

    ```
    me.sendMessage("My name is " + myName);
    ```

Always start the message with a quoted string (like "My name is ") and the plus sign, then add in your variable. Don't forget the semicolon at the end of each statement.

Finally, add a line to play a sound effect, using the float values you just declared:

```
me.playSound(me.getLocation(), Sound.GHAST_SCREAM, volume, pitch);
```

Save the file and then run the build.sh in the Simple directory.

```
$ cd Desktop
$ cd Simple
$ ./build.sh
Compiling with javac...
Creating jar file...
Deploying jar to /Users/andy/Desktop/server/plugins...
Completed Successfully.
```

Stop and restart your server, then connect from the Minecraft client. Run your new command, /simple, and marvel at the messages on your console (and the sound effect!).

---

3. Io is pretty cool. It has more than 400 active volcanoes. See http://en.wikipedia.org/wiki/Io_(moon).

Once that works, try changing the values for volume and pitch. Crank volume up to 1.0f for a terrifying scream. For pitch, try a very low value, like 0.1f for more of a growl, and higher (10.0f?) for a piercing shriek.

After you type the new value in the Java source code, don't forget to take these steps:

1. Save the file.
2. Compile and install with ./build.sh.
3. Stop and restart the server.
4. Reconnect your Minecraft client.
5. Type /simple in the client and enjoy the display and sound effect.

Here's what mine looks like:

(No, I'm not *really* 99, but I'm not going to tell you my real age, or my bank account number, or....)

If you need to see my code for hints, take a look at code/MySimple/src/mysimple/MySimple.java.

Organize Instructions into Functions

So now that you can store all kinds of data in variables, next you need to learn how to write instructions to do fun actions with all that data, from printing messages to flinging flaming cows in Minecraft.

As you've seen, you can also tell Java to do things. In Java, you organize lines of code (instructions) inside a pair of curly braces, like { and }. You give that section of code a name, and those instructions will be run in order, one line after another. We call that a *function* (sometimes we'll call it a *method*; for now they mean mostly the same thing).

Why do we bother with functions at all? Couldn't we just have one big list of instructions and be done? Well yes, we could, but it can get very confusing that way.

Think of a list of instructions and ingredients to make a cake with frosting:

- Blend together and bake
- Flour
- Butter
- Sugar
- Milk
- Eggs
- Vanilla
- Cocoa powder
- Confectioner's sugar
- Butter
- Milk
- Mix together and spread on cake

Which part of the list is for the cake itself, and which is for the frosting? Maybe the frosting part starts at the cocoa powder. Then again, maybe it's a chocolate cake base with a vanilla frosting. The point is, it's hard to tell. It might work as is, but if you need to figure out what's going wrong it will be very hard. And if you need to make any changes, it will be harder still. Suppose you have some strange relatives who want their cake to have an orange-apricot glaze instead of chocolate frosting (I did mention they were strange). Where do you go in and make the changes?

Instead of one big list, suppose we had broken it up into two steps like this, where each one lists the ingredients and steps for just that part of the cake-making process:

- makeChocolateCake
- makeVanillaFrosting

Oh, now it's easy to see. If there's a problem with the cake, you know where to look. If you want to do a different icing, you can easily change it to this:

- makeChocolateCake
- makeOrangeApricotGlaze

That's pretty much the idea behind functions. They are a way to gather instructions and data together into groups that make sense. But functions have an extra fun ability: you can use the same function (list of instructions) with slightly different data. For example, you could have one function named makeFrosting and call it with different flavorings:[4]

```
makeFrosting(flavor)
    sugar
    butter
    mix in "flavor"
    spread on cake
```

Then you could use that same function, passing in slightly different data as needed:

```
makeFrosting(vanilla)
makeFrosting(chocolate)
```

That's why we use functions: to make long lists of instructions (code) easier to read and understand, and to reuse sets of instructions with slightly different data.

You could say functions make programming a piece a cake. But back to Minecraft.

Defining Functions in Java

Every bit of code we write in Java will be in a function; that's how Java works. We've seen functions already, right from the very first plugin.

Back in the HelloWorld plugin, we declared a bunch of functions that Minecraft calls when the game is running: the short ones for onEnable and onDisable, and the main one for onCommand.

We call these particular functions in a plugin the *entry points*. These are the functions that the Minecraft server will call when it needs to. You can provide code, if necessary, for all of these—or just for some, depending on your plugin.

onLoad	Called when the server loads up the plugin, but before it's enabled
onEnable	Called when the server enables this plugin
onDisable	Called when the server disables this plugin or shuts down
onCommand	Called when the user types in a command in the Minecraft chat with a slash, "/"

---

4. When you write out an idea that's codelike but isn't really a programming language, we call it *pseudo-code*. Just in case you see that term somewhere, now you know what it means.

In our usual onCommand, we're calling other functions. Here's the section from HelloWorld:

```
public boolean onCommand(CommandSender sender, Command command,
                    String commandLabel, String[] args) {
  if (commandLabel.equalsIgnoreCase("hello")) {
    String msg = "[Server] That'sss a very niccce EVERYTHING you have there...";
    getServer().broadcastMessage(msg);
    return true;
  }
  return false;
}
```

There's a call to equalsIgnoreCase(), a call to getServer(), and a call to broadcastMessage().

Java knows you're calling a function because of the parentheses after the name of the function. It will expect that someone defined a function based on the name and it will give that function your message. We call the stuff you pass to functions *arguments*. When arguments are given to a function, the function knows them as *parameters*. We say the values are *passed in* or the function is *called with* these values. All these words and phrases are referring to the same concept.

For example, the getServer() function doesn't take any arguments. You still use the parentheses characters, (and), so that Java knows it's a function. That getServer() call returns something (I'm guessing it's a Server), and we're calling the Server's broadcastMessage() function, passing in a string argument named msg. With me so far?

You can define a function yourself. Here's an example that defines a new function named castIntoBlackHole. Watch closely, because you'll be doing this on your own next.

```
public static void castIntoBlackHole(String playerName)
{
    // Do something interesting with the player here...
}
```

There is a bit more noise here than in the cake example. Let's see what all this stuff means.

- *public* means that any other part of the program can use it, which for now you want to be the case.

- *static* means you can call this function all by itself (not like a plugin; we'll see the difference and what that means in the next chapter).

- *void* means this function is going to run a couple of instructions, but not give you any data back—it won't "return" any values to the caller.

- *castIntoBlackHole* is a name we just made up; it is the name of the function, and the () characters indicate that it is a function and will take the arguments we've listed. You always need the parentheses, even if the function doesn't take any arguments.

In this case, it takes one argument we named *playerName*, which it expects to be a String. For each argument your function accepts, you need to specify both a variable name and its type. Your function can take multiple arguments; you use a comma to separate each pair made up of the type and variable (like we did back in the onCommand in HelloWorld).

The braces, { }, are where the code for this function goes. You can put as much code in a function as you want, but a good rule of thumb is to not make it any longer than maybe 30 lines. Shorter is always better; if you find yourself writing very long functions, you will want to break those up into several smaller functions to help make the code easier to read.

Here's an example of a function that returns a value; it will triple any number you give it:

```
public static double multiplyByThree(double amt)
{
    double result = amt * 3.0;

    return result;
}
```

This function calculates a result and uses the return keyword to return that value to the caller. You would call the multiplyByThree function and assign the returned value to variables like this:

```
double myResult = multiplyByThree(10.0);

double myOtherResult = multiplyByThree(1.25);
```

Now myResult will be 30.0, and myOtherResult will be 3.75.

Try This Yourself

You're going to write a function named howlong() to calculate how many seconds you've been alive:

```
public static int howlong(int years) {
  // Write this function...
}
```

The function will take a number of years and return a number of seconds. We'll cheat a bit to make this easy, and convert years to seconds. (See the footnote if you need a hint.)[5]

You'll add this new function to the Simple plugin, and call the function to print out its value just like we did with your name and age.

Define the function where the top arrow is pointing:

```
   }
public void onDisable() {
   Log.info("[MySimple] Server stopping.");
   }


   ←——————— Add function definition here


public boolean onCommand(CommandSender sender, Command command,
                         String commandLabel, String[] args) {
   if (commandLabel.equalsIgnoreCase("mysimple")) {
    if (sender instanceof Player) {
     Player me = (Player)sender;
     // Put your code after this line:

     int my_age = 99;
     int my_age_doubled = my_age * 2;
     double day_on_io = 152853.5047;
     String my_name = "Andy Hunt";
     |
       ←——————— And call it here
     me.sendMessage("My age " + my_age);
     me.sendMessage("My age doubled " + my_age_doubled);
     me.sendMessage("A day on Io " + day_on_io);
     me.sendMessage("My name " + my_name);

     // ...and finish your code before this line.
     return true;
     }
```

And add the call to the function howlong down where my cursor is, at the second arrow. Assign it to an extra-big integer (a long) and pass in an age (I'll use 10 here) like this:

```
long secondsOld = howlong(10);
```

Then print it out to the player just like the rest of the sendMessage() calls do.

---

5. In other words, multiply the number of years by the number of days in a year, multiplied by the number of hours in a day, multiplied by the number of minutes in an hour, and finally by the number of seconds in a minute.

If I compile and install it with ./build.sh, stop the server and restart it (or reload the server), and then run the /simple command in Minecraft, my test with 10 years gets me 315,360,000 seconds:

```
$ cd Desktop
$ cd Simple
$ ./build.sh
Compiling with javac...
Creating jar file...
Deploying jar to /Users/andy/Desktop/server/plugins...
Completed Successfully.
```

Did you get the same answer? You can see the full source code that I put together at code/Simple2/src/simple2/Simple2.java.

Note that there are a couple of different ways to accomplish even this simple function. There usually isn't just one "correct" way to write code.

That's a good start, but there's more to Java than just variables and functions. The Java language has certain special *keywords* that you can use to direct how and when to run various bits of code. We've seen some of these already, including public and static, which describe the code. Now we'll look at keywords, including if, for, and while, that let you control how code is run.

Use a for Loop to Repeat Code

Computers are much better at repetitive tasks than humans are; you can tell the computer to do something ten times in a row and it will do *exactly* that, ten times, a hundred times, a million times, whatever you want. One way to do the same thing a bunch of times is to use a for loop. for is a Java keyword that lets you loop over a section of code a fixed number of times.

The for loop is a basic control structure in Java—a way to control the order of execution of your lines of code. If you need to make a bunch of blocks or spawn a lot of creepers in a Minecraft world, you'll use a for loop. If you need to loop through all the players that are currently online, you'll probably use a for loop (although there are nicer ways of doing that, which we'll see a little bit later).

For example, this snippet of code from the guts of a plugin will spawn ten pigs at your location. Saddle up!

```
//... somewhere inside a plugin:
for (int i=0; i < 10; i++) {
  spawn(myLocation, Pig.class);
}
```

In this case, the for statement will run the instructions in its braces ten times, so spawn will be called ten times, creating ten pigs.

The for statement has three parts inside the (), separated by semicolons. Here's what they do:

int i=0;

> The first part declares and *initializes* the looping variable. Here we'll use i as our loop counter, and it always starts off at 0—you'll see why later, but Java always counts starting at 0.

i < 10;

> The loop *test*. This tells us when to keep going with the loop (and more importantly, when to stop). This loop will keep running the code in the following braces as long as i is less than 10. Right now, that would mean forever, so we need the third part:

i++;

> The loop *increment*. This is the part that keeps the loop moving along. Here we are incrementing the variable i by 1 each time through the loop. Remember, i++ is shorthand for i=i+1. Either way, you are taking the value of i, adding 1 to it, and saving that back as the new value of i (you can use that kind of shortcut anywhere, by the way, not just in loops).

Use an if Statement to Make Decisions

An if statement lets you make decisions in code and optionally run a piece of code depending on whether a condition is true. This is how you make a computer "think."

It's just like the real world. We run on "if" statements all the time. If your age is >= 16, you are allowed to drive. If the door is unlocked, you can open it, or else you cannot. If the command given to Minecraft is equal to "hello", then send a message. If your health drops to zero, you're dead.

This is what it looks like in Java:

```
if (something) {
    // run this code...
}
```

The part in parentheses (something) can be anything that turns out true or false; in other words, a Boolean condition (more on that in just a second).

If you need to, you can also put code in to run if something is true *and* specify what to run if it's false:

```
if (something) {
    // run this code if something is true
} else {
    // run this code if something is false
}
```

For example, here's a fragment of code that will say something different depending on whether you're named Notch, by checking a String variable myname:

```
if (myname.equalsIgnoreCase("Notch")) {
    say("Greetings from Notch!");
} else {
    say("Notch isn't here.");
}
```

if statements (with or without the else) are critical to programming: that's how you can get the computer to make decisions and pretend to "think." Pretty powerful stuff, but really simple to use.

Compare Stuff with Boolean Conditions

if statements decide what to run based on whether something is true. What's true?

Besides numbers and strings that we've seen, you can also make a variable that keeps track of whether something is turned on, like a toggle switch.[6] In Minecraft, we'll use this to determine all sorts of things: if a player is on the ground or not, if a string matches another string, whether to use a game event or ignore it, and much more.

---

6. Photo by Jason Zack at en.wikipedia

Java calls this kind of variable a boolean, and it can be assigned true or false, or you can give it math expressions using any of these operators, all of which return either true or false:

==   Equal to *(two equals signs)*

!=   Not equal to

!   Not *(so "not true" is false, and "not false" is true)*

<   Less than

>   Greater than

<=   Less than or equal to

>=   Greater than or equal to

&&   And *(true if both things are true)*

|| Or *(true if one thing is true)*

For example, given these variables

```
int a = 10;
int b = 5;
String h = "Hello";
boolean result = true;
boolean badone = false;
```

Java will figure out these comparisons:

- a == 10 is true
- b == 6 is false
- a < 20 is true
- b >= 5 is true
- a > 100 is false
- result is true
- !result is false *(pronounced "not result"—"not" returns the opposite of a value)*
- result && badone is false *(pronounced "and"—true only if both are true)*
- result || badone is true *(pronounced "or"—true if either is true)*

But this next one won't do what you think it should; it will not be true:

```
h == "Hello"; // Gotcha!
```

That one is tricky. For strings and objects (more on that in the next chapter), you want to use an equals function instead of the double equals sign (==), like this:

```
h.equals("Hello"); // is true
// or
h.equalsIgnoreCase("hELLO"); // is true
```

We've used equalsIgnoreCase before, to check the user's chat command in HelloWorld, and we'll use it a lot more as we go along.

Use a while Loop to Repeat Based on a Condition

You use a for loop when you need to run a piece of code a fixed number of times. But what if you aren't certain just how many times you need to loop? What if you wanted to loop as long as needed, as long as some other condition is still true? In that case, you'd use a while loop. A while loop will keep executing a piece of code as long as the Boolean condition is true:

```
while (stillHungry) {
    // ...
    // Something better set stillHungry to false!
}
```

In a way, it's kind of a mix between an if statement and a for loop: it loops over code the same way a for loop does, but it keeps looping as long as the condition is true, testing the condition like an if does.

And yes, if you forget to change the value to false, while will continue forever, and your entire Minecraft server will be stuck until you kill it or reboot or lose power, whichever comes first.

Try This Yourself

Now it's time for you to create a loop yourself. Let's go back to MyHouse.java, in ~/Desktop/code/BuildAHouse/src/buildahouse, and instead of creating just one house with this call:

```
BuildAHouse.buildMyHouse(width, height);
```

write a for loop that will run ten times, with the buildMyHouse call in the body of the for loop. That will make ten houses. Your own mini city!

Edit MyHouse.java and add your for loop, and then build and install the plugin as usual:

```
$ cd Desktop
$ cd BuildAHouse
$ ./build.sh
Compiling with javac...
Creating jar file...
Deploying jar to /Users/andy/Desktop/server/plugins...
Completed Successfully.
```

Stop and restart your server, connect with your client, and type /buildahouse again. You now have a set of ten row houses.

Next Up

In this chapter you've learned something about Java syntax, from parentheses to squiggly brackets and semicolons. You know how to declare Java variables and use them to store important information. You can write Java functions that will act on your data, and you can control functions with if, for, and while statements.

Next we'll look at what happens when you package variables and functions together to make objects—the heart of a large system like Minecraft. Minecraft objects let you create plugins to manipulate everything in the Minecraft environment, from creepers to cows. Let's see how.

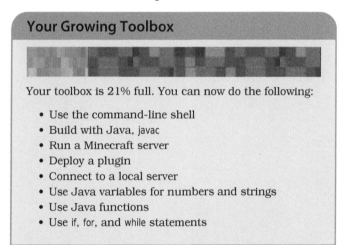

Your Growing Toolbox

Your toolbox is 21% full. You can now do the following:

- Use the command-line shell
- Build with Java, javac
- Run a Minecraft server
- Deploy a plugin
- Connect to a local server
- Use Java variables for numbers and strings
- Use Java functions
- Use if, for, and while statements

## CHAPTER 5

Plugins Have Objects

Your Toolbox

In this chapter we'll cover a bunch of new tools for the Java language:

- Use *objects*: bundles of variables and functions
- Use the right *import* for a package
- Use new to create objects

You may have heard of object-oriented programming or that Java is an "object-oriented language." That's what we're talking about in this chapter: using objects to represent elements of the Minecraft game, from players to cows.

You can do anything in code that you could do in the game, and then some. This comes down to working with mostly three kinds of things: blocks, items, and entities.

Everything in Minecraft Is an Object

The Minecraft world is filled with *blocks*. Every location in the game has a block, which might be made of air or another material. Blocks can exist in the world and in a player's inventory. Anything in a player's inventory is represented by an *item*.

In this world of blocks you have *entities*, which includes players, creepers, and cows. Items in motion are also entities—an arrow in flight or a snowball or a potion that's being flung. And all of these are objects.

Everything in our plugins is an object: locations, blocks, entities, cows, creepers, players, and even the plugin itself. All objects, all the time.

So now the real fun starts! You have variables holding data, and you have instructions expressed as functions, including some control statements to repeat bits of code or make decisions, and now we'll see how to put them all together into objects.

Try This Yourself

Let's try a little demonstration of objects in Minecraft. In the downloaded code there's a plugin called NameCow. Go there now and install that plugin:

```
$ cd Desktop
$ cd code/NameCow
$ ./build.sh
Compiling with javac...
Creating jar file...
Deploying jar to /Users/andy/Desktop/server/plugins...
Completed Successfully.
```

Stop and restart your server, connect your client, and you'll be able to run the new namecow command. This command will spawn a new cow and give it a name. In the Minecraft client, type the command followed by that cow's name:

```
/namecow Bessie
/namecow Elise
/namecow Babe
```

You'll see these cows appear in the game, and when you look at each one, you'll see its individual name appear.

This plugin spawns a new `Cow` object each time you run it. Each cow you spawn has internal variables that keep track of its unique state: the cow's own name, its position in the Minecraft world, its health, and so on.

While it's important that each cow is represented by its own separate object, that's not a good enough reason to use objects. So why do we use objects at all? There is a deeper reason.

Why Bother Using Objects?

Imagine you are a god of your own universe. You have spent a few eons arranging every quark, every atom, every molecule, all the way up to planets and galaxies, just the way you want it. Now the whole thing spins up, and you're responsible for every single subatomic particle in the whole universe, all at once. Even as a godlike being, trying to keep the universe going by dealing with every electron or every quark or even every molecule is just too much work (not to mention incredibly boring).

So instead, you deal with problems on the scale in which they occur. If it's a problem with a planet in the wrong spot, you move the planet. If you need to fiddle with a galaxy, you fiddle with the galaxy—not with every planet, and certainly not with every life form on every planet in every system.

Although it might sound grandiose, creating a program is very much like that. You're a very powerful creator of your own little universe. Maybe not exactly godlike, but you do have to face that same issue of dealing with things at a very low level, like atoms or molecules, and at a very high level, like creatures, mountains, planets, and galaxies. All at once—like in Figure 4, *Zoom in and out, from atoms to galaxies*, on page 68. When programming, you often have to zoom in to "atoms" and zoom out to "galaxies." They're all connected and have to make sense.

That's why we write code using objects. It's a way to organize data (in variables) and behavior (in functions) so that when we want to deal with a cow, we can treat it like a cow and not have to deal with each of the millions of atoms that make up said cow—or a biome, or a world, or a torch.

Even better, we can write code so that only a `Cow` has functions and data a cow needs. There's nothing worse than having assorted functions spilling out all over the place—you might end up with a torch that moos or a cow that lights up. Worse still, you'll end up with a huge pile of functions where you're not really sure *which* function can work with which piles of data.

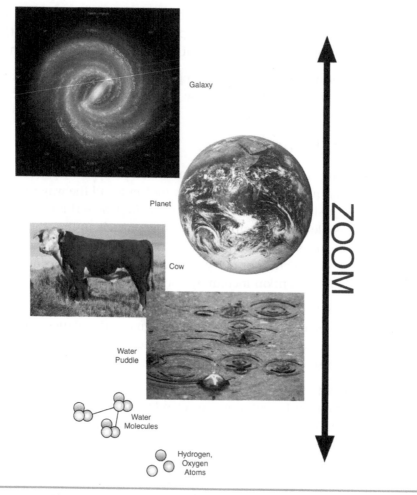

Figure 4—Zoom in and out, from atoms to galaxies.

For example, a Cow object in Minecraft has a lot of functions you can call. Here are a few of them:

- teleport(Location *location*)
- setFireTicks(int *ticks*)
- setBaby()
- setAdult()
- setBreed(boolean *canBreed*)

It also maintains some internal state: some variables to keep track of that individual cow's location, whether it's on fire, whether it's a baby or an adult, and so on.

These are all fine things you can do with a Cow object. But they wouldn't all make sense for a player, or an arrow, or a tree. Player objects can't breed, and you can't turn a Player into a baby, even if the player is acting like one.

You want to keep cow things in the Cow object, arrow things in the Arrow object, and so on. If you don't, then things can get awfully confusing awfully fast, and you might end up writing a pile of code that you can no longer understand or work with. So this is really just a matter of good hygiene, like keeping milk in the milk carton in the fridge, and not storing it in the pretzel bag in the closet. You don't even want to mix corn chips with potato chips, to continue with this metaphor.

Keeping separate things separate in different objects is the easy part.

The hardest aspect of programming is this problem of having to deal with very low-level details and very high-level details at the same time. We call these *levels of abstraction*. Let's face it: when you're writing code to deal with a player in Minecraft, it's not the actual person playing the game. Somewhere there is an actual person, sitting there, sweating, eating chips and listening to loud music. Your piece of code is an abstract representation of that real-life player; an abstraction that includes the data and behavior you need for the game.

And just as in the real world, each abstraction can contain parts. So you can choose to focus on molecules or planets as you need to—or in software, on the molecule objects or planet objects. You can zoom in and out to the level you need to be at, and work with the parts you want.

Let's take a closer look at what that means in Minecraft and Java.

Combine Data and Instructions into Objects

Suppose you were to write a game like Minecraft from scratch. You'd want to have a bunch of players in the game. Each one would have its own name, inventory, health points, and so on, but the structure of each player would be the same.

That is, every player object would have the same collection of variables (name, health, location, and so on) and the same functions that you'd want to run (set this player's health, teleport the player to a new location, that sort of thing). That's where objects come in. You'd create an object in Java to represent each player in the system. You'd write code to do things to a player, and that code would work no matter which specific player you were using at the time. That's exactly what the Minecraft folks did. Here's how the magic works.

In Java, you can define a pile of variables and a bunch of code that uses those variables, sort of like defining a recipe. You can then create and use an object that's built from that recipe. Java calls this kind of recipe a *class*. From that class recipe, Java will make running objects. Look at the following figure; here you have a few variables and some functions for a sample Player class, and some objects it can make.

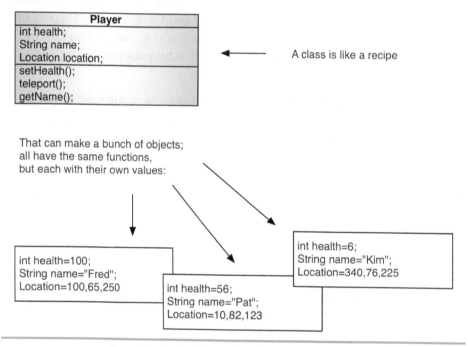

Figure 5—A class is a recipe for making objects.

It's just like building objects from Lego blocks: the blocks may all be the same, but when you follow the printed instructions that come with the kit, you can build a spaceship.

For instance, Minecraft keeps a pile of interesting data and functions related to each player who's online. Its "recipe" is defined by the class org.bukkit.entity.Player, which builds objects for an individual Player. Note that before you can use Player in your code, you must add an import statement at the very top of the file—in this case you'd do an import org.bukkit.entity.Player.

So how can we get at one of these player objects?

The Minecraft server knows who's online at any point, so we can ask the server for a list of Player objects. Or we can ask for a specific user by name, and it will give us a single Player object. Here's how.

Within a plugin, you can get access to the server using the function named getServer. That will give you an object representing the server. Once you have the server object, you can ask it for the player you want. You use getPlayer and call it with the name of the player you want.

That sequence of instructions looks like the following. (We're going to look at this in bits and pieces first, and end up with a complete running example.)

You start off with the imports that define the class recipes you'll be using:

```
// Up top
import org.bukkit.entity.Player;
import org.bukkit.Server;
```

Then later, in your plugin code, you can use variables of those types (Player and Server):

```
Server myserver = getServer();
Player fred = getPlayer("fred1024");
```

Imports

Each object recipe in Java lives in a package, like java.util or org.bukkit.entity, or something like that. You have to declare this package in an import statement at the very top of the Java source code file.

If you forget, you'll get an error from javac that says something like this:

cannot find symbol

You need to look in the Bukkit documentation or the Java documentation to find the full package name. We'll use a lot of the common ones in our examples, for Player, Server, Location, Entity, and various Java libraries. For your convenience, these are all listed in Appendix 7, *Common Imports*, on page 253.

Assuming that "fred1024" is online at the moment, we now have a variable named fred that represents the Player object. If Fred wasn't online, then the fred variable would be equal to the special value null, which is Java-speak for "there ain't one"—in other words, fred is not set to any object at all.[1]

Objects have parts. They contain stuff. An int, like 5, is just the number five. It can't do anything else; it can't store anything else alongside it. It just is what it is. But objects have functions and variables that you access with a period (.).

---

1. If fred was null and you tried to execute a function from fred, like fred.isSneaking(), you'd get an error and your plugin would crash.

So with fred in hand, you can get—and set—data for that player, using the period (.) to indicate which function or variable you want inside that object. Here are a few snippets of code that show what that looks like:

```
// Is fred sneaking?
boolean sneaky = fred.isSneaking();

// Hungry yet?
int fredsFood = fred.getFoodLevel();

// Make him hungry!
fred.setFoodLevel(0);

// Where's fred?
Location myloc = fred.getLocation();
```

The Player object has a function named isSneaking(), which returns a true or false, depending on whether that player is in sneaking mode.

Remember, that's the kind of thing you can use in an if statement:

```
if (fred.isSneaking()) {
    fred.setFireTicks(20); // Set him on fire!
}
```

There's also a getFoodLevel() function that returns an int telling you how hungry that player is. You can set the player's food level as well. The last snippet here shows how to get the player's current location in the world.

As you might guess, objects contain internal variables that their functions work with. For instance, in these examples the Player object for Fred has a location stored internally. We can get the value of Fred's location, we can set a new value, but at all times Fred has his own internal copy of his current location.

You can also run some interesting commands. For instance, you can execute a command as if you were Fred:

```
fred.performCommand("tell mary179 I love you")
```

Now Mary will think that Fred sent her a love note. Let's play with Fred's Location and see what other mischief we can create.

```
Location where = fred.getLocation();
```

Now the variable we named where will point to a Location object that represents Fred's location in the world.

Making Objects

You can also make a new location from scratch:

```
double x, y, z;
x = 10;
y = 0;
z = 10;
Location whereNow = new Location (fred.getWorld(), x, y, z);
```

Or do it in one step:

```
Location whereNow = new Location (fred.getWorld(), 10, 0, 10);
```

And that's how to make a new object in Java: by using the new keyword.

When you use new to create an object, Java will create the object for you and run its *constructor*: a function that's named the same as the class (for instance, public Location()). The constructor gives you the chance to set up anything in the object that needs setting. It doesn't return anything and isn't declared with a return type; Java automatically returns the new object after you've done your setup.

We'll discuss how to make our own object definitions a bit later in the book, but for now we'll use what Minecraft has given us plus our plugin skeleton.

And now armed with a location, you can whisk Fred away:

```
boolean ok = fred.teleport(whereNow);
```

If the teleport worked as expected, the variable ok will be set to true, and Fred will find himself...suffocating in bedrock (because y is zero). Ouch.

Plugin: PlayerStuff

Let's play around with a Player a bit more.

We're going to install the PlayerStuff plugin and change some of the object properties for players in the Minecraft world.

In the Player object, there are all kinds of interesting functions to get information about a player, and to set those values as well. Here are a few we'll look at:

sendMessage()

getPlayerListName() (can set it too)

setPlayerWeather(WeatherType *type*) (can get it too)

getExp() (get experience level; can set it too)

getFoodLevel() (can set it too)

We can send a message to a player, get some values, change the weather at a player's location, and more. Here's code for a full plugin that demonstrates some of these features. It provides the command "/whoami". For more advanced plugins, this approach could be a great way to debug in-game objects by displaying information about Minecraft objects. When you're writing code and it's not working, printing out a couple of values of different variables is a great way to find out what's going on.

Here's the code, which is the plugin directory Desktop/code/PlayerStuff. The full plugin has the necessary config.yml file and such:

PlayerStuff/src/playerstuff/PlayerStuff.java

```java
package playerstuff;

import java.util.logging.Logger;
import org.bukkit.WeatherType;
import org.bukkit.command.Command;
import org.bukkit.command.CommandSender;
import org.bukkit.entity.Entity;
import org.bukkit.entity.Player;
import org.bukkit.plugin.Plugin;
import org.bukkit.plugin.java.JavaPlugin;

public class PlayerStuff extends JavaPlugin {
  public boolean onCommand(CommandSender sender, Command command,
                            String commandLabel, String[] args) {
    if (commandLabel.equalsIgnoreCase("whoami")) {
      if (sender instanceof Player) {
        Player me = (Player)sender;
        String msg = "Your list name is " + me.getPlayerListName();
        me.sendMessage(msg);
        me.setPlayerWeather(WeatherType.DOWNFALL); // or CLEAR
        float exp = me.getExp();
        int food = me.getFoodLevel();
        me.sendMessage("Your experience points are " + exp +
                ", food is " + food +
                "\nwater falls from the sky "
                );
        return true;
      }
    }
    return false;
  }
}
```

Install that now:

```
$ cd Desktop
$ cd code/PlayerStuff
$ ./build.sh
```

Restart your server and reconnect your Minecraft client.

What happens when you type the command "/whoami" from the Minecraft client?

Here's what I get:

Let's walk through the code and see what's going on. After all the setup stuff, we're checking to see if the command label is equal to "whoami", and if it is we'll do our thing.

So we start off getting the player object me, and then the fun begins. Using the me object, we get the player's name and then send that as a message back to that player.

Then just for fun we'll make it rain (or snow) on the player by setting the weather to DOWNFALL.[2]

Next we'll get the experience points for the next level and the food level, and send those as a message back to the player. You can play around in this world for a while, and run "/whoami" to see if your food and experience have changed any.

It's just that simple: me is an object of type Player, and we can get values for various player values and send commands to me to do playerlike things, such as sending a message or setting the weather.

That's what objects are for.

---

2. You could make it stop by setting the weather to WeatherType.CLEAR instead.

Next Up

In this chapter you've seen how to use Java objects: how to import a Java package and class, how to use new to create objects, and how to change properties of objects that will affect the game (including making players hungry). We'll need all of that for the following chapters.

In the next chapter we'll take a closer look at how plugins are wired into Minecraft, how to add commands, and how to find things in the Minecraft world.

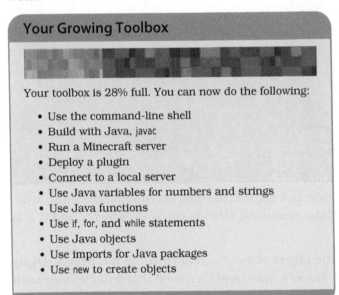

Your Growing Toolbox

Your toolbox is 28% full. You can now do the following:

- Use the command-line shell
- Build with Java, javac
- Run a Minecraft server
- Deploy a plugin
- Connect to a local server
- Use Java variables for numbers and strings
- Use Java functions
- Use if, for, and while statements
- Use Java objects
- Use imports for Java packages
- Use new to create objects

Add a Chat Command, Locations, and Targets

How Does Minecraft Know About Your Plugin?

We've been using a bunch of objects in the Minecraft code. For example, you know that a player is represented as a Player object and the server is a Server object.

So it shouldn't be too surprising to realize that our plugins are, in fact, Plugin objects. Bukkit has kindly defined a basic "recipe," a basic Plugin class that it knows about. Our job, as plugin writers, is to provide our own plugin code that fits into that framework.

As we've seen, the first line of a plugin declares the plugin's name and then adds the magical phrase extends JavaPlugin:

```
import org.bukkit.plugin.java.JavaPlugin;

public class MyFavoritePlugin extends JavaPlugin {
```

That makes JavaPlugin a parent of your class MyFavoritePlugin, just like the examples in the last chapter.

The Minecraft server already knows how to work with a JavaPlugin, and since that's your plugin's parent, it now knows how to work with your plugin—even though your plugin didn't exist when Minecraft was created. It's counting on the fact that you'll write a couple of functions that it knows how to call.

In addition to the plugin code itself, Minecraft needs a configuration file for the plugin, named plugin.yml. You saw a description of this back on page 35, while we were building plugins the first time. It tells the server which commands your plugin will handle.

With that configuration file and your code, the Minecraft server can run your plugin just like any other part of the game.

Plugin: SkyCmd

We're going to create a brand-new plugin called SkyCmd. In it, we'll create a command named sky that will teleport all nearby creatures (not players) fifty blocks up into the air. Very handy at night with skeletons and creepers about.

In the SkyCmd directory, plugin.yml has an entry for our new command, /sky. Here's the whole source file to the plugin:

SkyCmd/src/skycmd/SkyCmd.java
```java
package skycmd;

import java.util.logging.Logger;
import org.bukkit.Location;
import org.bukkit.command.Command;
import org.bukkit.command.CommandSender;
import org.bukkit.entity.Player;
import org.bukkit.plugin.Plugin;
import org.bukkit.plugin.java.JavaPlugin;
import org.bukkit.entity.Entity;
import java.util.List;

public class SkyCmd extends JavaPlugin {

  public boolean onCommand(CommandSender sender, Command command,
                           String commandLabel, String[] args) {
❶   if (commandLabel.equalsIgnoreCase("sky")) {
❷     if (sender instanceof Player) {
❸       Player me = (Player)sender;
        List<Entity> list = me.getNearbyEntities(50,50,50);
        for (Entity target : list) {
          if (!(target instanceof Player)) {
            Location loc = target.getLocation();
```

```
              double y = loc.getY();
              loc.setY(y+50);
              target.teleport(loc);
          }
      }
      return true;
    }
  }
  return false;
}
}
```

Compare this to our original, very simple HelloWorld.java file. Notice right at the top, the package statement and later the public class statement now each refer to SkyCmd instead of HelloWorld.

Let's take a closer look at how a plugin handles a chat command like /sky.

Handle Chat Commands

When the player types a command, your onCommand method will be called.

The player's command is passed to you in a string, which we've named commandLabel. So the first thing you need to do is check and see if the command the player typed is the one you want. How do you check to see if strings are equal? Down on the line at ❶ we'll use the string's function equalsIgnoreCase to check if the player typed "sky". (Remember, you can't use == on strings; you have to use either equals or equalsIgnoreCase, and most of the time you want to ignore the case, so "sky" will match "Sky", "SKY", and even "sKy".)

If we got a match for "sky", then we'll execute this next code block, in between the braces—{ and }.

The next thing we need to check is a little awkward; it turns out that the CommandSender that gets passed to us here may not be a Player. It could be a Player object, but it could be a Console instead, or who knows what else. We want to make sure it's really a Player, so we'll check for that explicitly at ❷, using the Java keyword instanceof. This tests to see if the thing passed in is really a Player. If it is, then we're going to do the bulk of the command starting at ❸.

This begins with another bit of magic, just like we saw with parent/child recipes at the end of Chapter 5, *Plugins Have Objects*, on page 65. Now that we've confirmed the variable sender is really of type Player (not just a Command-Sender or any other parent or child), we can convert it to the type Player, using a *cast* operator.

So the expression (Player) sender returns the variable sender, converted with a cast operator to the type Player so you can assign it to the variable me. It sounds messy, and it is a bit, but it's also something you can just copy and paste, as we'll be using this little recipe in almost every command plugin to get a Player object.

Now that we have a real Player object referenced by me, we can get the list of all nearby entities with me.getNearbyEntities(50,50,50);, which will get us all the entities within fifty blocks of us and return all of these entities in a List that we'll go through with a for loop.

We'll go over the details of lists in the next chapter, but first we'll look at how Location objects work. In this case, we're setting the variable target to each entry in the list of nearby entities as we go through the for loop. If the target is not a fellow player, then we want to fling it skyward, which we do by changing its location.

Location objects are important—that's how you get and set the coordinates of anything in Minecraft. Here's how we'll manipulate locations to fling the creatures up in the air.

Use Minecraft Coordinates

A Location stores three coordinates: x, y, and z, as the following figure shows.

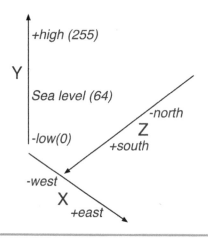

Figure 6—Minecraft coordinate system

The x value goes west (negative) to east (positive), the z coordinate goes north (negative) to south (positive), and y goes down (negative) to up (positive), with a y value of 0 being the bottom layer of bedrock, and 64 being sea level. That means that to make a player or other entity fly up in the air, you need to add some to the y value.

We'll get each target's current y value from loc and save it as y. Next we'll change the value in loc by adding 50. Here's the fun part: by calling target.teleport(loc) we tell the target to teleport itself to this new location. Finally, we return true to indicate that this was our command and that we executed it successfully.

Notice that if the caller wasn't a Player, or if the command typed wasn't "sky", we return false, indicating it wasn't our plugin's command.

Whew! That's a lot of stuff in a few lines of code. But give it a shot and compile and install it using build.sh just like we've been doing:

```
$ cd Desktop
$ cd code/SkyCmd
$ ./build.sh
```

Stop and restart your server, and try out the new command /sky for fun. Make sure you are in survival mode instead of creative mode,[1] and wait for night to fall and the creepers to come....

Try This Yourself

Well, that was fun! Let's try something a little different: adding a new command to this plugin, all on your own.

Add a new command to the SkyCmd plugin that will create ten squid—a squid bomb.

You'll check for a command string of "squidbomb" and if it matches, you'll use a for loop and the world's spawn function.

The spawn is documented to take a location and the thing you want to spawn:

```
me.getWorld().spawn(location, somethingToSpawn);
```

spawn returns an Entity, but we won't be using that right now.

So given a Player object (written here as me, just like we did in the SkyCmd plugin), you get its world with .getWorld() and call the function spawn on that world. You pass in a Location of where to spawn the thing, and then you have to indicate the Java class to spawn.

---

1. In the Minecraft game, you can do this by typing /gamemode c for creative or /gamemode s for survival.

For instance, to spawn a squid, you need to import org.bukkit.entity.Squid up at the top of the file. Then later in your function, pass Squid.class to the spawn function. With that we can make a simple "squid bomb":

```
import org.bukkit.entity.Squid

//... other parts not shown

    // Spawning some squid. Derp.
    for (int i = 0; i < 10; i++) {
        me.getWorld().spawn(loc, Squid.class);
    }
```

Use that in your new command in our SkyCmd plugin. Don't forget to do the following:

- Add your new command (squidbomb) to SkyCmd's plugin.yml configuration file (otherwise, you'll get "Unknown command" errors from the server).

- Recompile and install using build.sh.

- Stop and restart the server to pick up the change.

Before you make this change, the plugin.yml will look like this:

```
SkyCmd/plugin.yml
name: SkyCmd

author: AndyHunt, Learn to Program with Minecraft Plugins
website: http://pragprog.com/book/ahmine

main: skycmd.SkyCmd

commands:
    sky:
        description: Fling nearby creepers into the air

version: 0.1
```

You'll need to add a new command in the commands: section so that it looks like this:

```
commands:
    sky:
        description: Fly creepers up into the air
    squidbomb:
        description: Drop a fixed number of squid on your head
```

(Remember, don't use tab characters—only use spaces, and make sure that sky and squidbomb line up, and that both description lines line up too.)

Now, that's a little bit boring—all the squid kind of pile on top of each other. It might be better to randomize the location for each squid. Java provides a function, Math.random(), that will give us a random number that ranges from 0 up to (but not including) 1.

To get a random number from 0 up to 5, just multiply Math.random() by 5. So for instance, to get a new x-coordinate you might use an expression like loc.getX() + (Math.random() * 5). When multiplying and adding, parentheses are usually a good idea—in this case we want to multiply the random 0..1 by 5, then add that to the original x.

Now it's your turn again: improve the squid bomb by making a new location based on the player's location that you already have, and add a bit of randomness to the x- and z-coordinates. To get the squid to drop on you from above, add 10 to the y-coordinate.

Try going through this exercise all by yourself first. In case you get stuck and need some help, I made a whole new plugin for the squid bomb. You can see my code and config file in code/SquidBomb.

Find Nearby Blocks or Entities

Bukkit provides a very handy feature in org.bukkit.util.BlockIterator. A BlockIterator lets you find all the blocks along a line in the game. Most useful is probably the version where you pass in a LivingEntity (like a Player) and a maximum distance:

```
new BlockIterator (LivingEntity entity, int maxDistance);
```

That gives you a BlockIterator object, which you can use to retrieve blocks along the line of sight from that entity, like this:

```
BlockIterator sightItr = new BlockIterator (me, 100);
while (sightItr.hasNext()) {
    Block b = sightItr.next();
    // do something with this block, b
}
```

You might check each block along this player's line of sight and find the first block that isn't AIR. That would be the player's "target." Or we could set fire to each block along the way and then turn that target into LAVA.

Here's a plugin that does exactly that.

Plugin: LavaVision

This plugin runs a BlockIterator for the player, and checks each block along the way, setting a flame effect. The first block that isn't AIR is the target, so we'll set that to LAVA.

For extra punch, I've added an effect on each block we traverse:

```
me.playEffect(b.getLocation(), Effect.MOBSPAWNER_FLAMES, null);
```

The MOBSPAWNER_FLAMES gives us a nice set of flames along our line of sight.

I've also added a sound effect, using the Player object's playSound function, which takes a Location, a Sound, and floats for volume and pitch.

```
me.playSound(b.getLocation(), Sound.EXPLODE, 1.0f, 0.5f);
```

There's a list of possible effects in the Bukkit documentation under org.bukkit.Sound. I picked EXPLODE for drama. The next two numbers are specified to be float, not double, so I had to add the f modifier.

Here's the full code, with the iterator and sound effect:

LavaVision/src/lavavision/LavaVision.java
```java
package lavavision;

import java.util.logging.Logger;
import org.bukkit.command.Command;
import org.bukkit.command.CommandSender;
import org.bukkit.entity.Player;
import org.bukkit.plugin.Plugin;
import org.bukkit.plugin.java.JavaPlugin;
import org.bukkit.block.Block;
import org.bukkit.util.BlockIterator;
import org.bukkit.Material;
import org.bukkit.Sound;
import org.bukkit.Effect;

public class LavaVision extends JavaPlugin {
  public static Logger log = Logger.getLogger("Minecraft");

  public void onEnable() {
    log.info("[LavaVision] Start up.");
  }
  public void onReload() {
    log.info("[LavaVision] Server reloaded.");
  }
  public void onDisable() {
    log.info("[LavaVision] Server stopping.");
  }
```

```
public boolean onCommand(CommandSender sender, Command command,
                         String commandLabel, String[] args) {
  if (commandLabel.equalsIgnoreCase("lavavision")) {
    if (sender instanceof Player) {
      Player me = (Player)sender;
      BlockIterator sightItr = new BlockIterator (me, 100);
      while (sightItr.hasNext()) {
        Block b = sightItr.next();
        me.playEffect(b.getLocation(), Effect.MOBSPAWNER_FLAMES, null);
        if (b.getType() != Material.AIR) {
          b.setType(Material.LAVA);
          me.playSound(b.getLocation(), Sound.EXPLODE, 1.0f, 0.5f);
          break;
        }
      }
      return true;
    }
  }
  return false;
}
}
```

Install this plugin in the usual way:

```
$ cd Desktop
$ cd code/LavaVision
$ ./build.sh
```

Stop and restart the server, and in Minecraft look around and pick a target. Type the /lavavision command and watch the lava bubble.

Next Up

In this chapter you've seen how to add a new command to a plugin. Now you can start adding your own new ideas to existing plugins, and you can work with locations and blocks in the game. But as soon as you start dealing with a bunch of locations or a bunch of blocks, you have a problem: how does Java store lists of things like that, and how do you work with "piles" of data that you might need to find by name or in order?

In the next chapter we'll add a command for remembering information: stuff you'll need to keep track of. We'll talk more about variables in Java: who can see them and who can't, and—most importantly—how to keep and work with piles of data.

In short, we're going to look at how to keep track of stuff.

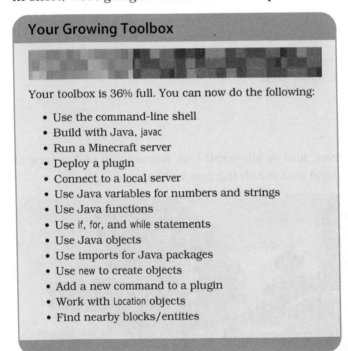

Your Growing Toolbox

Your toolbox is 36% full. You can now do the following:

- Use the command-line shell
- Build with Java, javac
- Run a Minecraft server
- Deploy a plugin
- Connect to a local server
- Use Java variables for numbers and strings
- Use Java functions
- Use if, for, and while statements
- Use Java objects
- Use imports for Java packages
- Use new to create objects
- Add a new command to a plugin
- Work with Location objects
- Find nearby blocks/entities

## CHAPTER 7

Use Piles of Variables: Arrays

Your Toolbox

Is your head full yet? I hope not, because you have a few fun things left to learn. In this chapter we'll add these abilities to your toolbox:

- Use local variables that exist only within a block
- Use class-level global variables that can be accessed from anywhere in the class
- Keep piles of data in arrays

Now that we can create a plugin command to do something, we need to take a look at how to remember stuff—in other words, how to better use Java variables to keep track of values. We'll see when to use which kind of variable and how to work with piles of data in different ways (things like lists of Player objects), and we'll build a couple of cool plugins along the way.

Variables and Objects Live in Blocks

Variables live inside of *blocks*. We've seen and been using blocks all along: blocks are the bits of code written between braces—{ and }.

Java is a "block structured" programming language. It's descended from a family of languages going back to the ancient Algol of the 1960s, a line that extends from the mother of all programming languages, C, its children C++ and Objective-C, and down to its half-cousin-stepchild Java. After Java was around, Microsoft came out with C#, which is (totally coincidentally) nearly identical to Java. All of these languages work more or less the same way.

In these languages, you work with blocks of code. Things like if statements work with blocks of code. Objects we define (like our plugins) are blocks of code. The whole structure of the language is based on blocks of code within braces.

And that's where variables live. For instance, in the HelloWorld plugin, look at this section where we create and send a message:

```
if (commandLabel.equalsIgnoreCase("hello")) {
    String msg = ChatColor.RED + "[Server] Hello, Minecraft World!";
    getServer().broadcastMessage(msg);
    return true;
}
```

In the body of this if statement we are declaring and assigning a variable named msg. It's a *local* variable—it lives only while this particular code block is running, between its declaration and the closing brace (the } symbol). You cannot use this msg variable before that, or anywhere else in your program. You might have another variable named msg somewhere else, but it will be a totally different variable, with different values. This msg is visible and usable only locally, in this one block of code. We say that its *scope* is local.

The parameters that you declare in a function are considered local as well. Remember the declaration for the onCommand function:

```
public boolean onCommand(CommandSender sender, Command command,
                String commandLabel, String[] args) {
```

The variables sender, command, commandLabel, and args are all available within this function, but aren't visible anywhere else. They are local.

Most of the time local variables are all you need. In fact, local variables are pretty safe to use. No other part of the program can use or change them, and it's very clear what line of code set a local variable's value and where it is used.

Global Variables

But you can make variables that have a wider scope and aren't just local (and we're going to need to do that for our plugins in this chapter).

Maybe you've declared a variable that many different functions can use. Maybe your entire class, or even the entire program and all your libraries, can see it and change it. We call that a *global* variable.

We've seen this before—in fact, from the very first HelloWorld plugin, which has a class-level static variable declared right at the top:

```
public class HelloWorld extends JavaPlugin {
    public static Logger log = Logger.getLogger("Minecraft");
    ...
}
```

We make the call to the Logger system and ask it for the Minecraft logger object. It returns that to us, and we assign it to our variable named log. log is of type Logger, which is what the documentation tells us it needs to be, but note that we've added the word static to this declaration.

Static here means two things:

- You access the variable using the name of the plugin without a plugin object. In this case, HelloWorld.log will work from anywhere, inside or outside an object.

- The static variable (log) is common to all HelloWorld objects, and lives on, outside the lifetime of any local variables in any object.

That means that any of the functions within a HelloWorld object can come and go, and their local variables can come and go, but the static variables will still be there and still remember their values.

Since log is the very first thing we declare inside our plugin, and it's not inside a function itself, all the functions in our plugin—everything inside this top pair of { and } characters—can use it. It's not local to any one function.

Here's where we first use log in HelloWorld.java:

```
...
public void onEnable() {
    log.info("[HelloWorld] Start up.");
}
...
```

Notice that we don't need any kind of extra declaration; we can just use log.

Global variables like these, however, can be mighty dangerous.

Why are they dangerous? Precisely because *anyone*, anywhere, can change the value of that variable on you. Maybe you know they did it, but maybe you don't. Even if "they" is "you," weeks from now if something goes wrong, you have to go and examine every single piece of code in the system to try to find out which piece of code set the variable badly, and why. That's a lot of work and creates a lot of opportunity to mess things up.

But sometimes you really do need a global variable like that. You may not want anyone else to change it, but maybe a lot of different pieces of code need to refer to it. The log is a good example: it's a shared service that all plugins and the server itself use. We all need access to the logging object, and we need it in a variable that won't go away. Unlike a local variable, we want it to be visible for all the functions in our plugin, and stick around as long as the plugin is around.

Here's a recap of our story so far:

- A block of code is written inside { and }.

- Variables you declare inside the body of a block of code are local to that block of code. They go away when the function finishes and returns.

- A function's parameters are local to that function.

- Variables declared as static will outlive any local variables declared within functions.

Here's a quick plugin that gives us a /caketower command. The idea is that it will build a tower of cake blocks. But there's a subtle problem in the code involving local and global variables, and the tower may not turn out the way you expect. Let's take a look.

Plugin: CakeTower

CakeTower/src/caketower/CakeTower.java
```java
package caketower;

import java.util.logging.Logger;
import org.bukkit.Location;
import org.bukkit.Material;
import org.bukkit.command.Command;
import org.bukkit.command.CommandSender;
import org.bukkit.entity.Player;
import org.bukkit.plugin.Plugin;
import org.bukkit.plugin.java.JavaPlugin;


public class CakeTower extends JavaPlugin {
  public static Logger log = Logger.getLogger("Minecraft");

  public static int cakeHeight = 100;

  public void onEnable() {
    log.info("[CakeTower] Start up.");
  }
  public void onReload() {
    log.info("[CakeTower] Server reloaded.");
  }
  public void onDisable() {
    log.info("[CakeTower] Server stopping.");
  }
```

❶ (marker pointing to `public static int cakeHeight = 100;`)

```
   public boolean onCommand(CommandSender sender, Command command,
                            String commandLabel, String[] args) {
     if (commandLabel.equalsIgnoreCase("caketower")) {
       if (sender instanceof Player) {
         Player me = (Player)sender;

         me.sendMessage("1) cake height is " + cakeHeight); // Print it

         cakeHeight = 50;

❷       int cakeHeight;
         cakeHeight = 5;
         me.sendMessage("2) cake height is " + cakeHeight); // Print it

         makeCakes(me); // Print it
         return true;
       }
     }
     return false;
   }

   public void makeCakes(Player me) {
     me.sendMessage("3) cake height is " + cakeHeight);
     Location loc = me.getLocation();
     loc.setY(loc.getY() + 2);
     loc.getWorld().getBlockAt(loc).setType(Material.STONE);
     for(int i = 0;i < cakeHeight;i++) {
       loc.setY(loc.getY() + 1);
       loc.getWorld().getBlockAt(loc).setType(Material.CAKE_BLOCK);
     }
   }
 }
```

When run, this code will print out the value of cakeHeight three times. Notice that there are two declarations of the variable cakeHeight, one at ❶ and another at ❷.

What will this code print out, and how many cakes will end up in the tower?

Try to figure it out first. Then compile and install using build.sh as usual.

What Happened?

Welcome to the wonderfully confusing world of *shadowing*.

In this piece of code, a variable named cakeHeight is declared at the top of the plugin. This is the variable you would expect to access anywhere within the plugin—starting on that line and ending at the matching closing brace, }.

But then on the line at ❷ we declare another variable with the very same name. From this point until the next closing brace, }, any time we mention cakeHeight we'll be working with this local one, not the class-level one. This local version *shadows* the class version. So when we set it to 5 and then print it, we're modifying this local version.

Calling makeCakes then uses the class version to build the tower. The makeCakes function has no knowledge of the shadowed variable inside the onCommand function. So you end up with fifty blocks; not a hundred, and not five.

Moral of this story: don't do this. As you can see, shadowed variable names can be very confusing. Give your variables unique, memorable names.

Try This Yourself

Since the cake tower doesn't quite work as expected, let's fix it!

Change code/CakeTower/src/caketower/CakeTower.java to use just the one local variable cakeHeight, not the class-level variable, and pass it in to makeCakes.

Now that you know where variables live and can be used, let's look at a couple of different ways you can use piles of data, using Java data collections.

Use a Java Array

While variables with individual values are useful and common, sometimes you need more than that. You need to keep track of all the players in the system, or one player's inventory items, or a to-do list, or a grocery list, or a homework list.

Java has you covered. There are several different ways to keep and access piles of data. We're going to focus on a few: the simple Array, the classier ArrayList, and the remarkably handy if somewhat alien HashMap (covered in the next chapter). First up, the Array.

There are actually a few different Array-like collections in Java, including Array, Vector, LinkedList, and ArrayList types. They each work differently on the inside, are stored slightly differently, and perform differently with large or small data sets, but the idea is the same for all of them.

Arrays are probably the simplest of these piles of data. Arrays are mostly used when you have a small list of values that you want to create directly in code and then use. Arrays are *fixed length*—you can't grow or shrink them. They aren't as useful if you need to add, delete, and move things around a lot in the list (for that, we'll use an ArrayList, which is up next).

You'll usually employ an Array when you want to access its values by an index, or run through all the values and do something to them with a for loop.

You can declare an Array using square brackets, and load it up with values using braces. Here's an example of a list of Strings.

```
String[] grades = {"A", "B", "C", "D", "F", "Inc"};
```

You can access individual elements from the list using brackets:

```
String yourGrade = grades[2];
```

In this case, yourGrade will be a C. Hey, wait a minute—why is that a C, and not a B? That's because Java, like the C language and its predecessors, starts counting at 0. The first element in any list is 0. The second is 1. The third is 2, and so on. You'll get used to it. Think of accessing the first element as adding 0 to the start of the list, and the second element as adding 1 to the start of the list.

That's exactly how an Array is stored in memory in the computer. Just a bunch of values all in row. Since the first entry in the Array is right at the start of the memory, it has no offset. The second value is one over from the start, the third is two over from the start, and up you go.

You can tell the length of an Array by looking at its length field (note this is not a function call; there are no parentheses):

```
int numGrades = grades.length;
```

numGrades will be set to 6. That means that each of the six values will be numbered 0 to 5. The index of the last element is always length-1 (in this case, 6-1, or 5).

Instead of sticking in all the values hard-coded as we did, you could make an Array that's a fixed size, then stuff values into it. Here's what that looks like with a list of int values:

```
int[] quizScores = new int[5];
quizScores[0] = 85;
quizScores[1] = 92;
quizScores[2] = 63;
```

Getting values out looks just like putting values in, only the other way around. Using the code we just looked at, you retrieve the values like this:

```
int myBestQuiz = quizScores[1];
int aBadDay = quizScores[2];
```

To get all the values, you can use an old-fashioned for loop:

```
for (int i=0; i < 5; i++) {
    me.sendMessage("Quiz score #" + i + ": " + quizScores[i]);
}
```

Remember that Array is a fixed size; if you try to retrieve a value that's past the end of the array (like quizScores[15]), your plugin will throw an error and crash. In this case, since we define the quizScores array to have a size of 5, you can safely store and retrieve values at index 0, 1, 2, 3, and 4. That's why we use i < 5 in the middle, instead of <=.

It's a lot safer to use the Array's .length field instead of hard-coding a number like "5." So it would be better to write that loop like this:

```
for (int i=0; i < quizScores.length; i++) {
    me.sendMessage("Quiz score #" + i + ": " + quizScores[i]);
}
```

In a little bit we'll discuss an even better way to loop through all the values in an array.

Let's do the same thing now, but with Minecraft blocks.

Here's an example of code for a quick plugin that builds a tower of different block types. I'm using a block's setType to change its type into one of several different materials.[1] Let's walk through this and see what's happening.

---

1. The codes for different materials are in the Bukkit docs at http://jd.bukkit.org/rb/doxygen/d6/d0e/enumorg_1_1bukkit_1_1Material.html.

Plugin: ArrayOfBlocks

ArrayOfBlocks/src/arrayofblocks/ArrayOfBlocks.java

```java
package arrayofblocks;

import java.util.logging.Logger;
import org.bukkit.Location;
import org.bukkit.Material;
import org.bukkit.command.Command;
import org.bukkit.command.CommandSender;
import org.bukkit.entity.Player;
import org.bukkit.plugin.Plugin;
import org.bukkit.plugin.java.JavaPlugin;


public class ArrayOfBlocks extends JavaPlugin {
  public static Logger log = Logger.getLogger("Minecraft");

  public void buildTower(Player me) {
    Location loc = me.getLocation();
    loc.setX(loc.getX() + 1); // Not right on top of player

    Material[] towerMaterials = new Material[5];

    towerMaterials[0] = Material.STONE;
    towerMaterials[1] = Material.CAKE_BLOCK;
    towerMaterials[2] = Material.WOOD;
    towerMaterials[3] = Material.GLASS;
    towerMaterials[4] = Material.ANVIL;

    for (int i=0; i < towerMaterials.length; i++) {
      loc.setY(loc.getY() + 1); // go up one each time
      loc.getWorld().getBlockAt(loc).setType(towerMaterials[i]);
    }
  }

  public boolean onCommand(CommandSender sender, Command command,
                           String commandLabel, String[] args) {
    if (commandLabel.equalsIgnoreCase("arrayofblocks")) {
      if (sender instanceof Player) {
        Player me = (Player)sender;
        // Put your code after this line:
        buildTower(me);
        // ...and finish your code before this line.
        return true;
      }
    }
    return false;
  }
}
```

Install the ArrayOfBlocks with build.sh, reload the server, and try the /arrayofblocks command. You should see something like this (you might need to turn around to see it):

Notice that I put the guts of the command in its own function, buildTower, instead of in the onCommand itself.

This is just a simple Array of length 5 that we are loading up with values one at a time. The for loop goes from index 0 to 4 and changes the block to the new material in our list.

Try This Yourself

Now it's your turn.

You're going to make a small change to reverse the order of the tower's elements, so that the anvil is on the bottom and the stone is on the top.

Change the for loop around to do this. Instead of going from 0 to < 5, change the loop to go from 4 down to >= 0. Hint: subtraction might work better than addition in this case.

Rebuild, reload, and try the /arrayofblocks command again.

Now you know how to work with for loops and indexes, but to be honest, this is an old corner of Java, and it's a tad musty. Array objects are handy, but there's perhaps a better choice.

Use a Java ArrayList

An ArrayList in Java also keeps track of a list of values, just like a simple Array does. ArrayLists are a little messy to declare but simple enough to use, and much more flexible and a bit safer than plain old Array objects. You can add and delete from the ArrayList as many times as you want; it's not a fixed length and will grow or shrink as needed.

Here's an example of an ArrayList that will hold Player objects:

```
List<Player> myPlayerList = new ArrayList<Player>();
```

There's a lot more gunk in there than we've seen up to now. First of all, I've called our new list myPlayerList. Note that funny syntax with the angle brackets, < and >. You have to specify the kind of list you're making (twice, in fact). Java 7 improves on this a little; you don't have to repeat it on the right-hand side and you can say List<Player> whatever = new ArrayList<>(). Also, in a small bit of weirdness, notice that although it's List on the left, it's ArrayList on the right. The reason for that is...because Java. (Okay, the reason is that List is the parent and ArrayList is one particular child.) Moving on now.[2]

With a list you've created, you can do a lot of fun things, like adding and removing values from the list, retrieving values, and checking to see if a value exists. Here's a bit of sample code:

ListPlay/src/listplay/ListPlay.java

```
public void listDemo(Player me) {
  List<String> listOfStrings = new ArrayList<String>();
  listOfStrings.add("This");
  listOfStrings.add("is");
  listOfStrings.add("a");
  listOfStrings.add("list.");

  String third = listOfStrings.get(2);
  me.sendMessage("The third element is " + third);

  me.sendMessage("List contains " + listOfStrings.size() + " elements.");

  listOfStrings.add(3, "fancy");

  boolean hasIt = listOfStrings.contains("is");
  me.sendMessage("Does list contain the word 'is'? " + hasIt);

  hasIt = listOfStrings.contains("kerfluffle");
  me.sendMessage("Does the list contain the word 'kerfluffle'? " + hasIt);
```

---

2. "Because Java" is a bit of an Internet joke; see http://www.theatlantic.com/technology/archive/2013/11/english-has-a-new-preposition-because-internet/281601 for details.

```
    // Print out each value in the list
    for(String value : listOfStrings) {
      me.sendMessage(value);
    }
```

❼
```
    listOfStrings.clear();
    me.sendMessage("Now it's cleared out, size is " + listOfStrings.size());

    hasIt = listOfStrings.contains("is");
    me.sendMessage("List contains the word 'is' now is " + hasIt);
  }
```

Try This Yourself

Read that over and see if you can figure out what it will do when run.

Does it all make sense? Let's go through the code and see what's going on.

First, at ❶ there's the new to create a list that will hold Strings. So far so good. Next, starting at ❷ we're adding a couple of strings to this list, one at a time, using the List function add(). With these added to the list, we can now try to get some data out.

On the line at ❸ we're getting the third element of the list—by asking for the list index of 2. Remember, it's zero-based counting, just like Array, which we talked about earlier. The third element is the string "a".

Next we check to see how many elements are in the list, using the function size() at ❹, and it tells us there are four.

One of the advantages of an ArrayList over an Array is that you can easily add and remove values—even in the middle of the list, as seen here on the line at ❺, where we're using add() and passing in an index of 3. That will add this value at index 3 in the list and move all the other values down one.

You can also remove values, re-add values, and so on, as much as you like. No matter how we add or shuffle values around in the list, we can check to see if a particular value is in the list without having to look through the whole list, as with the call to contains that looks for the word "is" at ❻. Cool, it's in there. After that we'll try again with a value that *isn't* in there. And indeed, the contains returns false for "kerfluffle".

You've seen how you could get a single value by index using the get function, but what if you want to go through the list one by one?

You could use a for loop as we did with Array, but that's old-fashioned, ugly, and error prone.

Instead, you can use a *for-each* construct. The statement for(String value : listOf-Strings) acts like a for loop that iterates over the collection listOfStrings, and in the body of the loop it will set the variable value to each entry as it goes through. We first saw this back in SkyCmd.

Whew! That's a lot of explanation for a few short lines of code. But it's a powerful idea, and we're going to use this in a plugin in just a bit.

Finally, what happens when we clear out the list entirely (at ❼)? Not much interesting, as it's empty now.

Plugin: ArrayAddMoreBlocks

Let's play with this a bit. We'll start with the ArrayOfBlocks plugin but change it to use an ArrayList instead of an Array. We'll call the new plugin ArrayAddMore-Blocks.

Since we can add to the array list easily, let's make it static:

```
public static List<Material> towerMaterials = new ArrayList<Material>();
```

Then, thanks to the wonder of ArrayList, we can add a couple of blocks to the new tower each time we call /arrayaddmoreblocks:

ArrayAddMoreBlocks/src/arrayaddmoreblocks/ArrayAddMoreBlocks.java
```
public void buildTower(Player me) {
  Location loc = me.getLocation();
  loc.setX(loc.getX() + 1); // Not right on top of player

  towerMaterials.add(Material.GLASS);
  towerMaterials.add(Material.STONE);
  towerMaterials.add(Material.WOOD);

  for (Material material : towerMaterials) {
    loc.setY(loc.getY() + 1); // go up one each time
    loc.getWorld().getBlockAt(loc).setType(material);
  }
}
```

If you stay in the same place it will keep adding to that same tower, and if you move around it will keep making new ones, taller each time you call it.

To reset the list, you use the clear() function, and I've set up a separate command to do just that:

```
if (commandLabel.equalsIgnoreCase("arrayclearblocks")) {
  towerMaterials.clear();
}
```

The full plugin is in code/ArrayAddMoreBlocks. Build, reload, and try that now, building and clearing some towers.

Try This Yourself

Now change the code and add a couple of different building materials. Then try changing it to use just one material, like GLASS perhaps. Or make a nice mix of GLASS and STONE. You're in control.

Next Up

In this chapter you've learned the difference between local and global variables. You can use a simple Array or the more flexible ArrayList to store a pile of data, and traverse it using a for-each iterator.

Arrays are great if you don't really care about finding one of the objects in the array by itself. However, if you care about objects by name—like a Player —then you'll need something a little fancier.

In the next chapter we'll cover how to use a HashMap to store data by name (or by Location, or by anything else you might need).

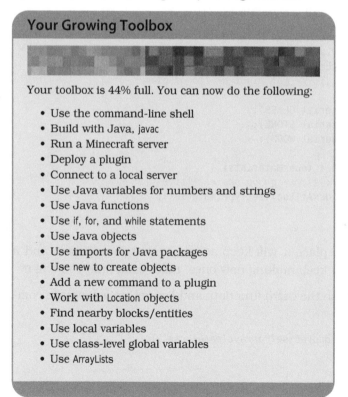

Your Growing Toolbox

Your toolbox is 44% full. You can now do the following:

- Use the command-line shell
- Build with Java, javac
- Run a Minecraft server
- Deploy a plugin
- Connect to a local server
- Use Java variables for numbers and strings
- Use Java functions
- Use if, for, and while statements
- Use Java objects
- Use imports for Java packages
- Use new to create objects
- Add a new command to a plugin
- Work with Location objects
- Find nearby blocks/entities
- Use local variables
- Use class-level global variables
- Use ArrayLists

## CHAPTER 8

Use Piles of Variables: HashMap

Your Toolbox

In this chapter we'll get a little fancier with piles of data and plugin structure, and add these abilities to your toolbox:

- Keep piles of data in hashes
- Use private to hide your private data, and use public for things other people should see and use

Use a Java HashMap

HashMap is a funny name. The "hash" part refers to how it works internally; it really has nothing to do with how you use it.

But the "map" part is about what you'd think: it maps a key, which can be anything, to a value, which can also be anything.

Other languages might call this a *dictionary* or an *associative array* or some kind of *associative memory*. They all mean the same thing. In the simple array we looked at, you use an integer as the index. But with a HashMap, you can use any object as the key, especially Strings (see Figure 7, *A Hashmap*, on page 102).

We'll use this a lot in the plugins. It's a great way to keep track of players, cows that you've spawned, or anything else you want. Although it kind of works like an array, you don't use it the same way. Back when we looked at an array you learned that you can get and set a value with an index like this:

```
myList[9] = "Andy";
String who = myList[9];
```

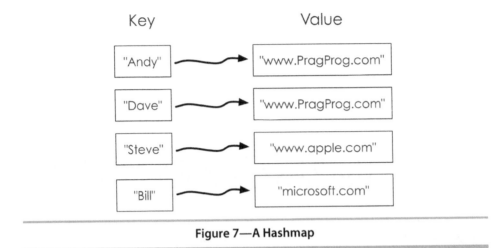

Figure 7—A Hashmap

But you can't use that kind of assignment and bracket notation with a HashMap. Instead you use its put and get functions. On the plus side, though, now you can use anything as a key. Most of the time you'll probably use a String. So suppose you have a HashMap cleverly named myHash.

```
myHash.put("Andy", "www.PragProg.com");
// Works like myHash["Andy"] = "www.PragProg.com";

String myUrl = myHash.get("Andy");
// Works like myUrl = myHash["Andy"];
```

Now myUrl will have the value of "www.PragProg.com".

HashMaps are a great way to store a lot of data that's indexed by a string, just like a dictionary. You look up a word and get a bunch of data. You can also use a HashMap to store a bunch of named properties for an object. The nice part about this is that the property names are just Strings. You could add new properties or delete them while the plugin is running—something that's tough to do with hard-coded function or variable names.

Let's play with these a bit. Here's a small standalone program where we can experiment with a HashMap. Maybe you'll make a plugin that implements some kind of *Hunger Games*–style contest, where you'd want to have a score for each player. You'd keep track of each player's score using a HashMap, like this:

HashPlay/src/hashplay/HashPlay.java
```
❶ HashMap<String, Integer> currentScores = new HashMap<String, Integer>();

public static void addToScore(HashMap<String, Integer> allScores,
                    String playerName,
❷                   int amount) {
```

```
❸    int score = allScores.get(playerName);
❹    score += amount;
❺    allScores.put(playerName, score);
}
```

You'd use it like this:

HashPlay/src/hashplay/HashPlay.java
```
currentScores.put("Andy", 1001);
currentScores.put("Bob", 20);
currentScores.put("Carol", 50);
currentScores.put("Alice", 896);
addToScore(currentScores, "Bob", 500);
me.sendMessage("Bob's score is " + currentScores.get("Bob"));
```

Compiling and running that in a plugin gives us the expected answer of 520 for Bob. Let's go over the code:

On the line at ❶ you see the call to new() that creates a new HashMap for us to use. Since the HashMap has to know what we're going to use for a key and a value, we have to pass in the type names using the angle brackets (< and >), just as we did for an ArrayList. Except here we need to pass in two types: one for the key (which is a String), and one for the value (an Integer).[1]

With a new HashMap named currentScores in hand, we can go through and create some test entries in our hash with player names and their scores. This time, though, we'll do something a little different.

We're going to make a new helper function that will increment a player's score. You can see this starting at ❷. It's a simple function that does three things, but it's a good habit to get into. Any time you have to do a series of steps a couple of times, don't write them out and copy and paste. Instead make a function to do the work for you, then just call the function when you need it.

Our function addToScore() is declared to take three arguments: the HashMap of all scores, the string with the player name, and the integer value to add to the score. With this data, we're doing three steps:

1. Get the current score for the player whose name is in playerName (on the line at ❸).
2. Increase that score by the amount you passed in as amount (at ❹).
3. Save that newly incremented score back into the hash (at ❺).

---

1. Why Integer and not int? Because Java. When using collections like HashMap and ArrayList, you have to refer to primitive types (int, float) by their class names, Integer and Float. The magic of *autoboxing* takes care of converting from Integer to int and so on. Just use the capitalized full names in the angle brackets, and life goes on.

Note that we're not returning any particular value from this function, as it's declared to be void, just like main is. Instead it's modifying the global currentScores HashMap.

Most of the time, though, you'll want functions that return a useful value. For instance, here's a short, trivial function that adds 10 to any number you pass in.

```
public static int addTen(int originalNumber) {
    int newNumber = originalNumber + 10;
    return newNumber;
}
```

All we've done differently is specify what kind of value we're going to return (int in this case) instead of using void in the declaration. Then we use the keyword return with the value that we want to return to our caller. Usually you want to call return as the very last thing in your function. That's because it specifies what value to return *and* performs the return right then and there. No more code will be run in your method after it hits the return. You're done.

Try This Yourself

Modify the HashPlay.java source so that no one's score can go below 0 or above 1,000. Use a helper function that returns a value to clamp the score to be between 0 and 1,000.

You can see my solution in HashPlayClamp/src/hashplay/HashPlay.java. In fact, you might see another subtle trick in there: instead of making the helper function public, I declared it to be private. What's that all about?

Keep Things Private or Make Them Public

Most of the time so far, we've used the Java keyword public when making static variables and defining functions and plugins. That tells Java that the thing we're defining should be publicly accessible—all of our own plugin code can use it, and any other plugin in the system can use it as well (like when we use Logger).

There is another option, though. You can create functions or variables or even helper objects that *no one else* can see. Instead of public, you can make them private.

In programming, there's a simple rule. So simple it's the kind of thing you'd tell a five-year-old: don't expose your privates.

Stack vs. Heap

You may have noticed that sometimes we create and directly assign a simple value to a variable, like int a = 25, and sometimes we use the new keyword to create an object, like a plugin.

These two different kinds of objects are stored differently. *Immediate values* like integers and floats are kept on Java's list of function calls that you're making. That list is called a *stack*. It's like a stack of pancakes. Each new function call throws a new pancake on the stack, and when it's done you remove that pancake and you're back to the previous one. When a function is finished, its "pancake" is thrown away, and any of its local variables disappear.

But objects that you create with new are kept off in a big pile of memory we call the *heap*. They can stick around after your function is gone, if you want them to (like a plugin does).

You just need to keep a variable somewhere that points to your object; that variable can be local and passed around, or global. Java keeps track of how many different variables reference the object created with new. Once no one is using that object anymore, it gets tossed in the trash. And then when the system feels like it, it empties the trash and your object is gone. (Java even calls that "garbage collection.")

In other words, if you're using a function or something that *only* you should use, then mark it as private to make sure that no one from the outside can use it. Why would you need to do that?

Suppose that somewhere in your plugin you have a function to mark a player as a super, high-level, über-Wizard. You wouldn't want any other plugin to call that function on a player of its choosing. So where normally you'd declare the function in the plugin like this (leaving out all the other bits):

```
public class WizardingWorld extends JavaPlugin {
    ...
    public void makeSuperUberHighWizard(Player p) {
        ...
    }
    // Any other plugin can call makeSuperUberHighWizard()
}
```

you can instead make it private, like this:

```
public class WizardingWorld extends JavaPlugin {
    ...
    private void makeSuperUberHighWizard(Player p) {
        ...
    }
    // Only functions here can call makeSuperUberHighWizard()
}
```

In general, if you're making a function that you're using internally within this plugin, and other plugins shouldn't call directly, then make it private.

If you want other plugins to see and use it, then make it public.

We'll start using private for our helper functions now.

Plugin: NamedSigns

Let's put a couple of these ideas together and make a plugin that uses helper functions (with and without return values), private functions and variables, some low-level array access, and a hash that will store names and locations.

This plugin lets you create signposts in the game and name them. You can then put text on any one of the signposts by name. For example, suppose I make two signs, named one and two, by typing these commands in the chat window:

```
/signs new one
/signs new two
/signs set one Hello!
/signs set two Goodbye!
```

I'd see something like this:

Now I can go in and change either sign's text at will just by issuing another signs set command, like this:

```
/signs set two Adios!
```

Let's start with the plugin in all its glory, then look at the interesting pieces.

NamedSigns/src/namedsigns/NamedSigns.java

```
package namedsigns;

import java.util.HashMap;
import java.util.Iterator;
import java.util.Map;
import java.util.logging.Logger;
import org.bukkit.Location;
import org.bukkit.Material;
import org.bukkit.block.Block;
import org.bukkit.block.Sign;
import org.bukkit.command.Command;
import org.bukkit.command.CommandSender;
import org.bukkit.entity.Player;
import org.bukkit.plugin.Plugin;
import org.bukkit.plugin.java.JavaPlugin;

public class NamedSigns extends JavaPlugin {
  private static Logger log = Logger.getLogger("Minecraft");
❶ private static Map<String,Location> signs = new HashMap<String,Location>();

❷ private void usage(Player me) {
    me.sendMessage("Usage: signs new name");
    me.sendMessage("       signs set name message");
  }

  private boolean parseArgs(Player me, String [] args) {
❸   if (args.length < 2) {
      usage(me);
      return false;
    }
    if (args[0].equalsIgnoreCase("new")) {
      return makeNewSign(me, args);
    }
    if (args[0].equalsIgnoreCase("set")) {
❹     if (args.length < 3) {
        usage(me);
        return false;
      }
      return setSign(me, args);
    }
    return false;
  }

  // signs new sign_name
❺ private boolean makeNewSign(Player me, String [] args) {
    Location loc = me.getLocation();
    loc.setX(loc.getX() + 1); // Not right on top of player
    Block block = loc.getWorld().getHighestBlockAt(loc);
    signs.put(args[1], block.getLocation());
```

```java
    block.setType(Material.SIGN_POST);
    log.info("Made new sign named " + args[1]);
    return true;
  }

  // signs set sign_name line1
❻ private boolean setSign(Player me, String [] args) {
    String name = args[1];
    String msg = args[2];
    if (!signs.containsKey(name)) {
      // No such named sign
      me.sendMessage("No sign named " + name);
      return false;
    }
    Location loc = signs.get(name);
❼   Sign sign = (Sign)loc.getWorld().getBlockAt(loc).getState();
    sign.setLine(0, msg);
    sign.update();
    log.info("Set sign named " + name + " to " + msg);
    return true;
  }

  public boolean onCommand(CommandSender sender, Command command,
                           String commandLabel, String[] args) {
    if (commandLabel.equalsIgnoreCase("signs")) {
      if (sender instanceof Player) {
        Player me = (Player)sender;
        return parseArgs(me, args);
      }
    }
    return false;
  }
}
```

There's a lot of code here, but it's really just a handful of simple parts and things we've seen already. These are the major pieces:

- A private static HashMap at ❶.

- A private helper function that returns nothing (void) at ❷. This function prints a usage message to the player. We'll call it if we find out the player didn't type in the command correctly.

- A private helper function that returns true or false (a boolean) at ❺. This function will create new signs.

- A private helper function that returns true or false (a boolean) at ❻. This function will change the name on existing signs.

- A check of the length of the args array on the lines at ❸ and ❹. Since the user may not have typed in enough words for us to use, we have to check that the length is long enough and indicate an error otherwise.

- A wee bit of magic at ❼. This is how the Bukkit docs say to get a org.bukkit.block.Sign object from a org.bukkit.block.Block.

That's the gist of it. Now let's go through each of those pieces in detail.

The signs HashMap

First off, we set up a HashMap named signs to keep track of Locations by name (a String). When we're creating a new sign, we'll stuff its location in the hash, using the name the user gave us. When we go to set text on a sign, we'll get the sign's location back out of the hash by using the name.

The parseArgs Function

Since there are a couple of things to check for when the user types in a command, I've split that out into its own function instead of doing it right in the onCommand.

Notice we're using a parameter from onCommand that we haven't used before: String[] args. These are any arguments that the player types in with the command in the chat window. For example, if I type in

```
/signs
```

that will be passed to onCommand as the commandLabel, and args will be empty (length of zero). If I type

```
/signs set one Hello!
```

then commandLabel will still be "signs", args[0] will be "set", args[1] will be "one", and args[2] will be "Hello!".

We know that we need at least two values in the args array: it will either be "new name" or "set name something". So if we don't have at least two, we'll send a nice message to the player and return false.

Remember that with arrays, you have to check that the array is long enough; otherwise you'll get a lengthy error message from the server that ends up with something like this:

```
Caused by: java.lang.ArrayIndexOutOfBoundsException: 1
        at namedsigns.NamedSigns.makeSign(NamedSigns.java:26)
        at namedsigns.NamedSigns.onCommand(NamedSigns.java:47)
        at org.bukkit.command.PluginCommand.execute(PluginCommand.java:44)
        ... 15 more
```

Safe in the knowledge that we have *at least* two values in the args array to work with, let's see what the player actually typed in.

The "/signs new" Command

Here's the part for the "new" command:

NamedSigns/src/namedsigns/NamedSigns.java

```java
// signs new sign_name
private boolean makeNewSign(Player me, String [] args) {
  Location loc = me.getLocation();
  loc.setX(loc.getX() + 1); // Not right on top of player
  Block block = loc.getWorld().getHighestBlockAt(loc);
  signs.put(args[1], block.getLocation());
  block.setType(Material.SIGN_POST);
  log.info("Made new sign named " + args[1]);
  return true;
}
```

First we grab a handy block next to the player (getX() +1) and get the highest block at that location with getHighestBlockAt(). That way we won't be putting the sign underwater or in bedrock or anything.

Next we save this block's location to the hash, using the name the player gave us (args[1]).

Finally we set that block's type to Material.SIGN_POST. Now it's a sign.

The "/signs set" Command

And here's the part for the "set" command:

NamedSigns/src/namedsigns/NamedSigns.java

```java
// signs set sign_name line1
private boolean setSign(Player me, String [] args) {
  String name = args[1];
  String msg = args[2];
  if (!signs.containsKey(name)) {
    // No such named sign
    me.sendMessage("No sign named " + name);
    return false;
  }
  Location loc = signs.get(name);
  Sign sign = (Sign)loc.getWorld().getBlockAt(loc).getState();
  sign.setLine(0, msg);
  sign.update();
  log.info("Set sign named " + name + " to " + msg);
  return true;
}
```

First off, we need to make sure there are at least three values in args ("set", the name of the sign, and the word to put on the sign).

Next, notice that we're setting two local variables, name and msg, to args[0] and args[1]. Why bother? Aren't they the same thing? Yes, they are, but it's a lot easier to read name instead of reading args[1] and trying to remember that 1 is the name and 2 is the message.

Next we'll check that we really have an entry in the hash for name, and if not we'll complain to the player. Otherwise we can safely get the location for the sign block.

Next is the bit of magic. We can get the block at the right location, but it's still a block—an org.bukkit.block.Block. A Block doesn't know anything about the functions of a Sign. A Sign is one kind of Block, so we'll have to convince Java to make an org.bukkit.block.Sign out of it.

The Bukkit documentation tells us to call getState() on the block, and then cast that using the cast operator (Sign) to make a proper sign. With the sign variable in hand we can call the two Sign functions we need: setLine() and update().

setLine() puts a line of text on the sign at the given index (0 in this case), and update() makes sure that the sign is redrawn in the client so you can see the new text.

It might look like a fair bit of code, but if you look at each piece one at a time, it's not so hard. In fact, now it's your turn to make some changes.

Try This Yourself

As we have it here, the plugin only sets the first line of the sign, but you can have up to four lines per sign. Modify the plugin so that if the user types in extra words, you'll pass each word to sign.setLine(). Remember: if it can hold four lines, then they are numbered 0, 1, 2, and 3. We've got the setLine(0) already, so you'll need to add the others if args is long enough.

Next Up

In this chapter we've seen how to use a HashMap to keep track of important game data by name or other object, and how to make functions private so that other plugins can't access them, or public so that they can.

In the next chapter we'll do more than just respond to user commands. We'll see how to listen to the Minecraft server and respond to game events as they happen, and even create a few of our own.

Your Growing Toolbox

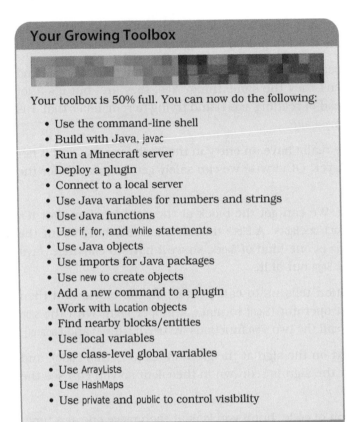

Your toolbox is 50% full. You can now do the following:

- Use the command-line shell
- Build with Java, javac
- Run a Minecraft server
- Deploy a plugin
- Connect to a local server
- Use Java variables for numbers and strings
- Use Java functions
- Use if, for, and while statements
- Use Java objects
- Use imports for Java packages
- Use new to create objects
- Add a new command to a plugin
- Work with Location objects
- Find nearby blocks/entities
- Use local variables
- Use class-level global variables
- Use ArrayLists
- Use HashMaps
- Use private and public to control visibility

## CHAPTER 9

Modify, Spawn, and Listen in Minecraft

> **Your Toolbox**
>
> With this chapter you'll add these abilities to your toolbox:
>
> - Modify blocks in the world
> - Modify and spawn new entities
> - Listen for and react to game events
> - Manage plugin permissions
>
> This is exciting! Now you have most of the basic tools you need; you can alter the world and react to in-game events.

Now we're going to go beyond issuing simple commands and dropping squid bombs, and look at a wider range of things you can do in Minecraft. By the end of this chapter, you'll be able to affect behavior in the game without having to issue *any* commands at all.

All you have to do is listen—you'll see how, by learning about Minecraft events. We'll listen for events, act on them, and even schedule our own events to fire sometime in the future.

From your plugin code, you can change existing blocks and entities, and you can spawn new ones. We'll look at exactly how to do that:

- Modify existing blocks: change things like location, properties, and contents
- Modify existing entities: change properties on a Player
- Spawn new entities and blocks

We've done some of this already—we've changed a Player's location, and we've spawned more than a few Squids. Let's take a closer look at what else you can do with the basic elements in the Minecraft world, and then we'll see how you can react to in-game events to affect those elements and create new ones.

Modify Blocks

The basic recipe for a block object in Minecraft is listed in the Bukkit documentation under org.bukkit.block.Block.[1]

There are many interesting functions in a Block, and we won't cover them all, but here are a few of the most useful and interesting things you can do to a block:

- getLocation() returns the Location for this block. Only one block can exist at any location in the world, and every location contains a block, even if it's just air.

- getType() returns the Material this block is made of.

- setType(Material type) sets a new Material for this block.

- getDrops() returns a list of items (actually a Collection of ItemStack lists) that would fall if this block were destroyed.

- breakNaturally() breaks the block and spawns any items, just as if a player had done the breaking. Returns true if the block was successfully destroyed, and false if it wasn't.

Let's play with that a bit.

Plugin: Stuck

Let's look at a plugin that will encase a player in solid rock (the full plugin is in code/Stuck). When you issue the command stuck with a player's name, that player will suddenly be encased in a pile of blocks. (If you're alone on the server, your player name might be the wonderfully descriptive name "player.")

We'll start by looking at pieces of this plugin, and then put it all together.

All the interesting parts are in a separate helper function, named stuck. The main part of the plugin should look pretty familiar by now:

Stuck/src/stuck/Stuck.java
```
package stuck;

import org.bukkit.Location;
import org.bukkit.Material;
import org.bukkit.World;
```

---

1. http://jd.bukkit.org/rb/doxygen/d9/d48/interfaceorg_1_1bukkit_1_1block_1_1Block.html

```
import org.bukkit.block.Block;
import org.bukkit.command.Command;
import org.bukkit.command.CommandSender;
import org.bukkit.entity.Player;
import org.bukkit.plugin.Plugin;
import org.bukkit.plugin.java.JavaPlugin;

public class Stuck extends JavaPlugin {
  public boolean onCommand(CommandSender sender, Command command,
                           String commandLabel, String[] args) {
    if (commandLabel.equalsIgnoreCase("Stuck")) {
      if(args.length == 1) {
        Player player = getServer().getPlayer(args[0]);
        if (player != null) { return stuck(player); }
      } else {
        sender.sendMessage("Usage: /stuck playerName");
      }
    }
    return false;
  }
```

In onCommand we'll try to get the named player, which may or may not work. If it doesn't work (if there's no player online with that name), we'll fall out of the if/then/else stuff and end up returning false from onCommand.

If it does work (that is, if we found the player), then we'll go ahead and call stuck, passing in the player object we got.

Here's the beginning of the stuck function:

Stuck/src/stuck/Stuck.java
```
public boolean stuck(Player player) {
  World world = player.getWorld();
  Location loc = player.getLocation();
  int playerX = (int) loc.getX();
  int playerY = (int) loc.getY();
  int playerZ = (int) loc.getZ();
  loc.setX(playerX + 0.5); loc.setY(playerY); loc.setZ(playerZ + 0.5);
  player.teleport(loc);
```

The first thing we'll do inside of the stuck function is get the correct world and the player's current location in loc. Over the next few lines, we'll set up to teleport the player to the center of the block he or she is stuck in right now. That makes it easier to plunk blocks down all around the player.

And how are we going to do that, exactly? Well, we know that a player takes up two blocks. The location we got for the player is really where the character's legs and feet are. The block on top of that (y+1) is the player's head and chest. So we want a bunch of blocks, arranged like a stack of two blocks on all four sides of the player, plus a block underneath and one on top. That should be ten blocks in all, as you can see in the figure.

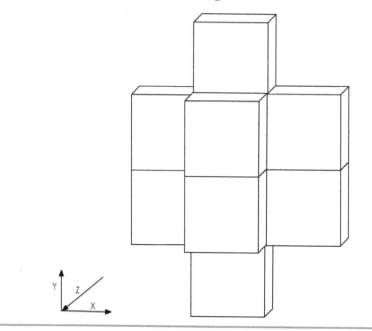

Figure 8—Trapping a player in blocks

We know where each of those blocks goes, based on the player's location. So we've got a case where we need ten sets of coordinates, each one offset from the player's base block. We need a list of lists.

And that's what you'll see next. It's an int array of ten elements, and each element is an int array of three offsets, one each for x, y, and z value:

Stuck/src/stuck/Stuck.java
```java
int[][] offsets = {
  //x,  y,  z
  {0,  -1, 0},
  {0,  2,  0},
  {1,  0,  0},
  {1,  1,  0},
  {-1, 0,  0},
  {-1, 1,  0},
  {0,  0,  1},
  {0,  1,  1},
  {0,  0, -1},
  {0,  1, -1},
};
```

We'll use a simple for loop to go through this list of offsets. The first element in the list is indexed at 0, and we'll go up to (but not including) the length of the list. By using the length of the offsets list instead of sticking in a fixed number, like 10, it makes it easier if we ever want to add extra blocks to the list (remember we're adding the playerX, playerY, and playerZ offsets from the preceding code):

Stuck/src/stuck/Stuck.java

```
    for(int i = 0; i < offsets.length; i++) {
      int x = offsets[i][0];
      int y = offsets[i][1];
      int z = offsets[i][2];
      Block b = world.getBlockAt(x + playerX, y + playerY, z + playerZ);
      b.setType(Material.STONE);
    }
    return true;
  }
}
```

So here we are, going through the list of offsets. At each list index (which is in i), we need to pick out the three elements x, y, and z. In each of the small arrays, x is first at index 0. The Java syntax lets you work with arrays of arrays by writing both indexes, with the big list first. Think of this set of numbers as a table or a matrix, with rows and columns, like you might find in an Excel spreadsheet. You specify indexes in "row-major order," which just means the row comes first, then the column. For each trip through the loop, we'll pick out an x, y, and z value from the list. That's the location of a block we want to turn to stone.

We get the block at that location we want—in this case, by adding the x, y, and z offset to the player's location (playerX, playerY, and playerZ from the code). With the block in hand, simply set its material to stone by using the constant Material.STONE. All the material types are listed in the documentation for org.bukkit.Material. You could, for instance, remove a block without breaking it—you'd set the block's material to Material.AIR.

Here's the code for the full plugin, all together:

Stuck/src/stuck/Stuck.java

```
package stuck;

import org.bukkit.Location;
import org.bukkit.Material;
import org.bukkit.World;
import org.bukkit.block.Block;
import org.bukkit.command.Command;
import org.bukkit.command.CommandSender;
```

```java
import org.bukkit.entity.Player;
import org.bukkit.plugin.Plugin;
import org.bukkit.plugin.java.JavaPlugin;

public class Stuck extends JavaPlugin {
  public boolean onCommand(CommandSender sender, Command command,
                           String commandLabel, String[] args) {
    if (commandLabel.equalsIgnoreCase("Stuck")) {
      if(args.length == 1) {
        Player player = getServer().getPlayer(args[0]);
        if (player != null) { return stuck(player); }
      } else {
        sender.sendMessage("Usage: /stuck playerName");
      }
    }
    return false;
  }
  public boolean stuck(Player player) {
    World world = player.getWorld();
    Location loc = player.getLocation();
    int playerX = (int) loc.getX();
    int playerY = (int) loc.getY();
    int playerZ = (int) loc.getZ();
    loc.setX(playerX + 0.5); loc.setY(playerY); loc.setZ(playerZ + 0.5);
    player.teleport(loc);

    int[][] offsets = {
    //x,  y,  z
      {0,  -1, 0},
      {0,  2,  0},
      {1,  0,  0},
      {1,  1,  0},
      {-1, 0,  0},
      {-1, 1,  0},
      {0,  0,  1},
      {0,  1,  1},
      {0,  0,  -1},
      {0,  1,  -1},
    };

    for(int i = 0; i < offsets.length; i++) {
      int x = offsets[i][0];
      int y = offsets[i][1];
      int z = offsets[i][2];
      Block b = world.getBlockAt(x + playerX, y + playerY, z + playerZ);
      b.setType(Material.STONE);
    }
    return true;
  }
}
```

Compile and deploy the Stuck plugin and give it a try. What happens if the player is standing on the ground or up in the air? What does it look like from the player's point of view, inside the blocks?

Try This Yourself

In the Stuck plugin, we've encased a player in the minimum number of blocks needed to enclose the player. But from the outside, it makes kind of a weird-looking shape.

So here's what you need to do: add extra blocks so that the player is encased in a solid rectangle, measuring 3 blocks wide, 3 blocks deep, and 4 blocks tall. Add the extra blocks to the list of block offsets, then recompile and deploy and see if you've put the extra blocks in the right places. From the outside, it should look like a solid, rectangular block.

Modify Entities

Entities, as you might expect, are quite different from blocks. For one thing, there are many more kinds of entities, and they have different kinds of abilities (and functions for us). With blocks, all you have to do is change the ID and perhaps add some additional information, but entities are more complicated.

To start off, all entities have the capabilities described in org.bukkit.entity.Entity, which include the following useful functions:

- getLocation() returns the Location of the entity.

- setVelocity(Vector velocity) sets its velocity.

- teleport(Location location) teleports the entity to a new location. It returns true if it was successful, and false otherwise.

- teleport(Entity destination) teleports the entity to the location of the *destination* entity. Way to crash a party.

Then, depending on the type of the entity, you might have other cool functions to play with. Living entities (org.bukkit.entity.LivingEntity), for example, have the following extra functions:

- launchProjectile(Projectile) lets you throw an egg, fire an arrow, toss a snowball, or launch other kinds of Projectiles. It returns the launched Projectile.

- getLastDamage() returns the amount of damage (as an int) just inflicted on this entity.

- setLastDamage(int damage) sets the damage value of the last damaging event. You could make it a lot or a little.

- damage(int amount) inflicts damage on this entity.

- getHealth() returns a double of this entity's health. It can be zero (dead) up to the amount returned by getMaxHealth().

- setHealth(double health) sets the health. Zero is dead.

You may have noticed that not all these functions are declared in LivingEntity itself. This is where Java gets a little messy. The familiar entity objects incorporate a lot of different parent recipes. For instance, a Cow is an Animals, but also an Ageable, a Creature, a LivingEntity, a Damageable object, and, of course, an Entity.

That means it uses functions from all these different parents. Because Cow inherits from Ageable, you get functions where you can alter a Cow property to change its age—make it a baby or an adult—let it breed or not, and so on.

A Player, on the other hand, does not use Ageable, so you can't turn players into babies, even if they're acting like them. Instead, a Player has a whole different set of functions available, including functions to change the weather, the time of day, and the player's experience level, food level, inventory, and so on.

Spawn Entities

You can use several functions to spawn different entities and creatures, as well as game objects—like an Ender Pearl.[2] To create new things in the world, we'll use functions defined in org.bukkit.World. There are a few useful ways to spawn things, depending on what you're making and how you want to specify it:

- spawn(Location location, Class whatToSpawn) is what we used to spawn squid previously. You can get the class to pass in by using the class function on the class name itself, like this: Cow.class.

- spawnArrow(Location location, Vector velocity, 0.6, 12) returns a new Arrow. The hard-coded numbers 0.6 and 12 seem to make an arrow that flies nicely.

- spawnCreature(Location loc, CreatureType type) returns a LivingEntity.

- spawnEntity(Location loc, EntityType type) is used for nonliving entities; it returns an Entity.

---

2. In survival mode, right-clicking on an Ender Pearl will transport you to where it lands.

- spawnFallingBlock(Location location, Material material, byte data) means "watch out below." What you pass in for data depends on the material.

- strikeLightning(Location loc) lets you hurl lightning bolts, in case you fancy being Zeus.

Plugin: FlyingCreeper

Here's a plugin that shows spawning two entities: a bat and a creeper. We'll make the creeper ride the bat, and then turn the bat invisible using a potion effect. The result is a nightmarish, terrifying, flying creeper.

Here are the guts of the plugin:

```
FlyingCreeper/src/flyingcreeper/FlyingCreeper.java
Location loc = player.getLocation();
loc.setY(loc.getY() + 5);
Bat bat = player.getWorld().spawn(loc, Bat.class);
Creeper creeper = player.getWorld().spawn(loc, Creeper.class);
bat.setPassenger(creeper);
PotionEffect potion = new PotionEffect(
        PotionEffectType.INVISIBILITY,
        Integer.MAX_VALUE,
        1);
bat.addPotionEffect(potion);
```

Notice we're using the first version of spawn that we just saw, where we pass in a location and a class—in this case, Bat.class and Creeper.class.

All Entity objects have a setPassenger() function. In theory, you could even ride primed TNT. But I wouldn't advise it. Here we're going to have the creeper ride the bat by setting the bat's passenger to the creeper.

Next we need to turn the bat invisible to make the flying creeper look more convincing. Fortunately, all LivingEntity objects can use potion effects.[3] We'll create a new potion effect, which lets us specify the effect's type, duration, and magnitude:

```
PotionEffect (PotionEffectType type, int duration, int amplifier)
```

In this case, the type is PotionEffectType.INVISIBILITY and we want it to last forever, so we'll make the duration the largest possible value we can: Integer.MAX_VALUE. There is no integer larger. The magnitude doesn't really matter in this case, as you can't be any "more invisible," so we'll just use a 1.

---

3. All potion effect types are listed at http://jd.bukkit.org/rb/doxygen/d3/d70/classorg_1_1bukkit_1_1potion_1_1PotionEffectType.html.

Finally, we add that new potion to the bat, and it's invisible.

Congratulations! You are now the proud owner of flying creepers. Good luck, and stay low.

For extra credit, you could go back and modify the SquidBomb to generate a ton of invisible creepers instead of squid. That'd be fun.

We'll see some more examples of modifying and spawning entities in the next section, once we see how to listen for game events.

Listen for Events

Now we get to the best part. You know how to write code for commands the user types in and you know how to do things to affect the world. Now it's time to see how to monitor what's going on in the world so you can respond to gameplay automatically, without typing in a command or anything.

It works like this: you set up your code such that your functions get called when some interesting event happens. In your function, you can let the events happen or you can stop them.

We'll start off by listening for events right in our main plugin. In the next chapter we'll look at how to split that off into its own separate class and source code file.

Here's a skeleton of what we need to add to our basic plugin in order to incorporate a listener. There are four parts to it:

1. Import the event listener.

2. Declare that your plugin implements Listener.

3. Register to listen for events with registerEvents.

4. Add the magical tag @EventHandler to mark your function as an event handler, and list the event you want as an argument.

You'll see all four parts in this short example skeleton of a listener:

```
import org.bukkit.plugin.java.JavaPlugin;
import org.bukkit.event.Listener;
import org.bukkit.event.EventHandler;
❶ import // Some kind of event goes here //

   // Add "implements Listener" here:
❷ public class HelloWorld extends JavaPlugin implements Listener {

❸     public void onEnable() {
          // Register this plugin to listen to events
          getServer().getPluginManager().registerEvents(this, this);
       }

       // Here's one event listener:
❹      @EventHandler
       public void anyname(SomeEvent event) {
          // Some code goes here
       }
   }
```

First off, you have to import the class for the event you're interested in (you'd add this somewhere around ❶).

There are a *ton* of events available, all listed in the Bukkit documentation under org.bukkit.event. Suppose you're interested in doing something whenever someone in the game teleports. You'd want the EntityTeleportEvent class, so first thing here you'd import org.bukkit.event.entity.EntityTeleportEvent.

Then the declaration for the plugin needs to add the magic words implements Listener, as shown at ❷.

Next you need to add some code to your onEnable() function, as shown starting at ❸. This is a standard piece of boilerplate code that just says "make this plugin listen for events." You need this only once in this file; it will work for all events you'll use. Add it in, and off we go.

Finally we come to the event listener itself, starting at ❹. Yes, starting there, not on the line with public void like usual. That @EventHandler thing is a tag that tells Java that the next function is special. It's part of the function name. Always start off an event handler with that special declaration.[4]

The function for the listener itself can be named anything you want (shown here as anyname). But the argument list is important: the type of event you list here determines when this function will be called, or if it gets called at all.

An event handler for the EntityTeleportEvent would look like this:

```
@EventHandler
public void myTeleportListener(EntityTeleportEvent event) {
    // Some code here
}
```

I made up the name myTeleportListener, but that part doesn't matter—it's the EntityTeleportEvent that's important. According to the documentation, this event has several interesting functions we can use:

isCancelled()	returns true if this event has already been cancelled.
setCancelled(boolean cancel)	lets you cancel or uncancel this event. Pass in a true to cancel it, and a false to revive it.
getFrom()	returns the location the entity came from.
setFrom(Location from)	sets the location the entity came from.
getTo()	returns the location this entity is moving to.
setTo(Location to)	sets location this entity is moving to.

For instance, to prevent anything from teleporting anywhere, you could write this:

```
@EventHandler
public void myTeleportListener(EntityTeleportEvent event) {
    event.setCancelled(true);
}
```

Remember our SkyCmd plugin? We can use the same logic from that in this event listener; now everyone who teleports will be flung skyward. That piece would look like this:

```
@EventHandler
public void myTeleportListener(EntityTeleportEvent event) {
    Location midair = event.getTo();
    double y = midair.getY();
    midair.setY(y+50);
    event.setTo(midair);
}
```

---

4. Java calls this an *annotation.*

Plugin: BackCmd

Let's use some of these features in a complete plugin. Here's the full source for BackCmd that provides a single command named back. Go ahead and build and install it:

```
$ cd Desktop
$ cd code/BackCmd
$ ./build.sh
```

And restart the server.

Now teleport to a couple of locations, either by using the /tp command in creative mode or by right-clicking on an Ender Pearl in survival mode.

Now type /back, and you'll be teleported back to your last location.

This plugin will listen for events to keep track of where you've been, and let you return to previous locations in order.

BackCmd/src/backcmd/BackCmd.java
```java
package backcmd;

import java.util.ArrayList;
import java.util.HashMap;
import java.util.List;
import java.util.Stack;
import java.util.logging.Logger;
import org.bukkit.Location;
import org.bukkit.command.Command;
import org.bukkit.command.CommandSender;
import org.bukkit.entity.Player;
import org.bukkit.event.EventHandler;
import org.bukkit.event.Listener;
import org.bukkit.event.player.PlayerTeleportEvent;
import org.bukkit.plugin.Plugin;
import org.bukkit.plugin.java.JavaPlugin;
```
❶ `public class BackCmd extends JavaPlugin implements Listener {`
   `  public static Logger log = Logger.getLogger("Minecraft");`
❷ `  private static List<Player> isTeleporting = new ArrayList<Player>();`
   `  private static HashMap<String, Stack<Location>> playerTeleports =`
   `      new HashMap<String, Stack<Location>>();`

   `  public void onEnable() {`
   `    log.info("[BackCmd] enabling.");`
❸ `    getServer().getPluginManager().registerEvents(this, this);`
   `  }`

❹
```java
public boolean equalsIsh(Location loc1, Location loc2) {
    return ((int) loc1.getX()) == ((int) loc2.getX()) &&
           ((int) loc1.getZ()) == ((int) loc2.getZ());
}


@EventHandler
```
❺
```java
public void onTeleport(PlayerTeleportEvent event) {
    Player player = event.getPlayer();
    if (isTeleporting.contains(player)) {
      isTeleporting.remove(player);
    } else {
      Stack<Location> locs = playerTeleports.get(player.getName());
      if (locs == null) {
        locs = new Stack<Location>();
      }
      locs.push(event.getFrom());
      locs.push(event.getTo());
      playerTeleports.put(player.getName(), locs);
    }
}

public boolean onCommand(CommandSender sender, Command command,
                         String commandLabel, String[] args) {
  if (commandLabel.equalsIgnoreCase("back")) {
    if (sender instanceof Player) {
      Player player = (Player) sender;
      Stack<Location> locs = playerTeleports.get(player.getName());

      if (locs != null && !locs.empty()) {
        Location loc = locs.peek();
        while (equalsIsh(loc, player.getLocation()) && locs.size() > 1) {
          locs.pop();
          loc = locs.peek();
        }
        isTeleporting.add(player);
        player.teleport(loc);
        return true;
      } else {
        player.sendMessage("You have not teleported yet.");
      }
    } else {
      sender.sendMessage("You must be a player to use this command.");
    }
  }
  return false;
}

}
```

As this plugin is using event listening, here are the special things you need to do:

- At ❶, declare that this plugin implements Listener.
- At ❸, register the plugin for events.
- At ❺ add the EventHandler annotation and declare that this event listener will listen for PlayerTeleportEvent events.

Every time a player teleports, the onTeleport function will be called. The first thing we do is get the correct Player object, which is stored in the event that was passed in to us. Now we know who we're dealing with.

Next we're looking in the list named isTeleporting to find out whether this player is someone we are in the middle of teleporting. What's isTeleporting, you ask?

Ah, take a look up at the top of the plugin around ❷, and you'll see two variables declared to be private static. That means no one else can see them, and the values will stick around in between this command being run. So here we have isTeleporting and playerTeleports to keep track of players and the locations they've teleported to and from.

We're checking to see if our isTeleporting list contains this player already. If it doesn't, we'll add it—this player has just started teleporting. If the isTeleporting list already contains this player, then we should ignore this event (and remove the player from the list). That means we generated this event ourselves, and we don't want our own teleport to trigger the teleport, because it would keep doing that forever. So we throw this extra teleport event out.

If this player has teleported before, we'll get a locs from the playerTeleports hash (a hash of locations) using the player as a key. We'll add this location to the existing list. If this is the player's first time teleporting, we'll make a new list (of Locations) and add this location as its first entry.

But this is no ordinary list. It's a kind of list, alright, but it's a Stack, not a plain list. A Stack works like a stack of pancakes. You add to the top of the stack, and when you remove a pancake it comes off the top of the stack. That's the model we want for our list of places we've teleported. As you teleport, each location is added to the top of the stack—and it's the top one you want to go back to next, then the one under that, and so on.

To add an object to the top of a stack, you push it on. To get the value and remove the object at the top, you pop it off. To just check on the top value without removing it, you can peek at it.

So as players teleport around, we'll have a stack of each of their teleport locations, stored in a Stack in our playerTeleports variable, which we can get to by using the Player object as a key. You can see what this looks like in the following figure.

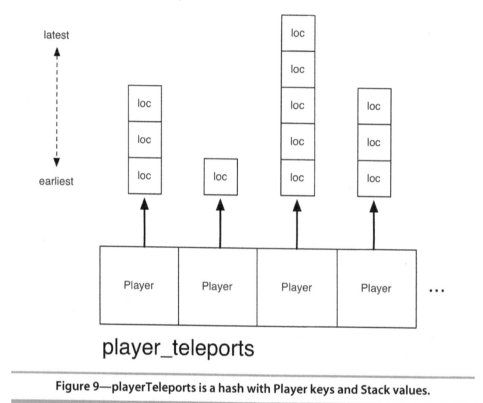

player_teleports

Figure 9—playerTeleports is a hash with Player keys and Stack values.

Finally, we get down to the onCommand. When we get a back command, we'll get the player's list of teleport locations (if there is one), and peek at the location on the top of the stack, saving that in loc for now.

Maybe we teleported to this spot and haven't moved yet. In that case, we'd want to go to the previous spot—not stay at this location. So we'll test for that: if we're still at the same location as the last teleport (or close to it), we'll remove that location from the locs list by using the pop, and set loc to the next location in the stack.

Either way, we've got a loc pointing to the spot that we want to teleport to. We'll add the player to the isTeleporting list and teleport the player to the new location.

Now what do we mean by "or close to it"? Notice that we're using a helper function named equalsIsh (declared at ❹). It's checking two locations to see if the x- and z-coordinates are within the same block. By casting the floating-point values to integer (using the (int) keyword), we're throwing out the fractional part of the coordinate. We're interested only if you're in the same block, not at a slightly different position within the same block.

Try This Yourself

For this exercise, you're going to create a brand-new plugin that uses a listener.

Create a plugin named FireBow. When you fire an arrow, it will change the arrow into a flying, exploding block of TNT. To do this, listen for a EntityShoot-BowEvent and spawn a new TNTPrimed entity at the same location as the arrow. Set the new TNT entity's velocity to the same as the arrow's velocity, as well. Don't forget to cancel the arrow event; that way, there will be no arrow—only flying TNT.

Hint: you can get the arrow from the EntityShootBowEvent event using event. getProjectile().

My example of code that does all this is in code/FireBow. Try it yourself first, from scratch, and if you get stuck take a look at the example. I added two commands that allow you to enable or disable the firebow behavior.

Check Permissions

Sometimes when writing a plugin, you might want to restrict the commands you've created—maybe only ops should run them, or maybe you have different kinds of players or teams, and each should only be able to run certain commands.

For instance, suppose you want to restrict the firebow commands to a select set of players. We'll invent a new name; let's call it FireBow.enable.

You can then use the hasPermission function in Player to determine if the current player is one of the chosen few:

```
player.hasPermission("FireBow.canEnable")
```

That will return a true or a false depending on whether the player has that permission.

In our FireBow plugin, it would look like this:

```
if (commandLabel.equalsIgnoreCase("firebow") &&
    player.hasPermission("FireBow.canEnable")) {
  enabled = true;
  return true;
}
```

If the command string is firebow *and* if the player has permission to run the command, then we'll set the necessary variable. Otherwise, it's as if the player didn't type the command at all.

You could break that out separately instead, and maybe take some other action when the folks without permission try to run a command:

```
if (commandLabel.equalsIgnoreCase("firebow")) {
  if (!player.hasPermission("FireBow.canEnable")) {
    player.sendMessage("You aren't allowed to use this command.")
  } else {
    enabled = true;
    return true;
  }
}
```

Setting and Managing Permissions

Setting and managing permissions can be a big deal if you're running a large server with lots of users. You might set up groups or classes of users in the server's permissions.yml file, or use additional plugins to help manage users.

For developing plugins and testing, though, you can just specify permissions directly in permissions.yml or use a simple plugin that manages basic permissions, such as PermissionsBukkit.[5]

The PermissionsBukkit plugin adds a bunch of in-game commands, including commands to set permissions for a player and to check what permissions someone has:

```
/permissions player setperm <player> <[world:]node> [true|false]
```

```
/permissions check <node> [player]
```

For example, in our plugin, to give jack37 permissions to use our /firebow command, you'd type the following commands in the console:

```
/permissions player setperm jack37 FireBow.canEnable true
```

Check out the Bukkit docs for more details.

---

5.   Located at http://dev.bukkit.org/bukkit-plugins/permbukkit

Next Up

We got a lot of new abilities in this chapter: you can now modify Minecraft blocks and spawn entities, manage plugin permissions, and, most importantly, listen for interesting events to happen in the game and react to them. That's the real heart of plugins that can change how the Minecraft world works by automatically acting on events as they occur.

In the next chapter we'll look at how to schedule events in the future, and make an exploding cow shooter. See you there.

Your Growing Toolbox

Your toolbox is 60% full. You can now do the following:

- Use the command-line shell
- Build with Java, javac
- Run a Minecraft server
- Deploy a plugin
- Connect to a local server
- Use Java variables for numbers and strings
- Use Java functions
- Use if, for, and while statements
- Use Java objects
- Use imports for Java packages
- Use new to create objects
- Add a new command to a plugin
- Work with Location objects
- Find nearby blocks/entities
- Use local variables
- Use class-level global variables
- Use ArrayLists
- Use HashMaps
- Use private and public to control visibility
- Modify Minecraft blocks
- Modify and spawn entities
- Listen for and react to game events
- Manage plugin permissions

## CHAPTER 10

Schedule Tasks for Later

Your Toolbox

In this chapter you'll learn more about objects, classes, and scheduling tasks that will run later. You'll add this knowledge to your toolbox:

- How to create a separate class
- How to schedule a task object to run later
- How to schedule a task object to keep running later

Your toolbox is nearly complete now. You can write some really cool plugins just based on what we've done so far.

Now we'll talk about how to make things happen in Minecraft that aren't in direct response to either an event or a user-issued command: how to schedule tasks that will happen sometime in the future—and even keep running—all on their own. This feature helps you implement things that seem to act all on their own, like attacking creepers or other enemies.

On the Java front, you'll also see how to make your own classes in separate files, and we'll take a look at some of the problems Java has with running multiple things at once.

What Happens When?

When we talk about running something "later," it exposes the ugly truth that the world doesn't stop changing just because your code is running. Computers can do more than one thing at once, and are doing that all the time. But most code isn't written that way.

Think about some of the plugins we've looked at so far. What would happen if, right in the middle of running that piece of code, another player typed the same command and that same code started running from the top?

Take a look at the following figure. Each arrow and code snippet represents a set of instructions that the computer is running at the same time. We call each separate set a *thread*—kind of like the thread of a subplot in a novel, or the thread of one conversation in the middle of many others at lunch.

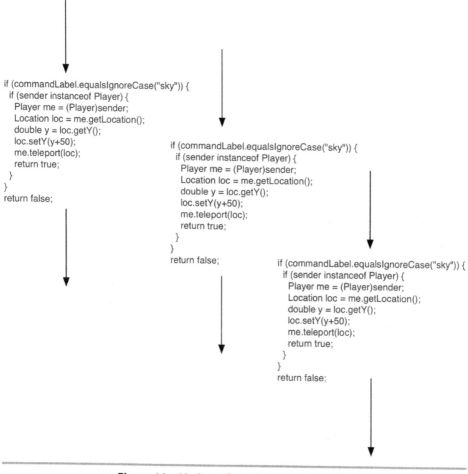

Figure 10—Various threads executing code

Normally you think of the computer running though your code once, as in the left part of the diagram. You'd think the computer executes instructions one after another, from top to bottom, and nothing else is going on at the same time. That would be one thread of execution (like one conversation).

But in fact that's not the case; the computer can be running a bunch of different threads of execution, apparently all at the same time. Can our code work that way? What would happen to our code if it were run by multiple threads?

If you're using only local variables and aren't trying to change anything in common in the Minecraft world, that would probably be fine—each version of the code as it's running would have its own copy of variables, and no harm done. But what if you're using a static variable, something like a big HashMap to keep track of players and values? Then you have two bits of code reading and writing from it at the same time, and that generally leads to disaster.

Imagine that you read the player's health as 50 in one thread, but then a second thread sets it to 0—killing the player. You don't know that, and you subtract 10 from the player's health and reset it to 40. Now the other thread thinks it's killed the player, but instead of 0 the health has "magically" been set to 40! That's a simple and innocent example, but far worse things can happen that could cause strange bugs or make your code—and the server —crash.

There are ways to write code that can be run by multiple threads safely; however, the Bukkit code was not built that way.

That's important enough to repeat: *the Bukkit library, and your code that uses it, is not built to be run by multiple threads.* It will break.

So when we want to run a piece of code "later," we can't actually let it run at some random time—we can't let it run at the same time as our code (or the Bukkit code).

Instead, we have to let Bukkit determine when to run the code. Then it can run it pretty much as if it were a player typing in a command or responding to an in-game event; it's the only thing running at the time. Bukkit calls that a *synchronous* task, and that's what you'll learn how to set up in this chapter.

But to set up a task, we'll first see how to make our own classes.

Put Code in a Class by Itself

First, let's be a little more precise in what we name things. In Java source code, you declare a plugin to be a public class, which is Java's way of saying, "This is a recipe. I can make objects of this class at runtime." While I've been loosely talking about recipes and parent recipes, I'm going to start calling them by their proper Java name: *classes*. "Recipes" are classes.

So far we've sort of cheated—we've been putting all new code in our one plugin class, in one source-code file. When the Minecraft server runs, it makes one object from that class file and uses that.

But if you look at other plugins out on the Internet, you'll notice that often a plugin is made up of several different classes, all working together. The main class file has the plugin itself, while other class files might contain listeners, or tasks to be scheduled, or any other kind of helper code that the plugin might need. We've been adding listeners right in our main class, but we aren't going to do that with schedule-able tasks; we'll define that code in its own class.

Mechanically, making another source-code file is easy. If you can hit your text editor's File -> Save (or something similar), you can make a new file. As long as you've saved it in the correct directory, the build system will see the new file and know what to do. But that's not enough. You need to know how to tell the plugin about the new file, and the new file about the plugin.

What Should I Put in a Class?

Beginning programmers might look at a class as just a box to toss functions and data into. Overall, that's a bad idea—just like a messy attic or garage, you end up with a lot of boxes full of junk spilling out and tangled up in each other.

Instead, any class you create should be responsible for just one thing. In other words, any class should have only one reason to change. If it's responsible for a lot of different things, then suddenly it's got a lot of reasons it may need to change: it's fragile, and fragile code leads to suffering.

For instance, in BackCmdListener we're making a separate Listener. The whole class is responsible only for listening to game events (an onTeleport event in this case).

Many plugins use a static variable to do that. In other words, they will use code in the main plugin to create a static variable that holds an object of the other class, and reference it that way. You can also just create an object from the class using new.

Using a Separate Listener

For example, suppose that in BackCmd we wanted to make the listener a separate class. We'd put the onTeleport method in a separate class file and name it something like BackCmdListener. Then in our main plugin, we'd change the top of the class declaration and take out the implements part, like this:

```
public class BackCmd extends JavaPlugin {
```

So the main plugin is no longer a listener. The separate class BackCmdListener is the listener now.

So later on when you want to use the listener, you can just create one using new:

```
pm.registerEvents(new BackCmdListener(), this);
```

It looks something like the following figure. The listener is in a separate file, and you create a listener object using the new keyword and pass that into registerEvents instead of the main plugin class, referenced by this.

So this is no longer the listener; a new BackCmdListener() is.

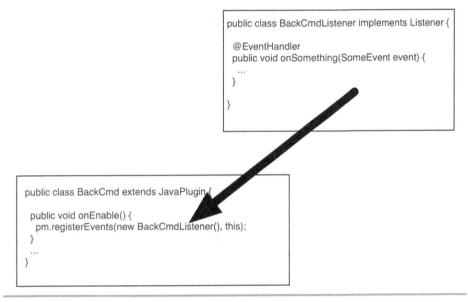

Figure 11—Using a separate listener class

You can look at the full code for the main plugin and the listener code in code/BackCmdListener/src/backcmdlistener, which has both BackCmd.java (the plugin) and BackCmdListener.java (the listener) files.

That seems easy enough and lets us use a separate file for the listener, which is the kind of thing we'll want to do when scheduling.

So let's see what it takes to make a task that we can schedule to run (when Bukkit thinks it's okay to run it) sometime in the future. We'll look at the bits and pieces first, and then put it all together in a cool plugin.

Make a Runnable Task

Here's the simplest code for a task that just sends a broadcast message. It may not do much, but you can use this piece of code as a starting template when making your own tasks.

Just add the code you want down in the body of the run function, change the package name, and add any imports you may need. (Remember, the common ones are listed in Appendix 7, *Common Imports*, on page 253, and you can find others in the Bukkit or Java docs.)

```java
package examplepackage;
import org.bukkit.Bukkit;
import org.bukkit.plugin.java.JavaPlugin;
import org.bukkit.scheduler.BukkitRunnable;

❶ public class ExampleTask extends BukkitRunnable {

    private final JavaPlugin plugin;

    public ExampleTask(JavaPlugin plugin) {
        this.plugin = plugin;
        // you can keep a reference to your plugin as I've done here,
        // or to any other variable you pass in
    }

    public void run() {
        // Do something interesting...
        plugin.getServer().broadcastMessage("Surprise!");
    }

}
```

In this case, you'd put this code in its own file, which must be named Example-Task.java (to match the name on the line at ❶).

So far so good, but what's up with this interesting-looking function that has no return type and is named ExampleTask—the exact same name as our class? Remember, that's called a *constructor*. That's the function Java calls when it's creating a new ExampleTask.

So to create an ExampleTask, you have to pass in a JavaPlugin to the new (which gets passed to your constructor). In other words, you have to give it your main plugin object. That way this task can get at all the Bukkit things it might need to, like the world, players, and so on.

Now that you have a task that will do something interesting (well, sort of), how do you schedule it?

Schedule to Run Later

Now back to your main plugin: once you have the task defined over in its own class, you can create an object of that class from your main plugin using new, and set it up to be run some number of server ticks in the future using runTaskLater().

```
BukkitTask task = new ExampleTask(plugin);
task.runTaskLater(plugin, 20);
```

plugin should be a variable that's set to your main plugin. If you're putting this code in a non-static function in your plugin, you can use the Java keyword this, which means "this plugin object." If you're putting this code in a static function, you need a static variable (like plugin) that has previously been set to the plugin. For example, in an object function (a *method*) like onEnable you'd set plugin = this.

You might want to hang on to the task variable, but it's not necessary. With or without it, you've created an ExampleTask whose run function will be run 20 ticks from now (which is about one second).

It will run that only one time, however, and never again.

Schedule to Keep Running

If you want a task that will *keep* running, then you use a slightly different scheduling function, runTaskTimer().

```
BukkitTask task = new ExampleTask(plugin);
task.runTaskTimer(Plugin plugin, long delay, long period);
```

So here you'd pass in a variable that holds your plugin, and two numbers. These numbers are declared as long, which is shorthand for a long int, which just means it can be a really big number.

This will run the given task after an initial *delay* (in server ticks), and will wait for a specified *period* (also in ticks) before running it again. It will run forever that way, until it cancels itself (or you cancel it).

We could change the previous example to delay for 1 second, then run the ExampleTask once each minute:

```
BukkitTask task = new ExampleTask(plugin).runTaskTimer(plugin, 20, 1200);
```

At 20 ticks per second, that's 1 second for the delay and 60 seconds for the period.

Plugin: CowShooter

Now we have enough parts to make a really fun plugin: the CowShooter. If you have a piece of leather in your hand in the game world, you can click to shoot a flaming cow out into the world. When the cow hits the ground, it will explode in a ball of flame, fire, and hamburger.

This plugin is a little different from what we've seen so far; there's no onCommand section at all. It's driven entirely by events.

One problem with a flaming cow is that it won't stay flaming forever, or even for very long. Normally a flaming cow will catch fire, then the cow dies and the fire goes out. That's not quite suitable for our purposes: we need the cow to stay on fire as long as it's flying through the air.

To make that happen, we'll schedule a task. The task will keep repeating as long as the cow is in the air, and in that task we can keep the cow alive and on fire until it hits the ground.

Here's the code for the main event listener:

```
CowShooter/src/cowshooter/CowShooter.java
@EventHandler
public void onInteract(PlayerInteractEvent event) {
  if (event.getAction() == Action.LEFT_CLICK_BLOCK ||
❶     event.getAction() == Action.LEFT_CLICK_AIR) {
    final Player player = event.getPlayer();
    if (player.getItemInHand().getType() == Material.LEATHER) {
      Location loc = player.getLocation();
      Vector vec = loc.getDirection();
      int mult = 3;
      vec.setX(vec.getX() * mult);
      vec.setY(vec.getY() * mult);
      vec.setZ(vec.getZ() * mult);

❷     final Cow cow = player.getWorld().spawn(loc, Cow.class);
      cow.setVelocity(vec);
      cow.setFireTicks(20);
      BukkitRunnable runnable = new CowTask(player.getWorld(), cow);
      runnable.runTaskTimer(this, 0L, 0L);
    }
  }
}
```

The PlayerInteractEvent event can mean any one of several different things, so first we'll need to check and see if this is a left click (either on empty air or on a block) at ❶.

How Do I Get a Piece of Leather?

For testing or just playing you might not have a piece of leather handy. Here's how to get one:

- Go into creative mode by typing /gamemode c.

- Press E.

- The icon in the upper-right corner is a search bar; click it.

- Start typing leather, and you should see the Leather material appear.

- Click it once, then click again on your hotbar (the bottom row of slots in the inventory) to put it there.

- Close your inventory by pressing the escape key, Esc.

- Press the corresponding number (1 through 9) to select the box where you put the leather.

When you try to go into creative mode you might see an error saying that you don't have permission. In that case, you'll need to "op" yourself—that is, give yourself operator privileges.

In the server directory, you'll see an ops.txt file, which is probably an empty file at this point. Just edit that file and add your name—you might be "player" or you might use your real account name.

Next we get the player's "item in hand" and check to see if the player is holding leather. If the answer is no, we just ignore the event and life goes on.

But if the answer is yes, we get the player's current location and the direction the character is pointing. We bump up the velocity by multiplying it by 3, as that seems to look pretty cool.[1] At ❷ we spawn a cow, set its velocity so it will go flying, and light it on fire.

Now, there's a problem with a flaming cow (or anything on fire, really). It won't stay on fire for long; it will burn up and die. So that's what our scheduled task will take care of: it will keep the cow alive and watch for it to land.

Here's the separate class that contains the runnable task:

CowShooter/src/cowshooter/CowTask.java

```
package cowshooter;
import org.bukkit.Bukkit;
import org.bukkit.World;
import org.bukkit.entity.Cow;
import org.bukkit.entity.LivingEntity;
```

---

1. Sometimes you just have to experiment.

```
import org.bukkit.plugin.java.JavaPlugin;
import org.bukkit.scheduler.BukkitRunnable;
public class CowTask extends BukkitRunnable {
    private World world;
    private Cow cow;
    public CowTask(World myWorld, Cow myCow) {
        world = myWorld;
        cow = myCow;
    }
    public void run() {
      if (cow.isOnGround()) {
        world.createExplosion(cow.getLocation(), 4f, true);
        cancel();
      } else {
        cow.setFireTicks(20);
        cow.setHealth(cow.getMaxHealth());
      }
    }
}
```

If the cow has hit the ground (tested with cow.isOnGround()), then we make the cow explode and cancel this task so it won't run again. We're done. But if the cow is still flying through the air, then we'll make sure it's still on fire with cow.setFireTicks(20) and bump up its health to the maximum to keep it alive a little longer. That actually looks a lot crueler in writing....

The result? You wave your leather as a magic wand, and shoot flaming cows that explode on impact.

The full code for both CowShooter.java and CowTask.java is in code/CowShooter/src/cowshooter.

Now isn't that a lot more fun than printing Hello, World?

Next Up

In this chapter you saw some Java mechanics, including how to create a new class and more on creating objects from classes. But the cool part is being able to run tasks in the background that keep running, which lets you implement cool things like flaming, exploding cows.

Next we'll cover how to save data and remember it despite the game being shut down, rebooted, or turned off.

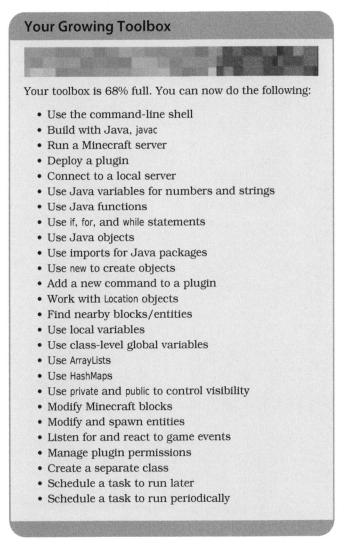

Your Growing Toolbox

Your toolbox is 68% full. You can now do the following:

- Use the command-line shell
- Build with Java, javac
- Run a Minecraft server
- Deploy a plugin
- Connect to a local server
- Use Java variables for numbers and strings
- Use Java functions
- Use if, for, and while statements
- Use Java objects
- Use imports for Java packages
- Use new to create objects
- Add a new command to a plugin
- Work with Location objects
- Find nearby blocks/entities
- Use local variables
- Use class-level global variables
- Use ArrayLists
- Use HashMaps
- Use private and public to control visibility
- Modify Minecraft blocks
- Modify and spawn entities
- Listen for and react to game events
- Manage plugin permissions
- Create a separate class
- Schedule a task to run later
- Schedule a task to run periodically

## CHAPTER 11

Use Configuration Files
and Store Game Data

Your Toolbox

Now we'll add some storage capability to your toolbox, and discover some more-advanced Java language features. You'll add these skills:

- Save and load user-editable configuration data from a local file
- Save and load your private game data from a local file
- Build up more-complex code from smaller functions
- Understand Java file functions
- Understand Java exceptions and annotations

Now we're getting someplace. From what you've learned so far, you can listen for events, schedule tasks to run later, keep data around in lists or hashes, and let your whole plugin use it as long as the server is up and running. That puts you in a good position to build some fun plugins. However, you're missing an important piece: servers don't run forever.

Any Minecraft server (including yours) can just stop running. You've stopped yours a bunch of times by now, just to install plugins! Even if you weren't installing new plugins, hardware can crash, or maybe you just closed your laptop. And once the server stops running, your plugin will forget everything it used to know. All its data is gone.

So we need to figure out how to save important data on disk somewhere, where we can save it often and load it back in when we need to.

It sure would be handy if we knew when the server was going down, and when our plugins were being loaded and run. Fortunately, the server is set up to call your plugin when these events happen. You've seen these entry points in our plugins ever since HelloWorld (and we've been using onEnable() to set up for listeners in the last two chapters):

```
public void onLoad() {
    log.info("[HelloWorld] Plugin loaded.");
}

public void onEnable() {
    log.info("[HelloWorld] Plugin enabled.");
}

public void onDisable() {
    log.info("[HelloWorld] Plugin stopping.");
}
```

I described these functions back in Chapter 6, *Add a Chat Command, Locations, and Targets*, on page 77; we've used onEnable already. Now we're going to start using onDisable() as well. To save and load plugin data from disk, we can use both of these functions.

As you may remember, when your plugin first gets loaded from disk, onLoad() will be called. At this point, the Minecraft worlds don't even exist! But if you need to do some setup before Bukkit does, then this is your chance (we won't be using it here, though).

When the server is going down or your plugin is turned off, onDisable() will be called, and that's your chance to save data. When the server comes up, you can use the onEnable() function to read data back in to your plugin (in addition to any other setup in onEnable()—for example, setting up listeners).

There are two different kinds of data that you might care about:

- Configuration data, which contains things you need to know about how the plugin should work. This is probably set only once and updated rarely, but it's read every time the plugin runs. You've probably used configuration files in other plugins or in the server setup for Minecraft itself.

- Game data, which contains things like player scores, inventory, and stuff that changes frequently as the game plays. That gets a little tricky, as we'll see shortly.

Let's look at each of these types of data and how to save and load them.

Use a Configuration File

Many plugins, and the Bukkit server itself, use *configuration files* to fine-tune and customize different values and select different behaviors. A configuration file is just a simple text file, designed to be read and edited directly by a person. The idea is that you can customize aspects of the plugin without having to fool around with the source code or recompile anything. End users, server operators, developers—everyone can use them. And now we will too.

We're going to modify a plugin to use a configuration file. Previously, on page 82, we built a plugin that dropped a bunch of squid on your current location— a "squid bomb." We're going to add configuration options to the SquidBomb plugin:

- The number of squid to drop
- The height from which the squid fall
- The ability to enable or disable setting the squid on fire (a new feature!)

Lucky for us, the Bukkit plugins come with a configuration-file mechanism built in and ready to use. Here's how it works.

The configuration file itself has to be named config.yml, and it looks something like this:

```
SquidBombConfig/config.yml
numSquids: 10
squidDropHeight: 0.0
setFire: false
```

The format used in this file is called YAML (which stands for "YAML Ain't Markup Language"), and it is designed to be a pretty simple format. In fact, you've been using it all along—it's the format of the plugin.yml file also.

Each line represents one setting and has just the name of the value you want to store (no spaces in the name, please), followed by a colon (:) and then the value. You can store strings, integers, Booleans (true or false), doubles, and so on. You can get fancier and nest sections, include lists and hashes, and more, but we'll keep it simple for now.

To use a configuration file in your plugin, start by making the file yourself, by hand. Be sure it's named config.yml and is in the plugin directory itself (not down underneath src with the Java files). It should be in the same directory as plugin.yml and src/.

I've gone ahead and created a config file and made the changes to SquidBomb in a new plugin called SquidBombConfig. Take a look at that plugin on disk; it starts off the same as the original SquidBomb, but you can see I've added the config file:

```
~/Desktop/code/SquidBombConfig$ ls
bin/          build.sh    config.yml dist/          plugin.yml src/
```

When you deploy your plugin, this file needs to be included. Fortunately, build.sh will include any .yml files in this directory, so both config.yml and plugin.yml will be packaged up when you run build.sh.

Next, let's look at how to modify the plugin code to use the config file. The important part is in the onEnable() function. As it first starts up, it'll go and grab values from the configuration file and set them into a few static variables for our plugin to use. Here's what I added:

SquidBombConfig/src/squidbombconfig/SquidBombConfig.java
```java
private static int numSquids;
private static double squidDropHeight;
private static boolean setFire;

public void onEnable() {
  FileConfiguration config = getConfig();
  numSquids = config.getInt("numSquids");
  squidDropHeight = config.getDouble("squidDropHeight");
  setFire = config.getBoolean("setFire");
  saveDefaultConfig();
}
```

First, we call getConfig() to get the configuration-file object for our plugin. (If there is no actual file yet, we'll get an empty object instead.) With this we can now make calls to get values out of the config file.

Each call to read data looks like config.get*Type*(), where *Type* is the type of the variable you're trying to get, so you have getInt, getDouble, getBoolean, getString, and such.[1] Using functions named get*XXX* and set*XXX* to read and save variables is a pretty standard part of Java.

We refer to these kinds of functions as *getters* and *setters*. Okay, perhaps not the most original names.

At the end of our function we'll call saveDefaultConfig() as a fail-safe. In case the actual configuration file goes missing, this will at least re-create it with default values.

Later in the plugin, we'll use these static, class-level variables instead of the hard-coded numbers we used in the previous version:

---

1. You have to use the camel-case version of the data type, so it's getInt, not getint; getBoolean, not getboolean; getDouble, not getdouble; and so on.

SquidBombConfig/src/squidbombconfig/SquidBombConfig.java
```java
double y = loc.getY();
loc.setY(y + squidDropHeight);
player.sendMessage("Spawning " + numSquids + " squids.");
//spawning some squids.
for (int i = 0; i < numSquids; i++) {
    player.getWorld().spawn(loc, Squid.class);
}
```

Easy peasy.

Try This Yourself

Go ahead and run build.sh on your new SquidBombConfig plugin and try the SquidBomb command—it should work exactly as it did in the previous version.

Now go to your server's plugin directory, and next to the deployed SquidBomb-Config.jar file you'll see a new SquidBombConfig directory. In that directory you'll find your new config.yml file:

```
~/Desktop/server/plugins$ cd SquidBombConfig
~/Desktop/server/plugins/SquidBombConfig$ ls
config.yml
~/Desktop/server/plugins/SquidBombConfig$ cat config.yml
numSquids: 10
squidDropHeight: 0.0
setFire: false
```

Here I used the command cat to dump out the contents of the file.

Go ahead and edit that file, and change the number of squid to something larger, say 50 or so, and change the drop height to maybe 10. Save the file, build the plugin, and restart or reload your server.

Now when you run the SquidBomb command, your target is inundated with fifty squid.

Congratulations! Your users now have the ability to tweak your plugin without needing access to the source code at all.

All these squid piling up are probably messing up your world a bit, so we need a way to quickly purge the world of all squid. To launch the Great Squid Purge, I added a command squidpurge to this plugin (we'll look at the source in just a second). Give it a try.

You can also change the behavior of plugins, not just change limits and quantities. Go back to the config.yml file and change setFire to true. Reload or restart the server, and now when you purge squid they'll be set on fire instead of just dying.

Fifty flaming squid.

Let's look at the full code for our final SquidBombConfig plugin.

Plugin: SquidBombConfig

```java
package squidbombconfig;

import java.util.Collection;
import java.util.Iterator;
import java.util.logging.Logger;
import org.bukkit.Location;
import org.bukkit.command.Command;
import org.bukkit.command.CommandSender;
import org.bukkit.configuration.file.FileConfiguration;
import org.bukkit.entity.Squid;
import org.bukkit.entity.Player;
import org.bukkit.plugin.Plugin;
import org.bukkit.plugin.java.JavaPlugin;


public class SquidBombConfig extends JavaPlugin {
  public static Logger log = Logger.getLogger("Minecraft");

  private static int numSquids;
  private static double squidDropHeight;
  private static boolean setFire;

  public void onEnable() {
    FileConfiguration config = getConfig();
    numSquids = config.getInt("numSquids");
    squidDropHeight = config.getDouble("squidDropHeight");
    setFire = config.getBoolean("setFire");
    saveDefaultConfig();
  }

  public boolean onCommand(CommandSender sender, Command command,
                          String commandLabel, String[] args) {
    if (commandLabel.equalsIgnoreCase("squidbomb")) {
      if (sender instanceof Player) {
        Player player = (Player)sender;
        Location loc = player.getLocation();
        double y = loc.getY();
        loc.setY(y + squidDropHeight);
        player.sendMessage("Spawning " + numSquids + " squids.");
        //spawning some squids.
        for (int i = 0; i < numSquids; i++) {
            player.getWorld().spawn(loc, Squid.class);
        }
```

```
        return true;
      } else {
        log.info("[SquidBombConfig] Console cannot use this command");
        return false;
      }
❶    } else if (commandLabel.equalsIgnoreCase("squidpurge")) {
      if (sender instanceof Player) {
        Player player = (Player)sender;
        Collection<Squid> squidlist =
          player.getWorld().getEntitiesByClass(Squid.class);
        for (Squid victim : squidlist) {
          if (setFire) {
            victim.setFireTicks(500);
          } else {
            victim.setHealth(0.0);
          }
        }
❷        return true;
      } else {
        log.info("[SquidBombConfig] Console cannot use this command");
        return false;
      }
    }
    return false;
  }
}
```

You can see where I've added the squidpurge command, starting at ❶ and going through until ❷. I'm getting a list of all squid in your world with player.get-World().getEntitiesByClass(Squid.class) and then traversing the list with an iterator, as we saw earlier. For each squid, depending on the setting in the config file, I can then decide whether to set it on fire, like this:

```
victim.setFireTicks(500);
```

or just kill it by setting its heath to zero suddenly:

```
victim.setHealth(0.0);
```

So with just a humble if statement and a config file, you can have your plugin users tune your plugin's behavior without modifying the source code. Sweet.

Store Game Data in Local Files

That's great for configuration data, but not so useful for game data—data that changes as the game plays on, like player scores and status, inventory, health, and things like that. We need to access data a little differently, and be able to write game data from the plugin as well as read it.

There are two main ways to go about this. One is to use a data file just like a config file but manage it ourselves, and that's what we'll do here. The other method is to use a full-fledged SQL database like SQLite or mySQL, but that's a lot more complicated than we have space to cover here. If you're dealing with hundreds of users, the file-based techniques here will work fine. But if you're dealing with millions of users on a large server, you'll need to look into the SQL techniques.[2]

So the first question that comes up is *where* we should write our data files for a plugin. Well, as you just saw, plugins that use a config file already have a directory where we can read and write files ourselves.

That makes it a lot easier for us. Now all we need to do is open and read in a file in the plugins/*plugin-name* directory.

The plugin's getDataFolder() function tells us the location of that directory so we can stay nice and tidy. getDataFolder() returns a File object, though, and what we really want is a string of that file's path name. getDataFolder().getAbsolutePath() will give us that.

It's polite to stay there and not spray files all over the server's disk. It's also customary to name the file with a .dat suffix to indicate that it is data. So we'll end up making a file named something like ~/Desktop/server/plugins/MyPlugin-Name/MyPluginName.dat for our data.

File reading and writing is a bit of a pain in Java. There's the problem of converting your variables into something writable, and then converting the file's data and structure back into Java variables. To top it off, the Java I/O (input/output) functions for reading and writing can be messy all by themselves. You could end up writing a lot of code to handle that.

So what can we do to make that a little easier? What if we started with a HashMap and stored everything we wanted in there (even lists and more hashes), and saved that one hash (which contains a whole mess) out to a file? Then all you'd need is a bit of code to load and save a HashMap to a file.

I've written a class named PermaMap that will do that for you. We'll take a quick fly-over at the very end of this chapter to see how it works on the inside, and look at some more-advanced Java while in there.

---

2. There's an official tutorial at http://docs.oracle.com/javase/tutorial/jdbc/basics/processingsqlstate-ments.html as well as some information on the Bukkit forums at https://forums.bukkit.org. But it's a much more advanced and confusing topic, even for professionals.

But first we'll cover how to use it with a simple plugin named SaveLocations. Then you'll be writing your very own class to use PermaMap to save the state of the more complicated BackCmd plugin.

Use PermaMap

PermaMap provides you with two functions, load and save. load takes a plugin and the name of the file you want to load from and returns a hash. save takes a plugin, the file name to save to, and the hash to save:

```
HashMap<String, Object> load(JavaPlugin plugin, String fileName)
```

```
boolean save(JavaPlugin plugin, String fileName, Map<String, Object> data)
```

The file name in both cases should be named after the plugin. For instance, we're going to hook this up in SaveLocations, so we'll use the file name "SaveLocations.dat". Notice we're not specifying the full path or any directories; the load and save will figure that out for you.

You'll probably want to load the PermaMap hash just once, in your plugin's onEnable section, and save it as often as you need to. You might want to save it in only the onDisable section, but in that case you could lose data if the server crashes or shuts down unexpectedly. If that's important to you, then you should save the hash any time you make a change to it.

There is one important limitation to PermapMap and many other storage approaches, however. This hash will save most normal Java objects, but will not save Minecraft-specific objects—things like Location or Player. You can save a player's name as a String, and save a Location as a set of double coordinates, but you can't save the Minecraft objects directly. That's because in order to be saved, an object has to know how to save itself, which is marked by having java.io.serializable as a parent. The Bukkit API objects don't do that, so we can't save or load them directly using Java.

That turns out to be a fair and reasonable limitation, because you really *should not* store Player objects, worlds, locations, or other "live" elements in the game.

Keep in mind that the game is still playing in real time. Players log off, they change locations, blocks change types, and things catch on fire, fall, and go in and out of inventory, all while your code is running. If you store a Player object on disk, or even in a list in memory, there's no guarantee that object will still be valid when you go to use it the next day or next week. In fact, odds are it probably *won't* be valid. All a player needs to do is disconnect and reconnect, and *bam*—the old Player object is no longer valid.

So instead of storing a Player object, just store the player's name. When you load the data back in and are ready to use it, check to make sure the player is actually online.

Let's see how to use this code within a plugin.

Plugin: LocationSnapshot

Here's a simple example of PermaMap being used in a new plugin, LocationSnapshot. In this plugin, we'll provide two new commands:

- /savelocations
- /loadlocations

You might want to use this kind of feature as part of a competition, where you can return everyone back to their starting points at the end.

The savelocations command, as you might expect, saves to disk the current locations of all online players. loadlocations reads them back in and teleports everyone back to those saved locations. We'll use the PermaMap functions to save and load a hash of Players and Locations.

This is a long plugin, so let's break it up and look at the pieces.

The plugin starts off in the usual way, and we'll keep the name of the data file in a string:

```
LocationSnapshot/src/locationsnapshot/LocationSnapshot.java
public class LocationSnapshot extends JavaPlugin {
  public static Logger log = Logger.getLogger("Minecraft");
  private final static String datafile = "locations.dat";
```

Why bother putting it in a string instead of typing it out literally (as "locations.dat") a few times? Because any time you have to type something repeatedly, you run a pretty good risk of typing it *wrong* the second or third time. In this case, the compiler can't help you: it doesn't know that there's a problem when you save to "loactions.dat" and read from "locations.dat". So you're there scratching your head over a weird bug where you never see the data you write. So we'll keep the name in a string instead, and mark the string as final. That means we can't change it, even by accident. And that's a good thing, because it should be named after the plugin and *shouldn't* be changed.

Now let's look at the save and the load. To keep things clean and start forming better habits, we'll put the code for each in its own function. So the logic for savelocations will look like this:

LocationSnapshot/src/locationsnapshot/LocationSnapshot.java

```java
private void saveLocations() {
  Player[] playerList = getServer().getOnlinePlayers();
  HashMap<String, Object> map = new HashMap<String, Object>();
  // For all players...
  for (Player player : playerList) {
    String name = player.getPlayerListName();
    Location where = player.getLocation();
    double coordinates[] = { where.getX(), where.getY(), where.getZ() };
    // Save the raw coordinates, not the Location
    map.put(name, coordinates);
  }

  if (!PermaMap.save(this, datafile, map)) {
    log.info("[Locations] Couldn't save file.");
  }
}
```

Here we run through the list of all online players and put the player's name and current location into a hash named map. The key in the hash is the player's name, so we can find that player again. The value we store is an array of the raw coordinates of the player's location, declared literally with the braces—{ and }.

Sometime later, when you type the loadlocations command, you'll run through the list of players that are online and look up their saved location, convert back to a proper Location, and teleport them there:

LocationSnapshot/src/locationsnapshot/LocationSnapshot.java

```java
private void loadLocations() {
  HashMap<String, Object> map = PermaMap.load(this, datafile);
  //Go through play list; if they are in the hash, teleport them.
  Player[] playerList = getServer().getOnlinePlayers();
  for (Player player : playerList) {
    String name = player.getPlayerListName();
    double[] coordinates = (double[])map.get(name);
    if (coordinates != null) {
      // Reconstitute a Location from coordinates
      Location loc = new Location(player.getWorld(),
        coordinates[0],
        coordinates[1],
        coordinates[2]);
      player.teleport(loc);
    }
  }
}
```

The "save" obviously needs to be done by going through the list of all players online, and it's easiest to do the same thing for the load as well. We *could* start with a list of all the players we saved in the hash, and then check to see if they are online, but it's probably easier this way. In either case, there may have been players that were online before and aren't now, or vice versa.

Now if there's an error saving the file, we'll log an error message but continue with our business. If there's an error reading the file, PermaMap assumes there simply isn't one, and we start off with a fresh, empty hash. You may want to treat errors differently; we'll talk more about this at the end of the chapter when we look at PermaMap's innards in more detail.

Note that we aren't saving Player objects or Location objects. Instead, we're storing player names (plain old String) and coordinates (Java double) of their Locations. When we are ready to teleport a player, we make a new Location object based on the coordinates we saved.

Use One Java Package

PermaMap is a general-purpose, reusable bit of code. You could use it from several different plugins.

Normally you'd put something general like PermaMap in a different package, and name the package "com.myname.utils" or similar. You'd then import PermaMap from all your plugins that use it.

However, because we want a plugin to be self-contained, it's easier to deploy by including the PermaMap.java source code right here in our package. That way, when it's installed there's no confusion as to where an extra package might be located; everything is in the one package we're installing.

Bukkit does have a mechanism to load multiple plugins and specify that one plugin depends on another plugin being loaded first, but we won't be working with that here.

Compile and install LocationSnapshot and give it a try. Connect from your client and run the "/savelocations" command. After you've saved locations, go into your server's plugin directory and take a look:

```
$ cd plugins/
$ ls
LocationSnapshot      LocationSnapshot.jar
$ cd LocationSnapshot
$ ls
locations.dat
```

And there's your data file. It's a binary file, so there's not much we can do from here except marvel that it was created.

Exit your client, stop the server, and restart everything. Go somewhere else in the game and try the /loadlocations command. You're back at the snapshot location (as is every other player on your server).

Plugin: BackCmd with Save

Using the same ideas as with LocationSnapshot, you're going to add data storage to the BackCmd plugin so that you can save the locations across server restarts. I'll provide the outline and function signatures, but you will be writing the bodies of the functions, the actual code to make it work. Buckle up!

Now, the BackCmd plugin is a little more complicated than our simple Location-Snapshot. As you may remember from the plugin on page 125, the BackCmd plugin tracks more than just a location per player; it tracks a Stack of Location objects for each player.

So instead of just converting a Location to double coordinates and back, you'll need to convert a Stack of Location objects to double coordinates and back. That's more than just a line or two of code; you'll need to iterate through each stack and build a new stack with the converted types, and I suppose you'll need something that looks like a Location but that you can safely save to disk. And while we're at it, you might want to handle Locations in different Worlds, something we didn't account for in LocationSnapshot.

To recap, here's your to-do list for the code you're going to write:

- Create an object like a Location that you can save to disk. Let's name it SavedLocation.

- Write a conversion function that takes a Location and makes a SavedLocation object.

- Write the other conversion function that takes a SavedLocation and makes a Location.

- Write a function to convert a Stack of Location objects to a Stack of SavedLocation objects.

- Write a function to convert a Stack of SavedLocation objects to a Stack of Location objects.

Don't be shy about adding log messages to help trace what the plugin is doing.

Okay, you have your hands full. I'll get you started.

Create a SavedLocation Class

Since you can't save Location objects directly to disk, you need to make an object that you *can* save to disk: a SavedLocation. You'll create a SavedLocation from a Location by making a new SavedLocation object like this:

```
SavedLocation saved = new SavedLocation(loc);
```

Let's get started writing some code. Go into the BackCmd plugin's src/backcmd directory and create a new file named SavedLocation.java. The first thing you'll need is a package statement:

```
package backcmd;
```

The start of your SavedLocation class will look like this:

BackCmdSave/src/backcmdsave/SavedLocation.java
```
import java.util.Stack;
import org.bukkit.Location;
import org.bukkit.Server;
import org.bukkit.World;

public class SavedLocation implements java.io.Serializable {
  public String worldName;
  public double x;
  public double y;
  public double z;

  public SavedLocation(Location loc) {
    // ...
  }
}
```

Go ahead and copy that into your new file, or type it in as we go.

First off, declare that the class implements java.io.Serializable. That's the missing piece that tells Java that objects of this class can be written to disk. Now, that means that any data you contain must also be Serializable, which all of the basic Java classes are. In this case, each of your SavedLocation objects will hold four pieces of data: a String for the name of the world of this Location, and the three coordinates, x, y, and z.

When you use new to create an object, Java will create the object for you and run the constructor. That gives you the chance to set up anything in the object that needs setting. And that's where you're going to start writing code.

Now it's your turn. Fill in the body of the constructor and set the object's internal variables (worldName, x, y, z) to the proper values from the Location named loc, which is passed in to this function. You may need to look at the Bukkit documentation for Location and World. Remember that because it's a constructor, you don't need a return statement or a return type. Just set the object's variables based on what's been passed in.

Make sure that much compiles, using build.sh as usual.

Convert to Location

So far, your SavedLocation class has the code so that you can build an object that contains a saveable version of a Location.

Now you need to go the other way. From your SavedLocation object, you need to write a function that returns a Location. If we have a SavedLocation object named saved, you'd end up calling it like this:

```
Location loc = saved.toLocation(getServer());
```

So you need to write a function named toLocation that will take a Bukkit Server and return a Location.

Add this declaration for the function in SavedLocation.java:

BackCmdSave/src/backcmdsave/SavedLocation.java
```
public Location toLocation(Server s) {
    //...
}
```

To create and return a new Location, you have to pass in a World. Fortunately, there's a function in Server that will return a World given its name. You could just pass in a World directly, but then every time you call this from a plugin you'd have to pass in getServer().getWorld() or keep a World variable hanging around. I think it's easier to pass in the Server in this case.

You have the world name and you have the x, y, and z, so you can make a new Location and return it.

Fill in the body of that function now, and make sure SavedLocation.java compiles okay.

Convert Stacks of Locations

Now it gets a little more complicated. Only a little. You need to copy some stacks back and forth. You know how to traverse a stack using a for-each construct. If locsStack is a Stack of Locations, you go through it like this:

```
for (Location loc : locsStack) {
    //...
}
```

So you need to create a new stack of the right type, go through the other stack and push entries onto the new stack, then return the new stack.

Since SavedLocation represents only a single location, you'll make these two conversion functions static (that is, not associated with any one object).

Here are the function declarations for you. Add these to SavedLocation.java:

BackCmdSave/src/backcmdsave/SavedLocation.java
```
public static Stack<SavedLocation> LocationStackToSavedStack(
        Stack<Location> locsStack) {
  //...
}
public static Stack<Location> SavedStackToLocationStack(Server s,
        Stack<SavedLocation> saveStack) {
  //...
}
```

Fill in the body of these functions now, and make sure SavedLocation compiles okay.

Add Save and Load to BackCmd

Now you have the lower-level mechanisms that will translate between Locations and SavedLocations, and stacks of each. Now it's time for you to add the code into BackCmd.java, which will call them.

Open up BackCmd.java and start making the following changes.

First, add a declaration for a file name to the top of the class:

BackCmdSave/src/backcmdsave/BackCmdSave.java
```
private static final String datafile = "BackCmdSave.dat";
```

Next, add the following code to save data in the onDisable function:

BackCmdSave/src/backcmdsave/BackCmdSave.java
```
// Create a Hash that we'll save
HashMap<String, Object> myHash = new HashMap<String, Object>();

// Load up our Hash from playerTeleports
for (String playerName : playerTeleports.keySet()) {
  Stack<SavedLocation> saveStack =
      SavedLocation.LocationStackToSavedStack(
                playerTeleports.get(playerName));
  myHash.put(playerName, saveStack);
}
// and save it to disk
if (!PermaMap.save(this, datafile, myHash)) {
  log.severe("Couldn't save plugin datafile");
}
```

Here you're making a new hash and iterating through the plugin's playerTeleports hash, getting the player's name and Stack of Locations. Passing that stack to LocationStackToSavedStack gives you a Stack of SavedLocations, which goes right into our new hash. Once that's done, use PermaMap to save the hash.

Read does mostly the same thing, but in reverse. Add this code to the onEnable function after it registers for events:

BackCmdSave/src/backcmdsave/BackCmdSave.java
```
// Load the Hash from disk
HashMap<String, Object> myHash = PermaMap.load(this, datafile);

// Put it into the playerTeleports hash
for (String playerName : myHash.keySet()) {
  Stack<Location> locsStack =
      SavedLocation.SavedStackToLocationStack(
              this.getServer(),
              (Stack<SavedLocation>)myHash.get(playerName));
  playerTeleports.put(playerName, locsStack);
}
```

This time we get the hash by loading it from disk. Going through that hash, use the player's name and his or her stack of SavedLocation, converted with SavedStackToLocationStack, and save that in the plugin's playerTeleports hash.

It looks a little messy with all the parameterized types and angle brackets, but in fact it's a lot simpler because we're breaking out all the conversion logic into its own functions, and then traversing the hashes here.

You're almost done.

Add PermaMap to BackCmd

Finally, you'll need to copy the PermaMap.java source file into your BackCmd/src/back-cmd directory from LocationSnapshot, and change the package statement (at the top) to BackCmd to match. So the top of your new copy of PermaMap.java should read as follows, just like in BackCmd.java and SavedLocation.java:

```
package backcmd;
```

Now compile and install the whole mess with build.sh, and you're good to go.

Test It

Assuming everything worked, you should be able to test it:

1. Start the server.
2. Connect from your client.

3. Teleport to a new place, either by using the /tp command or by throwing an Ender Pearl. Do this a few times.
4. Disconnect and shut down the server.
5. Restart and reconnect.
6. Now type the "/back" command in the client. Your history was saved and reloaded from disk, and you should be able to go back to each teleport point.

w00t.

Try This Yourself

You know what we need? A "clear" command so that we can clear out our teleport history.

Go ahead and implement that. It's a new command, so don't forget to add it to plugin.yml. In the code, all you need to do is to clear out the stack for the player in the playerTeleports hash. (You can use the stack's clear function for that.)

PermaMap: Save and Load a Java HashMap

In this section we'll look at PermaMap's innards to learn a little about Java file reading and writing, Java exception handling, and how to suppress warning messages. This section is optional, and you can skip it on first reading. But do come back and read it at some point.

Okay, now that the casual readers have moved on, let's take a look under the hood of PermaMap. The first thing PermaMap needs is some imports:

LocationSnapshot/src/locationsnapshot/PermaMap.java
```
import java.io.*;
import java.util.HashMap;
import java.util.Map;
import org.bukkit.plugin.java.JavaPlugin;
```

I cheated here. There are a bunch of packages under java.io that we'll need, so I simply said import java.io.* to grab *all* of them. The "*" character is magic—there isn't a package that's literally named "*"; instead, the "*" matches *all* the package names under java.io.[3]

Also, since we're using hashes, we'll need HashMap and its more generic parent class, Map, and we'll need the plugin class in order to find out where to write the file.

---

3. Grabbing all the packages with a wildcard can be a problem if two packages define the same class. For instance, both java.util.* and java.awt.* define a List class. You might not get what you expect.

Now let's start the class itself. In this case we need only two functions—one to save a hash and one to load a hash—so I used two static functions (see the sidebar for why I didn't make the class save itself).

> ## Don't Save Yourself
>
> Instead of saving a plain HashMap, I could have made a class that extended HashMap so that it was a subclass of HashMap and could save and load itself. But because it's a child of HashMap and not directly a HashMap itself, there's a drawback to that.
>
> If you change the class in any way—say, by updating the code in one of the functions—you won't be able to read the data back in. Instead, in the server log you'll get an exception that looks like this:
>
> ```
> 11:58:49 [SEVERE] java.io.InvalidClassException: backcmdsave.PermaMap;
> local class incompatible: stream classdesc serialVersionUID =
> -3076232018448774006, local class serialVersionUID = -4173171935782030929
> ```
>
> There are ways around that, but the whole enterprise starts getting a lot more complicated than it's worth.

Let's look at writing first, as that's very straightforward, but there is a new language feature we need to work with. Here's the function to save the hash to a file:

LocationSnapshot/src/locationsnapshot/PermaMap.java

```
public static boolean save(
      JavaPlugin plugin, String aFileName, Map<String, Object> data) {
  boolean result = true;
  try {
    String filename = plugin.getDataFolder().getAbsolutePath() +
              File.separator + aFileName;
    File file = new File(filename);
    file.getParentFile().mkdirs(); // Make parent dir if needed
❶   FileOutputStream foutput = new FileOutputStream(file);
❷   ObjectOutputStream stream = new ObjectOutputStream(foutput);
    stream.writeObject(data);
    stream.close();
  } catch (Exception e) {
    result = false;
    // Report error to log
    // if needed
    System.err.println(e);
  }
  return result;
}
```

The lines from ❶ to ❷ end up getting us a variable named stream that we can use to write to the file. That brings us to the real action: the line with stream.writeObject(data). That's going to write the data that was passed in (which is a kind of a HashMap) out to the file we opened.

After writing, you have to call stream.close(). That's important when dealing with files, and not just in Java. Many times when you write to a file, the computer doesn't actually write out to disk right away. It waits until it has a whole bunch of things to write and then does them all at once to be more efficient. The downside is that if you crash before that happens, the file might not get written all the way. When you close a file, it will flush any pending writes.

Now let's look at the other end and see what the load function looks like:

LocationSnapshot/src/locationsnapshot/PermaMap.java

```
❶ @SuppressWarnings("unchecked")
public static HashMap<String, Object> load(
            JavaPlugin plugin, String aFileName) {
  try {
    String filename = plugin.getDataFolder().getAbsolutePath() +
            File.separator + aFileName;
    File file = new File(filename);
    FileInputStream finput = new FileInputStream(file);
    ObjectInputStream stream = new ObjectInputStream(finput);
    Object pileOfBits = stream.readObject();
    stream.close();
❷    if (pileOfBits instanceof HashMap) {
      return (HashMap<String,Object>)pileOfBits;
    }
  } catch (Exception e) {
    // ignore read error
    System.err.println(e);
  }
  return new HashMap<String,Object>(); // Empty
}
```

It's pretty similar to save—the setup is the same, except now we're reading instead of writing, and we end up doing a readObject instead of a writeObject. But having read in the pile of bits from the disk, we need to do a little extra work to make those bits usable.

At ❷ we use the instanceof keyword to see if the pile of bits we read in actually is a kind of a HashMap (just like we use instanceof to make sure we have a Player in our usual onCommand). If it's not a map, then somebody wrote some garbage in our file or we're reading the wrong file somehow. We failed (and we'll log it).

Otherwise, if it is a map, we cast it to the actual type (HashMap<String,Object>) and return it. If we failed reading in the file (because it doesn't exist yet, perhaps), then at the bottom of this function we'll return an empty hash.

So if we fail to read in the file, what happens, exactly? What does this extra, mysterious code do?

Catch Exceptions in Java

See the code block bracketed by the try/catch keywords? Some of those functions are declared to "throw exceptions" when something goes wrong: if there are problems like there's no file to read, or there's an error writing the file because the disk is full. What's an exception?

An *exception* interrupts the code that's currently being run, throws away the rest of the function, and jumps straight to the catch block. It's sort of like if the fire alarm rang right now, you'd jump up and run out, and not finish reading the page.

For instance, if the call to new FileOutputStream throws an exception for some reason, the calls to writeObject and close will never be called. Instead, the two lines of code in the catch block will be run.

If there's no error, then the catch block will never be run.

To simplify things, our code here catches all exceptions and returns a simple true or false. That can be a very "beginner's" way to handle exceptions, though, and you shouldn't always catch all expressions. Instead, the question to ask yourself is "whose problem is it, and who can fix it?"

Normally, code that you're calling in a library has no idea what you're using it for. When something bad happens, it doesn't know what you need to do to handle the problem. Should the whole server exit? Should you return an error to the user? Do you need to change some variables and clean up whatever you were trying to do? Since the library code doesn't know, it doesn't try to fix it. It just raises an exception—it throws up its hands and gives up.

For instance, the constructor for FileOutputStream that we're using is declared to throw a FileNotFoundException:

```
public FileOutputStream(String name)
                throws FileNotFoundException
```

When you call that function, you have two choices. You can either accept the responsibility for dealing with any errors and catch the exception yourself, or you can throw up your hands as well, and pass the exception up to the caller. To pass the exception up, you just declare that *your* function also throws FileNotFoundException. Now it's someone else's problem.

In theory, however, exceptions should be used only for exceptional things. If you went to spawn a cow and instead got a creeper, that would be exceptional: an unexpected disaster. If you just added a player to a list of players and the length of the list was still zero, that would indicate a disaster in progress.

But trying to read a file that isn't there yet doesn't qualify as an exceptional disaster. It's a common occurrence. So we catch the exception (any exception at all) and return an empty hash. Now, that's the behavior I decided on for this particular plugin. That might not be appropriate in all cases. In your own plugins, if you really expected that data to be present and it's not, then that's a serious error. What will you do?

And what happens if you fail when trying to write a file? That might mean there's a more serious problem—you might be out of disk space on the server, for instance. What should you do?

If it were me, I'd want to shut down the server as gracefully as possible. A dead program does a lot less damage than a broken program that's still running. In writing code for most professional systems, that's almost always the best action to take: fail quickly and loudly.

But this isn't our server, necessarily; we've just made a plugin that someone else is running, and it would be rude of us to shut down their server just because we can't write a file. So in this case, we'll log an error message to the Minecraft console and struggle on.

Hide Compiler Warnings

The other new feature here is the odd-looking @SuppressWarnings("unchecked") annotation, which you can see on the line at ❶ of PermaMap.java.

We marked event listeners with an annotation in the last chapter, and we're marking this function with a different annotation. Here's why: Normally when you make a mistake in a program's source code, the compiler will complain with an error message and won't produce the .class file. But sometimes it *does* know what you're doing, and doesn't like it. In that case it prints out a more-or-less-friendly warning message to let you know that it's not happy.

Most of the time you should listen to those warnings very carefully. They are usually an indication that you really *do* have an error: the code itself might be perfectly legal, but it's probably not going to do what you want it to do.

However, in this particular piece of code, we get a warning message that comes from casting an Object that we read in from disk to its actual type:

```
if (pileOfBits instanceof HashMap) {
  return (HashMap<String,Object>)pileOfBits;
}
```

We *are* checking first to make sure it's the correct type, but the compiler still doesn't trust us (and doesn't know that we've done the check ourselves). So in this case, the @SuppressWarnings annotation prevents a bogus warning message.

Next Up

That was fun! And you're almost done. This is the last batch of Java techniques you needed. Now that you're able to save and load data, use Java file functions, and handle Java exceptions, you're in good shape.

In the next chapter we'll switch things up a bit, and instead of writing code, we'll look at a technique to help manage the code you write. You're going to set up a giant "undo button" for your plugin project code.

After that, you'll be ready to wrap up with a walk-through of how to design your very own plugin from scratch.

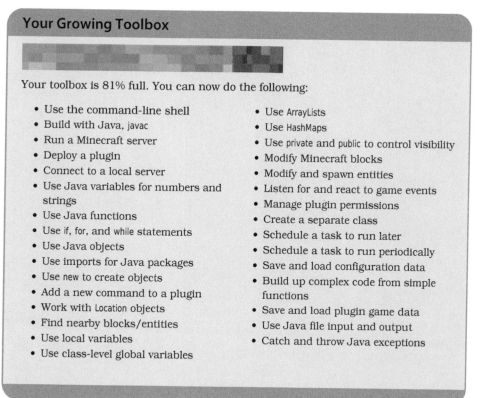

Your Growing Toolbox

Your toolbox is 81% full. You can now do the following:

- Use the command-line shell
- Build with Java, javac
- Run a Minecraft server
- Deploy a plugin
- Connect to a local server
- Use Java variables for numbers and strings
- Use Java functions
- Use if, for, and while statements
- Use Java objects
- Use imports for Java packages
- Use new to create objects
- Add a new command to a plugin
- Work with Location objects
- Find nearby blocks/entities
- Use local variables
- Use class-level global variables
- Use ArrayLists
- Use HashMaps
- Use private and public to control visibility
- Modify Minecraft blocks
- Modify and spawn entities
- Listen for and react to game events
- Manage plugin permissions
- Create a separate class
- Schedule a task to run later
- Schedule a task to run periodically
- Save and load configuration data
- Build up complex code from simple functions
- Save and load plugin game data
- Use Java file input and output
- Catch and throw Java exceptions

## CHAPTER 12

Keep Your Code Safe

Your Toolbox

In this chapter we'll add Git to your arsenal. With Git you can change your code without fear that you'll lose anything or mess anything up. Git gives you one of the most powerful tools of all: an "undo button" for your project. You'll add these skills to your toolbox:

- How to install Git
- Use Git to keep track of changes to code
- Go back to earlier versions of code (an "undo button")
- Maintain multiple versions of code at the same time
- Back up your code to the cloud

By now you might realize a certain frustrating moment when programming: everything was working just fine, but you added a couple of lines of code in a couple of different files, and now *nothing works anymore*. What changes did you make? Which one messed everything up? Was it in this file or that one?

Wouldn't it be great to be able to press a sort of giant "undo button," to toss out this set of changes that didn't work out so well, and go back to the code from a few minutes ago that was working alright so you can try again?

Have I got a treat for you.

You can use a tool named Git to do exactly that and more. Git acts like a huge memory of all the changes you make to your code. You can go back in time to any previous point, even if you've accidentally deleted a file or renamed it, moved code from one file to another, and so on—Git will track it all for you. In addition, you can set it up so that a copy of Git's memory can be backed up in the cloud, so even if your whole computer gets damaged or stolen, all of your source code and the full memory of it are safe. You can restore it to your new computer or a friend's computer and continue on.

You don't *have* to use this kind of tool, but I really, really recommend it. It's not hard to set up, and the first time it saves you from stupidly clobbering a file it will be worth it.

There are tons of tutorials and how-tos for Git on the Web, and a lot of books as well, but we'll take a quick pass at the basics here to get you started.

Install Git

First off, you need to download and install the Git software for Windows, Mac, or Linux from http://git-scm.com.

Once it's installed, you should configure it globally with your name and email address:

```
$ git config --global user.name "you@example.com"
$ git config --global user.email "Your Name"
```

Git on Windows

The Git distribution for Windows includes a well-intentioned but problematic version of the Bash shell. Readers tell me it doesn't work very well. In the Git installer for Windows, you'll want to choose "Run Git from Windows command prompt" instead of selecting the default "Git bash" option.

You set up Git once per project. Let's do that right now, in the CowShooter plugin. cd to the top-level CowShooter directory and type git init:

```
$ cd CowShooter/
$ ls
bin/        build.sh   dist/      plugin.yml src/
$ git init
Initialized empty Git repository in /Users/andy/Desktop/code/CowShooter/.git/
```

That creates a magical, hidden directory named .git where Git will store its memories—what Git calls your *repository*. You need to do this only once for each project, which in our case will be once per plugin.

Remember Changes

Now that you have Git, you need to tell it which of your files it needs to remember. You don't actually want all of them.

Typically you don't want to store .class or .jar files, as those can always be created again. You definitely want Git to remember all your .java source code, and your plugin-configuration and build-configuration files.

So first thing, let's clean up the plugin directory and get rid of the extra junk:

```
$ rm -f bin/*/*.class
$ rm -f dist/*.jar
```

That removed the generated .class and .jar files. Now you're left with a clean directory tree, with the files you want Git to remember and track changes for.

You use git add *files…*, where *files* can be individual file or directory names. Since for now you want everything in the current directory from here on down, you can just type git add .:

```
$ git add .
```

(Remember that "." means the current directory.) Now Git knows to watch all these files.

But it hasn't yet taken a snapshot of the current state of your files. To have it do that, you have to *commit* your changes:

```
$ git commit -a -m 'My first commit'
```

That command will record the current state of your source code in Git's repository. The -a means to commit changes in *all* the tracked files, and the -m lets you specify a *message*.

The message is very important: it's how you can tell what you were doing when you changed these files. If you use a wonderfully descriptive message like "I did stuff," then this won't help you any.

Let's play with that a moment. Create a new file in the CowShooter directory and name it README.txt. Put anything you want in the file: comments about the plugin, your own personal manifesto, nonsense text, whatever.

Now add the file and commit the add:

```
$ git add README.txt
$ git commit -a -m "Add my personal screed"
[master 50847c8] Add my personal screed
 1 file changed, 1 insertion(+)
 create mode 100644 README.txt
```

To see the history of your commit messages, you use git log:

```
$ git log
commit 50847c8a3e60dbfc8f441894202765eb23fbd9a5
Author: Andy Hunt <andy@toolshed.com>
Date:   Fri Jan 7 15:51:22

    Add my personal screed

commit aa58dfa87fa79b01e2c7ce172bbcdd41b7e962d6
Author: Andy Hunt <andy@toolshed.com>
Date:   Tue Jan 7 15:50:31

    First Commit
```

That shows the full log entries, with the long version of the commit identifier, the author, the date, and the log message. Those long random-looking strings (which are cryptographically interesting SHA1 hashes, in fact) identify each commit. But they are really long. Usually you can just use the first four to eight characters of the hash as long as that produces a unique string.

You can get a more concise report of the exact same information by using this:

```
$ git log --oneline
50847c8 Add my personal screed
aa58dfa First Commit
```

The shorter version of the commit hash is usually all you need.

So remember: when you create a new file and need Git to track it, don't forget to do the add:

```
$ git add myNewFile.java
```

And then do a commit to save a snapshot of all your files in the repository. You can always check to see what files Git knows about, which ones it doesn't, what's been committed, and what hasn't, by typing this:

```
$ git status
# On branch master
# Untracked files:
#   (use "git add <file>..." to include in what will be committed)
#
#       bin/
#       dist/
nothing added to commit but untracked files present (use "git add" to track)
```

Oops! I must have done a compile in there somewhere, because the bin and dist directories are back. That's fine, as we don't want Git to track them, but we also don't want Git to complain about them every time.

If these were files you cared about, you would just do the git add so that Git can track them. But in this case, we don't want Git to ever track these directories. We want it to ignore them. Here's how to make that happen:

1. Create a file named .gitignore in this directory (if there isn't one already; mkplugin.sh will make an empty one for you).

2. In the file, put the names of the files or directories you want to ignore.

3. Add the file and commit it.

In this case the .gitignore file will look like this:

```
bin
dist
```

Then we'll add it and commit just that one file by specifying the file name instead of the -a we usually use:

```
$ git add .gitignore
$ git commit .gitignore -m 'ignoring bin and dist'
[master cc0e424] ignoring bin and dist
 1 file changed, 2 insertions(+)
 create mode 100644 .gitignore
```

Let's see what git status tells us now:

```
$ git status
# On branch master
nothing to commit, working directory clean
```

Great! We got the reassuring message "nothing to commit, working directory clean." That message is what you want to see when you're finished coding for the time being.

Now add some text to the bottom of README.txt, save the file, and try git status again:

```
$ git status
# On branch master
# Changes not staged for commit:
#   (use "git add <file>..." to update what will be committed)
#   (use "git checkout -- <file>..." to discard changes in working directory)
#
#       modified:   README.txt
#
no changes added to commit (use "git add" and/or "git commit -a")
```

Ah, that's clever: Git recognized that you'd made some changes to the README.txt file and that those changes haven't been saved yet. A commit will fix that, and once again you can get the relaxing "nothing to commit, working directory clean" message:

```
$ git status
# On branch master
nothing to commit, working directory clean
```

So there's one important rule to remember:

Don't leave the scene until the working directory is clean.

An Easy Undo

Say you're going along and accidentally remove a file from your plugin directory. Or maybe you made a series of edits that turns out to be a really bad idea, and you want to go back. Oops. Have no fear: we've all done it.

In fact, let's do it now, deliberately—and see how to fix it, using the CowShooter plugin where you've set up a Git repository.

Bring up CowShooter/src/cowshooter/CowTask.java, and somewhere randomly in the middle of the file, type some nonsense like "Zombie cows are coming! Run for your life! Braaaainsss...." That will do for our example of making a mistake in a file. Java, of course, is not hip to our warning of the impending zombie-cow apocalypse, and has no idea what this means. Try to compile with build.sh, and you'll see a plethora of angry error messages like this:

```
src/cowshooter/CowTask.java:20: illegal start of type
    Zombie cows are coming! Run for your life! Braaaainsss....
                                          ^
src/cowshooter/CowTask.java:20: <identifier> expected
    Zombie cows are coming! Run for your life! Braaaainsss....
                                          ^
src/cowshooter/CowTask.java:22: ';' expected
    public void run() {
          ^
src/cowshooter/CowTask.java:22: invalid method declaration; return type required
    public void run() {
```

Argh! Something we typed blew up the compile. Now, if this were a real emergency you wouldn't know it was the bogus zombie warning text you just typed in.

So there's an interesting question: what has changed locally in your files that is different from the last time you did a commit (that is, took a snapshot)?

You can see what's changed by using git diff:

```
$ cd src
$ cd cowshooter
$ git diff CowTask.java
diff --git a/src/cowshooter/CowTask.java b/src/cowshooter/CowTask.java
index 4894201..556d0d3 100644
--- a/src/cowshooter/CowTask.java
+++ b/src/cowshooter/CowTask.java
@@ -16,6 +16,8 @@ public class CowTask extends BukkitRunnable {
        world = myWorld;
        cow = myCow;
    }
+
+Zombie cows are coming! Run for your life! Braaaainsss....

    public void run() {
        if (cow.isOnGround()) {
```

Reading this, you can see there's some gunk at the top and then it shows lines from the middle of CowTask.java, including two lines marked with plus signs (+). Those are the two lines that were added. Ah, that's where the problem is. Adding those lines was a bad idea; in fact, it would be nice just to scrap everything since the last commit, and restore this file to how it was before.

If you haven't committed a file yet, you can always get back to the last commit (like a save point in a game) by typing this:

```
$ git checkout MyMessedUpFile.java
```

Silently but surely, MyMessedUpFile.java goes back to the way it was. Anything you typed in since the last commit is gone. Vanished.

So in our case, we can do this:

```
$ cd src/cowshooter
$ ls
CowShooter.java CowTask.java
$ git checkout CowTask.java
```

And now CowTask.java is back to a known, running state, and we can even recompile:

```
$ cd ~/Desktop/code/CowShooter
$ ./build.sh
Compiling with javac...
Creating jar file...
Deploying jar to /Users/andy/Desktop/server/plugins...
Completed Successfully.
```

Great. So it's easy to throw out bad changes and get back to the last save point.

But what if you committed bad changes a while back, and only noticed the problem now? You can use the same checkout command, but this time specify which commit to fetch.

Let's try that now. Go back into CowTask.java and add the bad zombies line again. But now commit it with this:

```
$ git commit -a -m 'Added zombie warning'
[master e4ee198] Added zombie warning
 1 file changed, 2 insertions(+)
```

Now let's break it even worse. Find the two lines that say

```
private World world;
private Cow cow;
```

and delete them. Commit that as well:

```
$ git commit -a -m 'Deleted variable declarations'
[master 44b39f3] Deleted variable declarations
 1 file changed, 3 deletions(-)
```

Now let's see what the log says for CowTask.java:

```
$ git log --oneline CowTask.java

44b39f3 Deleted variable declarations
e4ee198 Added zombie warning
cc0e424 ignoring bin and dist
50847c8 Added my personal screed
aa58dfa First Commit
```

Your commit IDs, those magic numbers that are listed on each line, will be different from mine. But let's use mine for this example.

So in this case, we want to go back to the last known good version of this file. That would be where we logged the message about "ignoring bin and dist." That means we want to skip back past commits 44b39f3 and e4ee198, and check out this file at commit ID cc0e424, when life was happy:

```
$ cd ~/Desktop/code/CowShooter/src/cowshooter
$ git checkout cc0e424 CowTask.java
```

And silently but surely, CowTask.java reverts to its previous state, back before you added the zombie text and before you deleted those variables.

Now the file has actually been changed, just as if you'd edited it by hand, so be sure to commit this latest change with an appropriate message (perhaps something like "That was a bad idea; back to the drawing board."):

```
$ git commit -a -m 'That was a bad idea'
[master 0b6b051] That was a bad idea
 1 file changed, 3 insertions(+), 2 deletions(-)
```

Our bad code hasn't been forgotten; just like a bad day at school or a rotten quiz grade, it's part of history, as git log reveals:

```
$ git log --oneline CowTask.java
0b6b051 That was a bad idea
44b39f3 Deleted variable declarations
e4ee198 Added zombie warning
cc0e424 ignoring bin and dist
50847c8 Added my personal screed
aa58dfa First Commit
```

And if you really wanted to, you could even go back to the bad version of the code at commit 44b39f3 or commit e4ee198. That's part of Git's beauty: it remembers everything, good and bad, and you can always go back in time.

You can use this same idea for multiple files that were involved in the same commit—by specifying all the files you need instead of just the one. You can even do it across the entire project—just don't specify any file to git checkout, and it will operate on the whole project repository.

Visit Multiple Realities

Being able to revert to a previous commit is great; it's like time travel. You can always revisit your past. But why stop at just one past?

Git has a really neat feature called "branches." These aren't like branches on a tree, but more like branches in the space-time continuum: they are alternate realities, or alternate timelines like in science-fiction stories.

Here's how you might use branches: Suppose you have everything working, and maybe you've even released your plugin to the world. You want to experiment with a new feature or two, but you need the current version of your plugin around as well, in case there are any fixes you need to make for your users. You need two different timelines: one where the plugin stays as it is, maybe with a few fixes, and one where it's growing and gaining new features. Maybe you want another timeline as well, where you try implementing your features in a totally different way.

Not a problem!

You can create a new timeline easily using Git's branch command. branch by itself will list all the current branches in your project:

```
$ git branch
* master
```

There's only one branch by default. It's named master, and you're in that timeline. Now let's split the universe into two and make an alternate reality! It's simple:

```
$ git branch cow-plane
```

And now you've created a new timeline. But you're not in it yet; you're still in master. (Type git branch and you'll see the star is still next to master.) To switch into the other timeline, type this:

```
$ git checkout cow-plane
```

Yes, it's our good friend git checkout again. Powerful magic. It's now transported you to a different reality. Nothing you do here will affect the master timeline. You can edit files, delete files, add new files, commit changes—everything. And it's all in the cow-plane universe. You can go back to master at any time:

```
$ git checkout master
```

And now you'll see the world as it was in master's time, with none of your changes from cow-plane. Now you fix problems and release this version of the plugin, without any of the work-in-progress bits from your cow-plane timeline.

Try This Yourself

Let's try that for real in CowShooter. We're going to make a new branch, called play, make some changes in both the master and play branches, and merge changes from play back into master. Picture it like this:

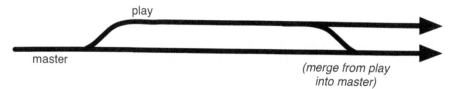

The master time stream is going along, minding its own business. We'll create a new branch to play on, and call it play:

```
$ cd ~/Desktop/code/CowShooter
$ git branch play
```

Then switch to that branch using git checkout:

```
$ git checkout play
Switched to branch 'play'
```

When in doubt as to where you are, just type git branch with no arguments, and it will tell you what branches exist and mark the one you're on with an asterisk (*):

```
$ git branch
  master
* play
```

So there are now two branches, and we're on play. Right now the content of the two branches is identical. Let's fix that.

Edit CowShooter.java. Right after the if statement to see if the player is holding leather, there's a bunch of lines of code to set a vector:

```
Location loc = player.getLocation();
Vector vec = loc.getDirection();
int mult = 3;
vec.setX(vec.getX() * mult);
vec.setY(vec.getY() * mult);
vec.setZ(vec.getZ() * mult);
```

That's kind of messy. Let's tidy that up. Create a new function above the public void onEnable and name it calculateVector. It will need to take a Location as an argument and return a Vector. Move those lines into the body of the function, and it will look like this:

```
private static Vector calculateVector(Location loc) {
    Vector vec = loc.getDirection();
    int mult = 3;
    vec.setX(vec.getX() * mult);
    vec.setY(vec.getY() * mult);
    vec.setZ(vec.getZ() * mult);
    return vec;
}
```

Then, where you took out those lines below, put in the call to calculateVector:

```
...
if (player.getItemInHand().getType() == Material.LEATHER) {
  Location loc = player.getLocation();
  Vector vec = calculateVector(loc); // Add this line

  final Cow cow = player.getWorld().spawn(loc, Cow.class);
  ...
```

Run build.sh to make sure it still works. Now suppose that it *didn't* work—you made a typo somewhere. Wouldn't it be nice to be able to go back and look at the original version? Seems easy enough:

```
$ cd ~/Desktop/code/CowShooter/src/cowshooter
$ git checkout master
error: Your local changes to the following files would be overwritten by checkout:
        src/cowshooter/CowShooter.java
Please, commit your changes or stash them before you can switch branches.
Aborting
```

Ah! Git does try very hard to make sure you *never* lose any code you've typed in. If Git can, it will merge your fresh, uncommitted changes and take them with you when you switch branches. But in this case the changes to move the vector calculation conflict with the master branch, and you haven't saved them anywhere else. Let's go ahead and commit our work in progress:[1]

```
$ git commit -a -m 'Moved vector calculation'
[play 411208c] Moved vector calculation
 1 file changed, 10 insertions(+), 5 deletions(-)
```

Now with that safely in a snapshot, let's take a look at the original:

```
$ git checkout master
M       src/cowshooter/CowShooter.java
Switched to branch 'master'
```

And now the version of CowShooter.java on disk is the version in the master reality. Take a look at it and see. One note of caution: Git changed the text file on disk. The version in your editor's buffer might be the old one. Most editors are savvy enough to realize when a file has changed out from under them, but how that's handled is up to the editor.

Now back here in master, let's change the cow shooter to shoot creepers instead.

In both CowShooter.java and CowTask.java, change the import from Cow (which we no longer need) to Creeper:

```
import org.bukkit.entity.Cow; // Delete this line
import org.bukkit.entity.Creeper; // Add this line
```

In CowShooter.java, change the spawn line to make a Creeper instead of a Cow:

```
final Creeper creeper = player.getWorld().spawn(loc, Creeper.class)
```

And now change the next few references to the cow variable to the new creeper variable:

---

1. You could also use git stash to keep temporary track of your changes.

```
creeper.setVelocity(vec);
creeper.setFireTicks(20);
BukkitRunnable runnable = new CowTask(player.getWorld(), creeper);
```

Great! Then over in CowTask.java, change our variable at the top:

```
private Cow cow; // Delete this line
private Creeper creeper; // Add this line
```

And again change all the references from cow to creeper to match.

Once it builds successfully, commit it for safekeeping:

```
$ git commit -a -m 'Changed to shoot creepers'
[master ea618af] Changed to shoot creepers
 2 files changed, 13 insertions(+), 13 deletions(-)
```

While we're working in master, it would be nice to bring these changes over to the play branch. For that, you can use a git merge:

```
~/Desktop/code/CowShooter/src/cowshooter$ git merge play
Auto-merging src/cowshooter/CowShooter.java
Merge made by the 'recursive' strategy.
 src/cowshooter/CowShooter.java | 17 ++++++++++++-----
 1 file changed, 12 insertions(+), 5 deletions(-)
```

Now take a look at the CowShooter.java file, and you'll see the changes from the play branch have been incorporated. master now contains the move to the calculateVector function and the changes from Cow to Creeper.

Having merged in changes from the play branch doesn't mean it's gone away. There's still a play branch out there and you can still play with it as long as you want. If you are really, truly done with it and never want to see that branch again, you can delete it:

```
$ git branch -d play
Deleted branch play (was f3e6538).
```

And it is unceremoniously deleted from reality, as git branch shows:

```
$ git branch
* master
```

Back Up to the Cloud

This is a fairly advanced topic. Feel free to skip it on your first reading. But do read it at some point—after all, hard disks fail, laptops break, and thumb drives get lost.

Git keeps a local copy of all of your files and all of your changes in its local repository, and you can set it up to keep a copy of your repository in the cloud as well. You choose when to send changes to the cloud by running the command git push. After a push, the remote repository in the cloud will have all the same content and changes you have locally.

To set that up, you'll need an account on a Git host.

The most popular one is GitHub, although many people like Bitbucket as well.[2] GitHub is the standard for code that you intend to share with others or make available as open source, while Bitbucket is better suited to private projects that you don't intend to share with the world.

Both offer really simple web interfaces to get you set up and running. For instance, once you create an account on GitHub, you can press the button to create a new repository, and you'll get a screen similar to the following:

Pick a name for your project, and select Public or Private.[3] Don't initialize the repository, as you already have one locally. Just press the Create Repository button, and *bang*—it's done.

Now you'll see instructions on what to do next.

---

2.   http://github.com, http://bitbucket.com
3.   Public repositories on GitHub are available for free, but private repositories cost money. Bitbucket, on the other hand, offers unlimited private repositories for free.

First, copy and save the URL to your repository at the top. In this example, that would be https://github.com/andyhunt/minecraft.git.

Since you already have a local repository, follow the instructions at the bottom for "Push an existing repository from the command line." Mine looks like this:

```
$ git remote add origin https://github.com/andyhunt/minecraft.git
$ git push -u origin master
```

The first command sets up a remote named origin and associates it with the given URL. Next, the push with the -u option sets the master branch to be tracked to origin. Now whenever you reach a good stopping point, you can run git push and all your code and changes will be safely saved in the cloud.

You (or anyone else if it's a public repository) can get a copy of all the code and the history of the changes by using git clone to clone a copy of the repository into an empty directory:

```
$ mkdir newcopy
$ cd newcopy
$ git clone https://github.com/andyhunt/minecraft.git .
```

Share Code

Distributing code via GitHub is a very popular way of sharing your code with the world. All you need to do is give out your GitHub project URL (in this example, https://github.com/andyhunt/minecraft.git). Now anyone in the world can use git clone to get a copy of your code, and they can make their own changes, compile it, install it, and so on.

One of the advantages of releasing your source code to the world is that other programmers can help add features and fix bugs.

Both GitHub and Bitbucket have nice web interfaces to help with that.

Friendly Code

When you're writing code to share with others—which means sharing with the whole world—you need to make a little extra effort to write "friendly" code:

- Neatness counts. Put braces where they belong; don't try and jam everything on one line or use inconsistent indentations. The format of the code can be as important as the code itself for human readers.

- Keep it tight. Don't make lines or functions hugely long.

- Comment your functions. Explain *why* a function is there, and *what* it's used for. Don't comment on *how* it does it—that's what the code is for.

- Honor naming conventions. Java prefers camel-case identifiers (like in the word *camelCase*), with embedded capital letters. Other languages may use names with underscores or other conventions. Name variables so that readers can easily understand what they are used for. Although single-letter variables (especially i) are often used for loop counters, that's not very descriptive. But it's even worse to use i (which is normally an index) as a string or a Location! Stick to the conventions.

Suppose one of your fans has code for a new feature she'd like you to include in your plugin. She'd fork (make a copy of) your repository on her own, and make the proposed changes in a named branch in her repository. Then through the magic of GitHub (or Bitbucket), she'd submit her changes in that branch to you as a *pull request*. That is, she's sending you a request to pull her branch into your repository and use it.

In the web interface, you can reply to pull requests with questions and comments, and have a whole discussion about the changes. If and when you want to incorporate them, just press the Merge Pull Request button. If the new code can merge in without any conflicts, you're done. Otherwise, click the Command Line button, and you'll get further instructions.

We've only scratched the very surface of Git: it's a really powerful and sometimes quite complicated tool. Whole books are devoted just to Git (including

Pragmatic Version Control Using Git [Swi08] and *Pragmatic Guide to Git [Swi10]*. But hopefully this is enough to get you started.

Next Up

Git is a powerful tool, not just because it gives you a project-wide "undo button," but because it allows you to experiment *with confidence*. You don't have to be afraid that you'll screw everything up. When you *do* screw everything up, Git lets you "unscrew" it back to the point where it all worked. With branches, you can even try a couple of different approaches in code. Not sure if you should use an array or a hash? Not sure if the listener should be in a separate class? You can use branches to try things out.

With that freedom in hand, you're ready for the final step.

git config --global user.email *email*	Set your email address
git config --global user.name *"Name"*	Set your user name
git init	Initialize a Git repo in the current directory
git add *files*	Add files (or directories) to be tracked by Git
git commit -a -m '*Commit message*'	Commit changes (-a all)
git log --oneline *files*	Show commit messages for one or more files
git status	Show what files you've changed, files you've created but Git doesn't know about (untracked), and so on
git diff *files*	Show differences between versions
git checkout *files*	Discard local changes for files (use with caution)
git checkout *name*	Switch to named branch
git branch	List all branches
git branch *name*	Switch to named branch
git remote add origin *url*	Add a remote repo as "origin"
git push -u origin master	Copy changes on the master branch to the remote named "origin"

Next, and finally, we'll look at how you can go about designing and building your own plugin from scratch.

Your Growing Toolbox

Your toolbox is 92% full. You can now do the following:

- Use the command-line shell
- Build with Java, javac
- Run a Minecraft server
- Deploy a plugin
- Connect to a local server
- Use Java variables for numbers and strings
- Use Java functions
- Use if, for, and while statements
- Use Java objects
- Use imports for Java packages
- Use new to create objects
- Add a new command to a plugin
- Work with Location objects
- Find nearby blocks/entities
- Use local variables
- Use class-level global variables
- Use ArrayLists
- Use HashMaps
- Use private and public to control visibility
- Modify Minecraft blocks
- Modify and spawn entities
- Listen for and react to game events
- Manage plugin permissions
- Create a separate class
- Schedule a task to run later
- Schedule a task to run periodically
- Save and load configuration data
- Build up complex code from simple functions
- Save and load plugin game data
- Use Java file input and output
- Catch and throw Java exceptions
- Use Git to keep track of changes to code
- Go back to earlier versions of code (an "undo button")
- Maintain multiple versions of code at the same time
- Back up your code to the cloud

## CHAPTER 13

Design Your Own Plugin

Your Toolbox

In this chapter you're going to design your own plugin. You'll add the last necessary bits to your toolbox. You'll learn the following:

- How to assign responsibilities to classes
- How to translate responsibilities into functions
- How to do a little design, a little coding, and a little testing, all as you go

You'll be able to start working on your very own plugins.

For all the plugins we've looked at so far, I've led the way and shown you what to do. In this chapter I'll give you some suggestions and hints to help you develop your own plugins from scratch. Together we'll go through the steps for a brand-new plugin and see how it works.

We're going to (more or less) follow these steps:

1. Have an idea: I want a plugin to do _____.
2. Gather your materials.
3. Lay them out.
4. Try each part.
5. Knit it all together.
6. Profit!

IMPORTANT NOTE: Even though I've laid out these steps in order, and we'll go through them in order, the real world doesn't usually work that way.

Creativity and invention rarely take a direct, linear path from idea to execution. Instead, you'll discover that something doesn't work the way you thought it did. The code you wrote is all wrong. Or the code is perfectly right but not what you need. That's all totally normal, and really it's what writing code is all about.

You may need to throw out anything you've done and do it over, up to and including the entire project. Hey, even the government does that with $100 billion projects, so we can do it too.

Professional programmers tackle this problem by taking very small steps: do one small, bite-size thing at a time, make sure *that* works, then go on to the next. Any time you realize that you've made a mistake or misunderstood something, go back and fix it right then and there. Don't think you'll remember to fix it later; you won't. Trust me on that one.

Let's dig in and design a new plugin. I'm going to go through these steps on my new plugin, and you'll do the same thing for *your* new plugin alongside of me. Yours should do something different. And it's okay if this takes awhile; this isn't the sort of chapter you'll whip through in one evening.

Have an Idea

Before you start, you need some idea of what you want to write. It may not be a great idea or a perfect idea yet, and that's okay. This is *soft*ware, after all, and you're allowed to change your mind. But we need to start somewhere.

So I think I'd like to figure out how to randomly generate "creeper cows." That is, cows that jump around and try to attack you, and that explode when they jump on you. That might be fun.

At this point, I have no idea how to even start such a thing.

Try This Yourself

What is your idea? Jot it down now. If you're stuck, take a look at plugins other people have written, or just browse the Bukkit documentation and see if something inspires you.

Gather Your Materials

Armed with an idea, the next thing to do is "gather your materials." If you were building a craft project, you'd gather all the raw materials (glue, wood, paper, googly eyes, plutonium) and tools (scissors, hammer, arc welder, cooling tower—whatever). We need to do the same. But what materials do we need?

Well, we need a first guess at what sort of data we'll require in the plugin, how to keep track of it, and what makes the plugin run—is it run from a command, or an event, or a timer? Here are some good questions to ask:

- What do you need to keep track of?

- How long do you need to keep it? (During a command, while the server is running, across server reboots on disk...)

- What are the triggers? (User-entered command, in-game event, internal state, timer, combination...)

- What parts of the game do you need to affect (blocks, players, potions, inventory, and so on) and what Bukkit or Java functions will you need to use for them?

- What can go wrong?

You may not have all the answers yet. But that won't stop us; let's get started (using my "creeper cow" idea).

What do you need to keep track of? We probably need to keep track of the cows we spawn. We might need to keep track of players that each cow is targeting and trying to attack, or maybe we'll figure that out for each cow as we go along. We don't know which yet. Anything else? Oh, we want to randomly create locations for the cows; do you remember what function to use to get random numbers in Java?

How long do you need to keep it? Since these are randomly generated attack cows, I don't think we need to keep track of them when the server shuts down—we'll just make new ones. We will need to keep track of them in memory while the server is running, though, so at a minimum we'll need some kind of a static list or hash of the cows we've spawned. Reread Chapter 7, *Use Piles of Variables: Arrays*, on page 87, or Chapter 11, *Use Configuration Files and Store Game Data*, on page 145, if you need a refresher.

What are the triggers? It would be kind of stupid to have to type in a command to get attacked by creeper cows, so we won't be using an onCommand function. Instead, we'll need an event to kick off cow generation, and maybe a timer to keep the cow attacking and make it eventually explode. We'll have to find some kind of suitable event to listen for. Have a look back at Chapter 9, *Modify, Spawn, and Listen in Minecraft*, on page 113, and Chapter 10, *Schedule Tasks for Later*, on page 133, for details.

What parts of the game do you need to affect? We'll need to move the killer cows around and blow them up, which we know how to do from the earlier plugins. We'll need to blow up the player that we're attacking. Can we just blow up when the cow is next to a player, or do we need to explicitly kill the player (by setting health to zero or setting the player on fire or something)? We'll need to experiment and see how that works.

What can go wrong? This is a question to ask yourself *constantly* when creating a plugin. For now it seems likely our cows could get confused when attacking and get stuck somewhere, or not have any player nearby to attack. So we'll need to deal with that. Also, it's probably a good idea to limit the number of cows we're going to spawn, so we don't accidentally create the Great Cow Deluge.

It's not much, but it's a start. Here's what we've gathered so far:

- A static list or hash of cows we've spawned

- The Java function to make a random number (what was that again?)

- An event to spawn cows

- The idea that each cow needs a timer so it has a chance to find players and attack them

- The idea that the cow needs to not get stuck in the terrain (what if there's no player nearby?)

- The knowledge that we may need to put a limit on the number of cows to spawn

Try This Yourself

Now go through these questions for the plugin you want to build, and come up with your own list of things you'll need—your "materials."

Include things you aren't sure about—there's no penalty if you end up not using them.

Lay Them Out

Before we create the plugin and start writing code, let's think about what might go where. In other words, will this fit all in one function or even one class, and if there are several functions or classes, what goes where? If there are additional classes, what do they need to know about us or each other? If you've forgotten some details of functions and objects, check back with Chapter 4, *Plugins Have Variables, Functions, and Keywords*, on page 41, and Chapter 5, *Plugins Have Objects*, on page 65, for a refresher.

So here are our questions:

- What goes where? What functions and classes do you need?
- Why do you need this function (or class)? What is it responsible for?
- Who else needs to know about this function or class (if anyone)?

One way of attacking this, especially on complicated plugins, is by using good old-fashioned index cards. (These are called CRC cards, where CRC is short for "class-responsibility-collaborators," invented by our friends Ward Cunningham and Kent Beck.) Divide each card into three parts: a title up top, a list of things it is responsible for on the left, and other classes it needs to work with on the right.

So our main plugin class, so far, would look like this:

Then there's the CreeperCowTimer, which will hold a cow and take care of the things an attacking cow needs to do:

Notice we haven't gotten into any detail of particular functions yet: you want to get a firm idea in your head of *why* a particular class needs to exist. What is it responsible for doing?

Then for each responsibility, take a stab at working out what it needs to do. So as not to get too hung up on Java syntax and issues (or those of any other programming language, for that matter), say what you want to do in steps, in plain English. Tell the story of *what* you want to do—don't worry about *how* yet.

Each of those steps will become a function. Or *at least one function*—you may want to further split that up into a couple of simpler functions and/or classes as needed.

1. Create our list of cows.
2. Spawn creeper cows and add them to our list.
3. Set up each creeper cow with a timer.
4. Listen for events to create and remove cows.

That part was easy. But what's a creeper cow to do? We said its responsibility is to "attack players." What does that mean? How about this:

1. Find the closest player. (There might not be one.)
2. Jump toward the closest player. (Don't die from the impact!)
3. If you hit the closest player, explode.

So for the CreeperCow plugin, let's take our list of gathered materials plus the list of steps, make up some function names, and see what we need to code:

CreeperCow (the main plugin class):

- listOfCows: A static list of cows we've created.

- Math.random(): We need a random number, and the Java docs say this will return a double between 0 and 1.[1]

- spawnCows(): Create some random number of cows, no more than some established limit. We'll create a CreeperCowTimer to hold each cow and set its timer going.

- eventListener(): A listener to call spawnCows().

CreeperCowTimer (one per cow):

- findClosestPlayer(): There might not be one.
- jump(Location loc): Jump means fly up into the air and don't die on impact.
- explode(): If we hit a player (or are close enough), explode and tell the plugin to remove this cow.

There's a lot we haven't figured out yet, but this gives us enough to start putting some code together. And *that* will help us figure out the remaining questions. And probably raise some new ones. Onward we go.

---

1. http://docs.oracle.com/javase/7/docs/api/java/lang/Math.html#random%28%29

Try This Yourself

Get a couple of index cards or some bits of paper, and jot down your main class and its responsibilities, and any parts of Bukkit it might need. If you need extra classes like we did here, either for a task runner or as a listener, or anything else you need to keep track of, create those cards as well.

For each responsibility, write a list of steps that reads like a story. Then go through your list of "materials" and take a first stab at making a list of functions and variables, asking the same questions we asked here.

Once you have your list together, it's time to start writing some code. But not all at once, as we'll see in the next section.

Try Each Part

We're going to start coding now, but as exciting as that is, we want to go slowly. Whether you're following along with me here or working on your own plugin, remember to take one small step at a time—don't rush it.

Let's begin by creating a new directory and the usual files that every plugin needs. Once again we'll use the mkplugin.sh script to get started:

```
~/Desktop/code$ ./mkplugin.sh CreeperCow
~/Desktop/code$ cd CreeperCow
~/Desktop/code/CreeperCow$ ls -a
.            .gitignore  build.sh    plugin.yml
..           bin/        dist/       src/
```

And we'll start right away by using Git to track our work (check back with Chapter 12, *Keep Your Code Safe*, on page 169, for a refresher if you need to).

The mkplugin.sh script thoughtfully made us a .gitignore that will ignore the bin/ and dist/ directories. So we'll add our first couple of files and commit them as a baseline:

```
~/Desktop/code/CreeperCow$ git init
Initialized empty Git repository in /Users/andy/Desktop/code/CreeperCow/.git/
~/Desktop/code/CreeperCow$ git add .gitignore build.sh plugin.yml src
~/Desktop/code/CreeperCow$ git commit -a -m First
[master (root-commit) 2e483f1] First
 4 files changed, 95 insertions(+)
 create mode 100644 .gitignore
 create mode 100755 build.sh
 create mode 100644 plugin.yml
 create mode 100644 src/creepercow/CreeperCow.java
```

(If you are hooked up to a remote repository, you can do a git push now, as well.)

Now on to the code.

We know that we need to create a static listOfCows and a spawnCows() method, and we'll need to listen for some events, so let's start with that in CreeperCow.java. Here's the interesting part (omitting other imports and the usual other stuff):

```
...
import org.bukkit.event.Listener;
import org.bukkit.entity.Cow;
import java.util.ArrayList;

public class CreeperCow extends JavaPlugin implements Listener {
  public static Logger log = Logger.getLogger("Minecraft");
  public static List<Cow> cowList = new ArrayList<Cow>();

  public void spawnCows() {

  }
...
```

We made the main plugin a Listener and added a cowList variable and the start of the spawnCows() function. Now before we go any further, let's test out *just that much* and see if it builds without errors, and run the (empty) spawnCows function.

Small steps, remember. We don't have an event listener yet (in fact, we don't even know *what* event we're going to listen for), so we'll use a trick.

We're going to add a command to onCommand() that's just for us—it's not for users, and we won't even include it in the plugin.yml when we're done. But we can use it to test what we're doing as we go along.

So let's wire that up first, even before we've added any code to spawnCows:

```
public boolean onCommand(CommandSender sender, Command command,
                         String commandLabel, String[] args) {
  if (commandLabel.equalsIgnoreCase("testSpawnCows")) {
    if (sender instanceof Player) {
      Player me = (Player)sender;
      spawnCows();
      return true;
    }
  }
  return false;
}
```

And add the command to the plugin.yml file:

```
name: CreeperCow

author: Andy Hunt

main: creepercow.CreeperCow

commands:
    testSpawnCows:
        description: Test cow spawning, for development use only
        usage: testSpawnCows

version: 0.1
```

Now we have the ability to log in to the game and run the /testSpawnCows command to watch our cows spawn and make sure that works.

We don't actually spawn any cows yet, but let's just try it now and make sure everything compiles, using build.sh, before we add any more code.

```
~/Desktop/code/CreeperCow$ build.sh
Compiling with javac...
Creating jar file...
Deploying jar to /Users/andy/Desktop/server/plugins...
Completed Successfully.
```

That's a good opportunity to make sure we've got the right imports and everything, and haven't made any typos. And since it's working, I'll do a git commit.

Try This Yourself

Now do this much yourself: create a new plugin directory with mkplugin.sh, get a Git repository set up for it, and add any functions and data that you think you need. Refer back to earlier parts of the book if you need a refresher on anything.

Add the testing commands to onCommand (and plugin.yml), even if you have real commands that you're going to add as well. Again, small steps. You want to make small functions that run by themselves, and get them right before continuing. Don't try and flesh out the functions yet; just start with empty function bodies like we did here.

Don't forget to do a git commit to "save your game" as you go along.

Filling in the Details: the spawnCows() Function

Now that we have a way to test it, let's move on to the guts of spawnCows() itself. We noted earlier that we need to do the following:

1. Create our list of cows.
2. Spawn creeper cows and add them to our list.
3. Set up each creeper cow with a timer.
4. Listen for events to create and remove cows.

Let's take this one at a time. We already made the simple static list of cows, so let's look at spawning.

We'll need to create some random cows. This raises a question: where should we put them? All over the game? Near where you are? Right on top of your friend's head? All of these choices may have their appeal.

When programming, one of the best things you can do when making decisions is to delay making them. In many cases, you don't know the "right" answer, and you may not know it for a while—or ever. But that's what function parameters are for: we don't have to decide the details right now. Instead of deciding on some particular detail, pass that detail in as a parameter. Now you don't have to decide, and the function can be used with all sorts of different details.

So we need to change the temporary declaration we had in place for spawnCows() and pass in something to indicate where we want these cows. What should that look like?

Let's start with a Location, and then a number of blocks square. The location will be one corner of a large square, and the square will then extend for some number in the x and z directions. So we'll change the function signature to look like this:

```
public void spawnCows(Location start, int size) {
```

(We'll need to import org.bukkit.Location; too.)

Then we can decide later what to pass in. For testing, we can pass in your Player location and a number you pick. Let's wire that up now.

Ah, one small hitch: onCommand() passes us the arguments to a user command as an array of String objects. We don't want a string to pass to testSpawnCows(), though—we want an int. How do you do that conversion, again?

A Google search for "java convert string to int" reveals the magic incantation:

```
int foo = Integer.parseInt("1234");
```

Now we can finish up the command to call spawnCows from our test command:

```
public boolean onCommand(CommandSender sender, Command command,
                         String commandLabel, String[] args) {
  if (commandLabel.equalsIgnoreCase("testSpawnCows")) {
    if (sender instanceof Player) {
      Player me = (Player)sender;
      spawnCows(me.getLocation(), Integer.parseInt(args[0]));
      return true;
    }
  }
  return false;
}
```

Okay, *now* it's safe to add the code to implement spawnCows, because we have a way to check it. Professionals work like this: write some way of checking your code before you write the code itself. We can't quite do it all automatically —we still have to manually log in to the game and visually confirm that we're spawning creeper cows, but it's a similar idea.

So we need to start making some cows! We'll use a for loop, the starting location, and the size to create a new location to spawn each new cow. How many cows to spawn? Oops. We didn't think about that. Better add that to the function signature:

```
public void spawnCows(Location start, int size, int number) {
```

and pass it in from the onCommand() for testing:

```
spawnCows(me.getLocation(),
  Integer.parseInt(args[0]), Integer.parseInt(args[1]));
```

Now we know how to do the for loop to create cows, and add them to our list of Cows. We can finally put the code in spawnCows:

```
public void spawnCows(Location start, int size, int count) {
  World world = start.getWorld();
  for (int i=0; i< count; i++) {
    Location loc = new Location(world,
      start.getX() + (Math.random() * size),
      0,
      start.getZ() + (Math.random() * size)
    );
    loc.setY(world.getHighestBlockYAt(loc) + 2);
    Cow cow = world.spawn(loc, Cow.class);
  }
}
```

To recap: we're multiplying the random number (0..1) by the size of the square, so that will give us a number between zero and the size of the square. We'll use that for an x and z of the location on the square, then ask the server for the highest block at that point and use that as the y. That's the location where we'll spawn the new cow.

Let's compile and build it, and test it out.

I'll log in to the game and try the command /testSpawnCows 10 8, which will spawn eight cows within a 10×10 block from my current location.

Hey, we made some cows! They aren't very frightening, though. They're just sitting there, as cows do. We need to get them to jump around and attack.

I've written some code, tested it, and now I'll do a git commit to save this state of the world before going on.

Try This Yourself

Your turn! Start fleshing out your functions just as I did here. Don't feel they have to do *everything* yet—just enough to get started (for instance, our cows here don't jump yet).

For each function you make, include a test command so you can try it from inside the game.

Make sure all your test commands work with as much as you have done so far. And don't forget to save your progress with Git.

Filling in the Details: CreeperCowTimer

Earlier we decided to put the code for the jumping, attacking, exploding cow into a new CreeperCowTimer class. Eventually we'll crank this up from an event in the main CreeperCow plugin.

But first off we need a function to make a cow jump and attack. We'll build and test that first.

Given a target and our cow's location, we create a new Vector by taking the difference in Location coordinates in the x and z directions: that gives us the displacement between the cow and its target. But that's too large a number for a velocity, so we then multiply it by a convenient number (0.1) that I found by experimenting. Finally we set that as the cow's velocity, which will make it jump along that Vector at that speed.

```
public class CreeperCowTimer implements Listener {

  import org.bukkit.event.Listener;
  import org.bukkit.entity.Cow;
  import org.bukkit.util.Vector;
  import org.bukkit.Location;

  private Cow cow;

  public void jump(Location target) {
    Location cowLoc = cow.getLocation();
    double multFactor = 0.1;
    Vector v = new Vector(
      (target.getX() - cowLoc.getX()) * multFactor,
      1,
      (target.getZ() - cowLoc.getZ()) * multFactor
    );
    cow.setVelocity(v);
  }
}
```

I'll do a git add on the new CreeperCowTimer.java file so my changes can be tracked.

Great. Now we need some way of setting that private cow object. We'll hook this up to the spawnCows function later, but right now we'll just pass in a cow that's been spawned already. For that, we'll use the constructor function:

```
CreeperCowTimer(Cow aCow) {
  cow = aCow;
}
```

Next we need to add a jump command to the plugin for our testing. Now we'll go back into the spawnCows function and add the spawned cows to the ArrayList. Then, in the jump command we can go through the list and get each of the spawned cows to jump toward us.

So we'll start with this:

```
Cow cow = world.spawn(loc, Cow.class);
cowList.add(cow);
```

Then we'll add a test command:

```
if (commandLabel.equalsIgnoreCase("testJump")) {
  if (sender instanceof Player) {
    Player me = (Player)sender;
    for (Cow c : cowList) {
      c.jump(me.getLocation());
    }
    return true;
  }
}
```

Oops, that's not going to work.

We shouldn't have kept a list of cows. We really need to keep track of Creeper-CowTimer objects, as that will get us the jump() function and the other guts that we need to write, as well as the Cow itself.

And if we do that, we should probably change the list to be a HashMap instead of an ArrayList so we can look up the CreeperCowTimer objects by their Cow, as that's what we'll get from events and spawning and such. We'll need to redo a few things now.

Make a list of things we need to change for this, and come on back once you have it.

Changes We Need

Here's what I came up with:

1. Change the import java.util.ArrayList; to import java.util.HashMap;.

2. Change the cowList from public static ArrayList<Cow> allCows = new ArrayList<Cow>(); to use a hash instead: public static HashMap<Cow, CreeperCowTimer> allCows = new HashMap<Cow, CreeperCowTimer>();. (Also, I renamed it so that the type of list isn't part of the name.)

3. Change the cowList.add(cow); to allCows.put(cow, new CreeperCowTimer(cow)); since you have to put in a hash.

4. Change the for loop to iterate through the HashMap so the new loop looks like this:

```
for (Cow c : allCows.keySet()) {
  CreeperCowTimer superCow = allCows.get(c);
  superCow.jump(me.getLocation());
}
```

Right about now this might feel frustrating.

That's okay: it's not important to get it right the first time. That rarely happens and doesn't gain you much. It *is* important to get it right the last time.

With these changes we can now test jumping. I'll fire up the server, connect from the client, and test by spawning just a single cow first. Then I can use the testJump command to see if it starts heading toward me:

```
/testspawncows 5 1
```

Great! Now for a few jumps:

```
/testjump
/testjump
/testjump
```

Ah, right. The cow died. We ran into that same problem back in the CowShooter plugin—we have to set the cow's health to the max using something like this:

```
cow.setHealth(cow.getMaxHealth());
```

But where should we do it? And what else do we need to finish up this plugin?

The current version is working but has a problem. Do a git commit to save the current state of the code at this point before we start making more major changes.

Knit It All Together

We need to add a few things from our list of materials and take care of a couple of problems.

First off, we need to fix the dying cows, so let's add an event handler to listen for EntityDamageEvent, and cancel the event if its cause is DamageCause.FALL.

When testing the spawn function and the jump, we used ourselves as the target. We need to do a little better than that, so we'll need to add a getClosest-Player() function to find the closest player to any given cow.

And as we saw earlier, we need to pick an event to use to spawn these creeper cows. There are probably a couple of ways to do that. You don't want to spawn cows all over the world; it would be great if there were some kind of event that gets sent when each new chunk of the world gets loaded into the server.

A quick look through the Bukkit documentation for events under org.bukkit.event.world reveals just what we need: a ChunkLoadEvent when a part of the world is loaded, and a ChunkUnloadEvent when it's deleted. So each time a new 16×16 chunk of the world gets loaded, we'll get an event. One minor nit: the chunk tells us which chunk it is in a grid of chunks; you have to multiply by 16 to get a real-world coordinate.

Our to-do list now includes these items:

- Add an EntityDamageEvent event handler so the cow doesn't die.
- Add getClosestPlayer so each cow can find a nearby target.
- Add ChunkLoadEvent to spawn cows in a 16×16 area.
- Add the ChunkUnloadEvent to remove cows from that chunk.
- Set up a task timer so each cow can find a target, jump, and explode if needed.
- Manage the cowList in all these functions (add to it on spawn, delete it on death or unload).

Phew! That's a bit of work. But all of these activities are using functions and skills we've used already, so I won't bore you with a lengthy play-by-play.

Here is the code in its entirety for you to read over and crib from as you need.

CreeperCow/src/creepercow/CreeperCow.java

```java
package creepercow;

import java.util.logging.Logger;
import org.bukkit.command.Command;
import org.bukkit.command.CommandSender;
import org.bukkit.entity.Player;
import org.bukkit.plugin.Plugin;
import org.bukkit.plugin.java.JavaPlugin;

import org.bukkit.entity.Entity;
import org.bukkit.entity.Cow;
import java.util.HashMap;
import org.bukkit.Location;
import org.bukkit.World;
import org.bukkit.Chunk;
import org.bukkit.event.Listener;
import org.bukkit.event.EventHandler;
import org.bukkit.event.entity.EntityDamageEvent.DamageCause;
import org.bukkit.event.entity.EntityDamageEvent;
import org.bukkit.event.world.ChunkLoadEvent;
import org.bukkit.event.world.ChunkUnloadEvent;

public class CreeperCow extends JavaPlugin implements Listener {
  public static Logger log = Logger.getLogger("Minecraft");

  private static HashMap<Cow, CreeperCowTimer> allCows =
    new HashMap<Cow, CreeperCowTimer>();

  private final static int CHUNK_SIZE = 16;

  public void spawnCows(World world, double x, double z, int size, int count) {
    for (int i=0; i< count; i++) {
      Location loc = new Location(world,
        x + (Math.random() * size),
        0,
        z + (Math.random() * size)
      );
      loc.setY(world.getHighestBlockYAt(loc) + 2);
      log.info("[CreeperCow] spawned cow at " + loc);
      Cow cow = world.spawn(loc, Cow.class);
      allCows.put(cow, new CreeperCowTimer(this, cow));
    }
  }
}
```

```java
public void cowDied(Cow cow) {
  log.info("[CreeperCow] cow died.");
  allCows.remove(cow);
}

public void onEnable() {
  log.info("[CreeperCow] enabling.");
  getServer().getPluginManager().registerEvents(this, this);
}


public boolean onCommand(CommandSender sender, Command command,
                         String commandLabel, String[] args) {
  if (sender instanceof Player) {
    Player me = (Player)sender;

    if (commandLabel.equalsIgnoreCase("testSpawnCows")) {
      Location loc = me.getLocation();
      spawnCows(loc.getWorld(), loc.getX(), loc.getY(),
          Integer.parseInt(args[0]), Integer.parseInt(args[1]));
      return true;
    }
    if (commandLabel.equalsIgnoreCase("testJump")) {
      for (Cow c : allCows.keySet()) {
        CreeperCowTimer superCow = allCows.get(c);
        superCow.jump(me.getLocation());
      }
      return true;
    }
    if (commandLabel.equalsIgnoreCase("testJump")) {
      for (Cow c : allCows.keySet()) {
        CreeperCowTimer superCow = allCows.get(c);
        superCow.explode();
      }
      return true;
    }
  }
  return false;
}

@EventHandler
public void onChunkLoad(ChunkLoadEvent event) {
  World world = event.getWorld();
  Chunk chunk = event.getChunk();

  if (Math.random() > 0.10) { // Only make a cow 1 in 10
    return;
  }
  log.info("[CreeperCow] Spawning");
  // The X and Z from the chunk are indexes;
```

```
    // we have to multiply by 16 to get an actual
    // block location.
    spawnCows(world, chunk.getX() * CHUNK_SIZE,
                     chunk.getZ() * CHUNK_SIZE,
                     16, 1);
  }

  @EventHandler
  public void onChunkUnload(ChunkUnloadEvent event) {
    Entity[] ents = event.getChunk().getEntities();
    for(int i = 0; i < ents.length; i++) {
      if (ents[i] instanceof Cow) {
        Cow cow = (Cow) ents[i];
        if (allCows.containsKey(cow)) {
          allCows.get(cow).cancel();
          allCows.remove(cow);
        }
      }
    }
  }

  @EventHandler
  public void onEntityDamage(EntityDamageEvent event) {
    Entity ent = event.getEntity();
    if (ent instanceof Cow) {
      Cow cow = (Cow) ent;
      if (event.getCause() == DamageCause.FALL) {
        if (allCows.containsKey(cow)) {
          event.setCancelled(true);
        }
      }
    }
  }

}
```

CreeperCow/src/creepercow/CreeperCowTimer.java
```
package creepercow;

import org.bukkit.plugin.java.JavaPlugin;
import org.bukkit.event.Listener;
import org.bukkit.entity.Cow;
import org.bukkit.entity.Player;
import org.bukkit.util.Vector;

import java.util.List;
import java.util.ArrayList;

import org.bukkit.Location;
import org.bukkit.scheduler.BukkitRunnable;
import org.bukkit.scheduler.BukkitTask;
```

```java
public class CreeperCowTimer extends BukkitRunnable {
  private Cow cow;
  private CreeperCow plugin;
  private BukkitTask task;

  CreeperCowTimer(CreeperCow parentPlugin, Cow aCow) {
    cow = aCow;
    plugin = parentPlugin;
    runTaskTimer(plugin, 10, 10);
  }

  public void run() {
    if (cow.isOnGround()) { // otherwise it's still jumping
      Location cowLoc = cow.getLocation();
      Player p = getClosestPlayer(cowLoc);
      if (p == null) {
        return;
      }
      Location pLoc = p.getLocation();
      double dist = distance(cowLoc, pLoc);

      if (dist <= 4) {
        explode();
      } else if (dist <= 20) {
        jump(pLoc);
      }
    }
  }

  public Player getClosestPlayer(Location loc) { //return -1 on failure
    List<Player> list = loc.getWorld().getPlayers();
    Player closestPlayer = null;
    double minDistance = -1;
    for(int i = 0; i < list.size(); i++) {
      Player p = list.get(i);
      Location ploc = p.getLocation();
      if (Math.abs(ploc.getY() - loc.getY()) < 15) {
        double dist = distance(loc, ploc);
        if (dist < minDistance || minDistance == -1) {
          minDistance = dist;
          closestPlayer = p;
        }
      }
    }
    return closestPlayer;
  }
  //
  // Find the distance on the ground (ignores height)
  // between two Locations
  //
```

```
public double distance(Location loc1, Location loc2) {
  return Math.sqrt(
    Math.pow(loc1.getX() - loc2.getX(), 2) +
    Math.pow(loc1.getZ() - loc2.getZ(), 2)
  );
}

// Explode yourself
public void explode() {
  plugin.cowDied(cow); // notify parent
  Location cowLoc = cow.getLocation();
  cow.getWorld().createExplosion(cowLoc, 6f, true);
  cow.setHealth(0.0);
  cancel(); // this task
}

// Jump this cow toward the target
public void jump(Location target) {
  Location cowLoc = cow.getLocation();
  double multFactor = 0.1;
  Vector v = new Vector(
    (target.getX() - cowLoc.getX()) * multFactor,
    0.5,
    (target.getZ() - cowLoc.getZ()) * multFactor
  );
  cow.setVelocity(v);
}
}
```

You might notice that I didn't actually implement everything I mentioned in my lists. For example, there's no check for spawning too many cows, and I don't kill the target player directly. I may end up adding those, or just let it be. Just because I *thought* I needed those elements doesn't mean I have to write them yet. I can always add them later if needed.

And I might run into other problems that I hadn't thought about. For instance, what happens to these cows when the server shuts down? The cows will still be in the world, but they won't be CreeperCows anymore, as the plugin doesn't keep track of them. Maybe I should despawn the cows on shutdown. Or maybe having extra cows isn't really a problem? Ah, software.

Try This Yourself

That was our journey with the CreeperCow plugin. Your journey with your plugin will probably be a little different. But try to follow these same general steps: figure out what parts you need, possibly using index cards, then write out a sequence in English of what should happen. Take all that and create your functions, pass around the data you need to, store the stuff you need to remember, and always add test commands so you can test each part separately.

Remember to remove the test commands before shipping your plugin to your friends. Or, for a bit of extra flash, set it up so that you need a special "Developer" permission to run the tests, and give yourself that permission.

And that's it! Your toolbox is now complete:

Your Growing Toolbox

Your toolbox is 100% full. You can now do the following:

- Use the command-line shell
- Build with Java, javac
- Run a Minecraft server
- Deploy a plugin
- Connect to a local server
- Use Java variables for numbers and strings
- Use Java functions
- Use if, for, and while statements
- Use Java objects
- Use imports for Java packages
- Use new to create objects
- Add a new command to a plugin
- Work with Location objects
- Find nearby blocks/entities
- Use local variables
- Use class-level global variables
- Use ArrayLists
- Use HashMaps
- Use private and public to control visibility
- Modify Minecraft blocks
- Modify and spawn entities
- Listen for and react to game events
- Manage plugin permissions
- Create a separate class
- Schedule a task to run later
- Schedule a task to run periodically
- Save and load configuration data
- Build up complex code from simple functions

- Save and load plugin game data
- Use Java file input and output
- Catch and throw Java exceptions
- Use Git to keep track of changes to code
- Go back to earlier versions of code (an "undo button")
- Maintain multiple versions of code at the same time
- Back up your code to the cloud
- Use CRC cards to think about classes and responsibilities
- Decompose responsibilities into functions
- Test as you go

Just the Beginning

It's been a fun trip, but we've barely scratched the surface. There is more Java you need to learn, and there's a lot more to Bukkit than we've covered here. Plus, there's a ton more to programming in general that you'll discover as you go along.

But I hope this has been a fun start for you. Don't stop now! Get a couple more books on Java or another language, on programming, on web design— whatever. Never stop reading and learning.

And when you make something really cool, email me and let me know.

Thanks for buying this book, and all the best,

Andy

andy@pragprog.com

How to Read Error Messages

Error messages from the Java compiler, the runtime system, and the Minecraft server try to be self-explanatory, but they don't always succeed. The javac compiler in particular can get more than a little confused and spit out unhelpful messages.

Please read through this whole section even if you aren't getting a particular error at the moment, as some of this information might help you decipher other error messages that aren't included here.

I've included some of the common error messages you might run into, along with some observations and commentary. If you run into an error that you just can't figure out, and it isn't listed here, try Googling for the text of the error message. Odds are that someone else has had the same problem at some point, and you can benefit from their experience.

Java-Compiler Error Messages

Java-compiler error messages usually look something like this:

```
src/helloworld/HelloWorld.java:21: cannot find symbol
symbol   : class CommandSender
location: class helloworld.HelloWorld
  public boolean onCommand(CommandSender sender, Command command,
```

Java is trying to tell you exactly where the error occurred and what it thinks the problem is.

The first bit of text is the name of the file where Java thinks the problem is located—in this case, the file src/helloworld/HelloWorld.java. Next is a number in between colons—that's the line number in the file (21 here). Next is the error message itself, "cannot find symbol." After that come the details specific to *this* error message, which in this example is the symbol that it can't find, and some more information about the location of the missing symbol.

So on line 21 of HelloWorld.java, Java doesn't know about the thing named CommandSender. Let's look at some possible causes.

javac: Cannot Find Symbol

"Cannot find symbol" means that the compiler has come across a word, a piece of text, that it doesn't understand.

This error can be caused by several problems. First, what happens if I just stick in an assignment statement like i = 10 without ever declaring what i is?

```
src/helloworld/HelloWorld.java:23: cannot find symbol
symbol  : variable i
location: class helloworld.HelloWorld
        i = 10;
        ^
```

The compiler has no idea what i is or what it should be, so it complains.

To fix it I can add a declaration like int i; above this code or on this same line as int i = 10;. Now the compiler knows that i is a local variable.

But what if I have declared the variable and I still get an error? For instance, in the call to onCommand, I'm declaring a parameter CommandSender sender. sender is my variable, of type CommandSender, but I get the same error:

```
src/helloworld/HelloWorld.java:21: cannot find symbol
symbol  : class CommandSender
location: class helloworld.HelloWorld
  public boolean onCommand(CommandSender sender, Command command,
```

This can indicate a missing or misspelled import statement. The compiler knows that sender is a variable of type CommandSender, but it doesn't know what a CommandSender is.

In this case, adding

```
import org.bukkit.command.CommandSender;
```

at the top of the file fixes the error. See Appendix 7, *Common Imports*, on page 253, for a list of common imports we've used in the book, or look it up in the Java or Bukkit doc.

javac: Missing Semicolon

```
src/helloworld/HelloWorld.java:6: ';' expected
import org.bukkit.command.CommandSender
```

We forgot the semicolon at the end of the import line. It should be this:

```
import org.bukkit.command.CommandSender;
```

However, this error message isn't always foolproof. For instance, if I leave off the opening brace, {, of a code block by mistake, like this:

```
public void onDisable()
  log.info("[HelloWorld] Stopping.");
}
```

I'll get a slew of errors, starting with "missing semicolon" and continuing on to the next several lines of code, past our initial error:

```
src/helloworld/HelloWorld.java:18: ';' expected
  public void onDisable()
                        ^
src/helloworld/HelloWorld.java:21: class, interface, or enum expected
    public boolean onCommand(CommandSender sender, Command command,
           ^
src/helloworld/HelloWorld.java:25: class, interface, or enum expected
      getServer().broadcastMessage(msg);
        ^
```

The compiler is confused: it thinks maybe we should have had a semicolon after onDisable(), but actually we needed an opening brace, {. Then it has no idea what's supposed to be happening, and it starts complaining that the *entire rest of the file* is not what it expected.

That's why in most cases you only want to read the first one or two errors and ignore the rest for the moment, as many of the following errors will disappear once you fix the first one.

javac: Illegal Start of Expression

This is a generic error message if we didn't tidy up an expression as we should have and the compiler isn't ready to start a new expression yet—for instance, if I leave off the closing brace at the end of a function:

```
public void onDisable() {
  log.info("[HelloWorld] Stopping.");
```

Again I'll get a bunch of errors, starting at the point of the missing brace and continuing way past it into the rest of the file:

```
src/helloworld/HelloWorld.java:21: illegal start of expression
    public boolean onCommand(CommandSender sender, Command command,
           ^
src/helloworld/HelloWorld.java:21: ';' expected
    public boolean onCommand(CommandSender sender, Command command,
                                                                   ^
```

```
src/helloworld/HelloWorld.java:21: ';' expected
  public boolean onCommand(CommandSender sender, Command command,
                                                                 ^
src/helloworld/HelloWorld.java:21: not a statement
```

Just remember that "illegal start" really means "didn't finish properly."

javac: Class Is Public, Should Be Declared in a File Named…

In my HelloWorld.java, I get creative and start to add another class declaration at the end of the file:

```
public class TooMany {
  // ...
}
```

This generates a very descriptive error message:

```
src/helloworld/HelloWorld.java:32: class TooMany is public,
should be declared in a file named TooMany.java
public class TooMany {
```

Remember that every public class must be in a separate file that is named for the class, in a directory named for the package.

However, you *can* declare a private class inside your public class within the same file. This can sometimes be helpful for small helper classes.

javac: Incompatible Types

In the BackCmd plugin version where we're saving player locations to disk, I made a typo: playerTeleports returns a Stack of Location objects. But I accidentally tried to assign it to a stack of Player objects, like this:

```
Stack<Player> locs = playerTeleports.get(player.getName());
```

That results in the fairly straightforward error message "incompatible types":

```
src/backcmdsave/BackCmdSave.java:98: incompatible types
found    : java.util.Stack<org.bukkit.Location>
required: java.util.Stack<org.bukkit.entity.Player>
        Stack<Player> locs = playerTeleports.get(player.getName());
```

Java says it found a Location where it was expecting me to use a Player. Of course that's backwards—that's not what I meant at all.

At times like this it really helps to think like the computer does (in this case, to think like the compiler does).

So imagine you're the Java compiler. You just completed reading a line of code through to the semicolon, and you're starting the next line. You see this first part:

```
Stack<Player> locs =
```

Ah! The programmer is declaring a variable named locs, and it's a generic Stack of Player objects. And we're about to assign an initial value to it.

Then the compiler sees the next part of the statement:

```
playerTeleports.get(player.getName());
```

You (the compiler), look up playerTeleports() and see that it returns a Stack of Location objects. Well, that won't do at all. Here the programmer says we've got a Stack of Players, and now the code is trying to assign a Stack of Locations. So from the point of view of the compiler, you expected a Player and instead got a Location.

The compiler, of course, is wrong.

That's because no compiler can really infer your *intent*. The compiler can only judge what you've actually done, not what you intended to do.

Always bear that in mind when trying to decipher compiler error messages: they are from the compiler's point of view, and it cannot read your mind. At least not yet. We're working on it.

At any rate, correcting the type of the Stack to match corrects the problem:

```
Stack<Location> locs = playerTeleports.get(player.getName());
```

Bukkit Server Error Messages

Bukkit will display error messages either in the server log (~/Desktop/server/server.log) or right in the Minecraft game console as you're playing. Here are the most common errors you might see with a new plugin.

Server Log: Plugin Won't Load

Most errors in the file server.log or in the server's console (in your screen session) are more straightforward than the compiler error messages. One of the most critical and common ones is this error:

```
[SEVERE] Could not load 'plugins/HelloWorld.jar' in folder 'plugins'
org.bukkit.plugin.InvalidPluginException:
java.lang.ClassNotFoundException: helloworld.HelloWorld
```

You've written a new plugin, and you're getting an error that it can't be loaded.

This usually means the package name and plugin name specified in your plugin.yml file don't match the package name and class name in the code. Check your spelling. Remember that the package name is customarily all lowercase, and that the class name is mixed uppercase and lowercase.

Minecraft Console: Unknown Command

If the plugin compiles okay but Minecraft gives you the "Unknown command" error, be sure to check your plugin.yml file to make sure the command is there and spelled correctly. Also check in your onCommand() function to make sure you've spelled the command correctly there when you're comparing strings.

How to Read the Bukkit Documentation

Many times you'll need to read the Bukkit documentation directly to find out how to do something in the Minecraft world involving a Block, a Player, an Ocelot, a Cow, a Creeper, or whatever. You need to find out what classes to use and what functions they offer. The Bukkit documentation lists this information for you, and we'll take a quick look here at how to find it.

Bukkit JavaDoc Documentation

The Bukkit JavaDoc documentation is centered on the system's classes, listed within their packages. Here you'll find the following:

- The package name, which is what you use in the import statement.[1]

- The class name, which is what you use to declare variables and create objects with new.[2]

- The functions (methods) in the class that you can run with () and parameters.[3]

- Parent classes or interfaces that it uses, which will include additional functions you can call.[4]

Point your browser to the Bukkit documentation, and all the hidden treasures of Bukkit are yours![5] Ah, but what does all this stuff mean? And where is everything?

---

1. Chapter 2, *Add an Editor and Java*, on page 15, and Appendix 7, *Common Imports*, on page 253.
2. Chapter 4, *Plugins Have Variables, Functions, and Keywords*, on page 41, and Chapter 5, *Plugins Have Objects*, on page 65.
3. Chapter 7, *Use Piles of Variables: Arrays*, on page 87.
4. Chapter 5, *Plugins Have Objects*, on page 65.
5. http://jd.bukkit.org/rb/doxygen/annotated.html

On the left side of your screen, there's a listing of all of the top-level package names in Bukkit, starting with org.

Throughout the doc, you'll see little triangles pointing to the right. Each one of these is a *disclosure button*. Press it, and all the children of that element will show up. So click on org's triangle, and you'll see bukkit; click on bukkit's triangle, and you'll see a whole bunch of packages, starting with block and command and continuing through entity and event.

Open up event, and there's a whole new list, including world. Opening up the package org.bukkit.event.world reveals the classes in that package:

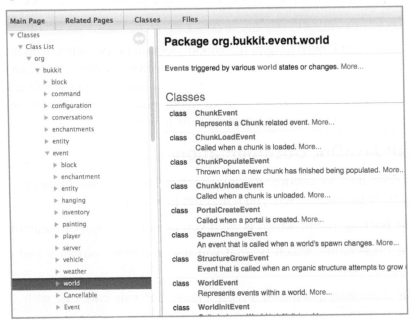

On the right you'll see a class named ChunkLoadEvent. You might be interested in that for a plugin that spawns creeper cows (Chapter 13, *Design Your Own Plugin*, on page 187). If you click on that class name, you'll see a listing of all the member functions ("methods") that ChunkLoadEvent provides (see Figure 12, *Class name showing member functions*, on page 219).

So given an object of ChunkLoadEvent type (let's call it "event"), you can call these functions, like getWorld(), which is shown here to return an object of type World and takes no parameters:

```
public handleEvent(ChunkLoadEvent event) {
    World home = event.getWorld();

    ...

}
```

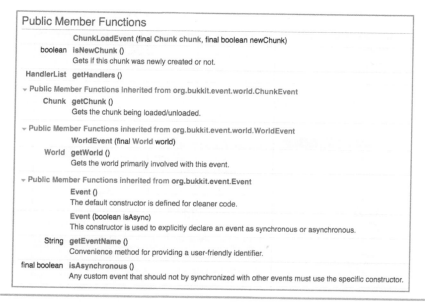

Figure 12—Class name showing member functions

Oracle JavaDoc Documentation

If you're looking for general Java class documentation, not just the Bukkit-specific classes, point your browser to Oracle's documentation on the Web.[6]

It looks pretty much the same as the documentation on the Bukkit site (see Figure 13, *JavaDoc for Bukkit*, on page 220).

In the upper-left corner, there's a scrolling list of the packages, including very useful ones like java.util and java.math. Under that is a list of interfaces (like classes, but without their own functions) and the classes in that package. In the right-hand pane is the documentation for the class you've clicked on. Here I've gone to the package java.util, the class ArrayList.

The class documentation is great when you know roughly what you want but need the specifics. But what if you don't know where to start?

The Wiki and Tutorials

Hopefully this book has given you a good idea of where to look for specifics about Blocks made of different Materials, and different kinds of Entity objects. But what about something we haven't covered?

---

6.   http://docs.oracle.com/javase/7/docs/api

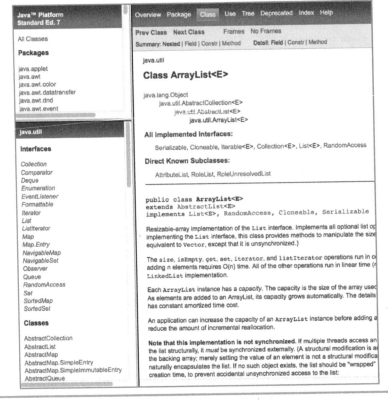

Figure 13—JavaDoc for Bukkit

In addition to the class-based documentation, the Bukkit site contains tutorials and detailed explanations of topics on its *wiki*.

A wiki is a set of web pages that anyone can edit. Wiki, short for a "wiki wiki Web," was invented by our friend Ward Cunningham. The idea is that anyone can add details or corrections. You may have heard of Wikipedia, which takes the concept to the next level and covers a huge swath of human knowledge.

The Bukkit wiki contains tutorials, how-tos, and various bits of additional information you might find helpful.[7] There's also a forum where you can ask questions and ask for help.

And don't forget about this book's forum at the Pragmatic Bookshelf website, where you can ask questions and post comments about this book itself, along with anything really cool you've discovered that you'd like to pass on.[8]

---

7. http://wiki.bukkit.org/Main_Page
8. http://forums.pragprog.com/forums/314

How to Install a Desktop Server

So you have your great new custom plugins running on the server on your computer, and you want your friends to be able to connect and play along.

There are two ways to go about that: set up your own personal computer for your friends to access, or set up a permanent server in the cloud. (See how in the next appendix, Appendix 4, *How to Install a Cloud Server*, on page 229.)

To use your own computer, remember that it needs to be powered on and running your Minecraft server for that to work. If you're okay with that idea, here's what you need to do.

There are two main issues to address:

- You need a mechanism for your friends to find your machine's address on the Internet.

- You to need to make sure that your Minecraft port, 25565, is open to the world.

What's a Port?

In this and the next appendix, you'll see references to network ports and Minecraft's default port of 25565. A port is just a number—an agreed-upon number that lets computers communicate over a network. For example, the Web uses port 80.

There are several ways to go about this. The easiest is to use a piece of software that does all the work for you. You can also take care of all the bits by hand, which is more fun but more work.

The Easy Way: LogMeIn

Hamachi is a product available from LogMeIn in a free version ("Unmanaged") for up to five users,[1] as well as a more feature-rich paid version ("Managed") for Windows and Mac computers.

It sets up an IP address for your friends to connect to. You don't need to mess with your firewall or router or anything locally; it just works. To set it up, first download the Unmanaged version and install it.

When you first run it, LogMeIn will ask you to join or create a network:

You'll want to create one. I named mine andys_minecraft_server:

And we're up and running!

---

1.   https://secure.logmein.com/products/hamachi/download.aspx

Now tell your friends to download the same software and join your network with the name you picked (like andys_minecraft_server).

They can join your network. When they right-click on your network name, they should select Copy IPv4 Address and use that in the Minecraft client to connect to you.

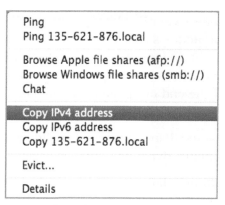

When you don't want your friends connected, just press the power-switch icon to turn your network off.

You're done.

The Harder Way: By Hand

To set up your computer to be open and findable on the Internet without the help of something like LogMeIn isn't magic, but it does take some work. Here are some advantages of doing it the "hard way":

- It's free.
- You can connect more than five users if you want.
- You can be available to the whole world, not just your friends.
- It's really interesting and useful stuff to learn.

You'll need to learn a little bit more about networking and how the Internet works. I'll outline the important steps here, but you may need to do some additional reading on your own. Most importantly, I can't give you exact step-by-step directions because every router (or cable modem, DSL modem, and so on) is different. But you can find that information online with help from Google or via informational sites like http://portforward.com.

Let's look at the steps.

First, your friends need to find your machine.

Static vs. Dynamic DNS

An IP address is a number that anyone in the world can use to connect to your server. An IP address is usually four sets of numbers with periods in between, like 93.184.216.119 (example.com) or 127.0.0.1 (your local machine, localhost).

Your ISP probably changes your IP address every so often; you aren't guaranteed to get the same IP-address assignment unless you pay extra for a *static IP*. If you knew to ask for a static IP, you probably already knew how to set up a domain name and DNS server to point to your IP (if not, and you want a static IP, check out the end of Appendix 4, *How to Install a Cloud Server*, on page 229).

But you don't need a static IP for your friends to find you. There's a trick that lets you use your changing, dynamic IP just as easily.

First off, if you don't know what your IP even looks like, point your browser to this URL: http://www.checkip.org.

And that's what your IP looks like to the outside world.

If that changes every few hours or every few days, that can be annoying, as you have to keep telling your friends what IP address to use to connect to you. But you're in luck! You can get set up with a *dynamic DNS* registration for free or at a low cost from places like http://dyndns.org or http://www.noip.com.

They'll get you set up so that your friends can use a friendly name to find you on the Internet—something like andyminecraft.dns.org.

Now that they can find your machine, you need to let them in.

Open Up Your Firewall

Windows, Mac, and Linux machines, as well as your cable modem or ISP's router, can all run firewall software, which is designed to block exactly what we're trying to accomplish here. The idea is that twisted, evil griefers are always trying to attack your machine and break in. So most machines run some kind of firewall to lock out every port except the ones you really want to have open and are expecting.

So first you need to make sure *your* computer is open to port 25565.

Windows:

> On Windows 8, start typing Firewall, and Metro will guide you through to "Allow an app or feature through Windows Firewall." See the Windows

online documentation for more.[2] On Windows 7, search under Control Panel for "Firewall" and "Allow a program through Windows Firewall":

Then enable public access for Java:

Mac OS X:

Open System Preferences and go to the Security & Privacy panel:

---

2.   http://windows.microsoft.com/en-us/windows-8/windows-firewall-from-start-to-finish

If the firewall is turned off (not enabled), then you're good to go. If it's turned on, make sure Java has permission to allow incoming connections:

Linux:

If you've set up a firewall using IPTables, make sure port 25565 is open.

However, opening up the firewall on your computer itself may not be enough.

To check if the Internet can get to your port, by point your browser to http://canyouseeme.org. That will come up with your publicly visible IP address. Type in the port to check as 25565, and press Check Port. If it works, you're good to go. If not, there's one more thing you might need to do.

If you are connected to the Internet through a router or cable modem, then *that* device may have a firewall as well. Also, even if it has the port open to the Internet, you need to forward the port traffic from the router to your local computer.

Port Forwarding

You need to exercise caution and restraint when changing settings on your router. If you change something you didn't intend to, you could end up mucking up the device and losing your Internet access. So stick to the plan here. However, every router is different, so I can't really give you specific step-by-step instructions. Here are the basics:

1. Log on to your router. You may already know the user name and password for it. If not, it may have a default user name and password that you can Google for.

2. On some menu it will have a section for *Port Forwarding*. On my router it was listed under "Gateway" and "Forwarding."

3. You need to tell it to forward port 25565 (both TCP and UDP if it asks) from the outside world (your external IP, as reported by http://www.checkip.org to your computer's *internal IP*.

Your computer has an internal IP address, which is used for communication between it and your router/cable modem. You can run a command on your computer to see what that address is:

Windows

Run ipconfig, and look for "IPv4 Address" under "Ethernet adapter" or "Wireless LAN."

Mac/Linux

Run ifconfig. It's probably listed under "inet" then "en1."

You might be able to Google for more specific information for your router setup, or check sites such as http://portforward.com for additional information.

One last complication: your internal IP address might change every so often, just like your ISP's IP address can change. If you're getting the IP address from a DHCP server on your router, you can also tell it to create a *DHCP reservation* so that you always get the same internal IP address.

Or just go in and change the port forwarding when (or if) your internal IP address changes.

If you're having friends in only occasionally and don't mind the setup hassle, this is a perfectly fine way to work. But if you want more than a few folks to connect, and you want the server up 24×7, you'll need to set up a server in the cloud, which is detailed in the next appendix, Appendix 4, *How to Install a Cloud Server*, on page 229.

Quality of Service

Many modern routers have a feature where you can specify the desired Quality of Service (often called QoS) for different ports/services. The idea is that you can set a high or low priority on different kinds of network traffic.

You might find that useful when running a local Minecraft server: you can set the Minecraft port to have a very low priority.

Putting the Minecraft port at the lowest setting will ensure that your own traffic gets priority over your friends using your server.

How to Install a Cloud Server

You can run a Minecraft server on your own computer, but there are some drawbacks to doing that. The biggest one is that your computer needs to be powered on and connected to the Internet 24×7. That's a little difficult on a laptop. Also, anything you're doing personally on the computer may slow down the Minecraft server and all your players—and anything the server is doing will slow down the other programs on your computer. So if a lot of folks want to connect to your server and play on it, you might prefer to set it up on a remote server in the cloud.

Setting up a Minecraft server in the cloud is very similar to setting up a server locally, with one important difference: you don't have physical access to the computer that's running your Minecraft server. That means no keyboard, no screen, no power switch or reboot button.

But no worries; you know how to use the command line, and that's all you need.

We'll see what this all means and how to work with it in this appendix.

What Is the Cloud?

Some say that "the cloud" is really just a big rack of computers in Virginia. That's actually not far from the truth, as Amazon and others do maintain large data centers in that area, plus in California and many other spots around the world. "The cloud" is just a bunch of computers somewhere on the Internet.

When people talk about a computers in the cloud, they mean a computer that is accessed only over the Internet, that you might not even know (or care about) the physical location of, and that someone else owns and maintains. As you can see, that's a pretty generic and flexible definition. A huge variety of cloud services is available, with an equally huge range of pricing, reliability, and what you get for your money. There are two major types of services you might be interested in:

- Minecraft-specific: The service provider does all the work of maintaining and administering the server. The provider will load or provide plugins, possibly handle griefers and attacks, and keep the server running. You don't have to do anything. You may be charged by the number of players online at once instead of being charged for the size of the server.

- Generic: The service provider supplies a running system and a login, but nothing else: you have to install Java and Bukkit, load and provide plug-ins, administer the server, reboot it if it gets hung up, and so on. You are usually charged based on the number of CPUs, the amount of RAM, and possibly the amount of network traffic used each month.

While you might want to look at a Minecraft-specific provider, it's a trade-off between ease of use and control. In this case you don't get much control over the server; you might have to ask to get plugins loaded, and the service might load only well-known plugins, not your development version.

Instead, what you probably want is known as a *virtual private server*, or VPS for short. There are tons of VPS providers on the Internet, with different pricing plans and packages, located in different countries with different hardware and features available. Just Google "VPS providers."

A VPS looks like an entire computer to you. You can log on and have all the files and processor to yourself. In reality, you're sharing a big piece of hardware with a bunch of other people. But everyone sees what looks like a whole computer that is all theirs. That means that as an administrator of the system, you can install any software you want. You can add user accounts, reboot, and set up your own domain name (like example.com or andy.pragprog.com).

The good news is that you can work on the remote server using a command-line shell, just like we've been doing all along, because your remote server is probably running Linux.

Remote Operating Systems

Virtually all VPS services offer one operating system for your server: Linux. Some providers, such as Microsoft with its own Windows Azure cloud service,[1] can offer Windows, and a small number offer Mac OS X. But these are rare and relatively expensive. The vast majority, including Amazon's cloud service,

---

1.   http://www.windowsazure.com

VPS Features

While pricing and features can vary a lot for VPS offerings, here are some commonalities and things to look for:

- Most VPS systems include a Web-based front end (one named cpanel is very popular) that allows you to reboot the system, add users, and that sort of thing.

- While a fast computer is always good to have, Minecraft is more sensitive to the amount of RAM you have available. You want a package with as much RAM as you can get—at least 2 GB (gigabytes), and often 4 or so.

- As I write this, several good providers have systems available for between $20 and $50 a month. That's a lot of money for a hobby, but you can help support the server by asking for donations from your players. Even a few dollars per player can fund your server. However, there might be issues with your government's laws and tax codes once you start taking money, so you should check with someone in your area who knows about such things before you start.

Some providers allow unlimited network traffic ("bandwidth"), and others set a cap. Just as with many cell-phone plans, if you exceed the bandwidth cap the provider will charge you more money.

Some providers may do the same thing with RAM or disk storage: you're allowed a certain amount, and if you exceed that they'll start charging you extra.

When comparing plans, just be sure to add up the extra fees that you might have to pay.

offer some "flavor" of Linux, a Unix-like, largely POSIX-compliant operating system.[2]

But Linux isn't just one thing. Linux is really a bundle of the core operating system plus all the extra bits: the windowing system, utilities, programming languages, and so on. A particular bundle is known as a *distribution*, and each one is a little bit different in terms of what's included, what's not included, how you install software, and how and when it gets updated.

These are some popular distributions, listed more or less in order of popularity:

- CentOS
- Ubuntu
- Fedora
- Debian
- Linux Mint

---

2. POSIX stands for Portable Operating System Interface, a standard for operating-system compatibility.

Before you panic over all these different bundles, realize one very important and comforting thing: the command-line shell, bash, works the same on each and every one of these distributions. All the commands we've used in this book, such as ls, cp, and cd, all work exactly the same no matter which Linux flavor you choose.

Ubuntu and CentOS seem to be the most common server distributions at the moment. Most VPS services will let you choose which distribution you want from a small selection of offerings.

The biggest difference you'll run into from one distribution to another is their package management: what tool you use to install software packages, and what packages are included by default.

Remote Access

To log in to your remote server's command-line shell, you need to use a set of programs known as SSH (which stands for "secure shell"). ssh is the command you run to connect to the server; it's the client. The server is running sshd (for "ssh daemon"), and that's what you connect to. Your server might already be running an sshd. We'll get to that shortly.

You can use ssh to connect to a server, and its companion program, scp, to copy files to the server (scp works a lot like plain cp).

ssh just needs to know the user name and server name or IP address you're connecting to, which you can specify like an email address, using the "@" sign:

```
$ ssh andy@example.com
Password:
```

Or if you don't have a name yet, you can connect using the IP address:

```
$ ssh andy@93.184.216.119
Password:
```

You may have been given an account name to use already, or you may need to make one using the web interface from your VPS provider.

You use the same sort of notation with scp to copy a file. Here we're copying a local text file named myfile.txt up to the server example.com, logging in as andy, and copying the file to my home directory ("~/").

```
$ scp myfile.txt andy@example.com:~/myfile.txt
Password:
```

(Again, you could also just use the IP, as in andy@93.184.216.119).

Notice that when you use ssh or scp without doing anything else, it will ask you for your password on the remote machine. Every time. That gets tiresome pretty quickly, so fortunately there's a better way to set up your remote login.

Set Up SSH Keys

This setup takes a couple of steps, but they are pretty straightforward. We'll go into the details next, but the overall steps are as follows:

1. Generate a special set of secret keys, including a "public key."
2. Copy the public key to the remote machine.
3. Make sure the public key is secured on the remote machine.

Once that's done, you can use ssh and scp without having to supply a password. That means you can use ssh and scp from shell scripts—which can be very handy when you need to do a bunch of things to the remote machine.

Here are the steps in detail.

First off, change to your home directory and use ssh-keygen to generate a set of RSA-style keys:[3]

```
$ cd
$ ssh-keygen -t rsa
```

When asked for a passphrase, press Enter—don't input text at this point. That command will make a subdirectory named .ssh under your home directory. Because of the leading dot (".") you won't normally see this directory listed with ls, but ls -a will show it:

```
$ ls -a
. .. .profile .ssh (and a bunch of other stuff)
$ cd .ssh
~/.ssh$ ls
id_rsa          id_rsa.pub      known_hosts
```

Your public key is id_rsa.pub, and you'll need to add that to a file named ~/.ssh/authorized_keys on the server.

To do that, make the .ssh directory on the server first. I'll show the login prompt on the server as Server $ so you can tell which machine I'm on.

```
$ ssh yourname@example.com
Password:
Welcome to My Awesome Minecraft Server
Last login: Mon Feb 16 12:16:57 from xyzzy-plugh
Server$ mkdir .ssh
```

---

3. RSA is a public-key-style cryptographic system, named for its inventors.

Changing Your Prompt

The environment variable PS1 sets your prompt string for bash. In that string, you can use \w to print out the current directory. So if you set

```
$ PS1='Server \w\$ '
```

your prompt will come back as

```
Server ~$
```

Stick this in your bash startup file to make the change permanent (as we saw back in Chapter 2, *Add an Editor and Java*, on page 15).

Now back on your computer, copy the id_rsa.pub file (or whatever your .pub file is named) up to the server using scp, putting it in the .ssh directory and renaming it authorized_keys:

```
$ scp id_rsa.pub yourname@example.com:~/.ssh/authorized_keys
```

That will copy the file to your .ssh directory under your home ("~"), and name it authorized_keys. If you want to later, you can add keys from other machines into this file (that's why "keys" is plural). But for now you just have this one entry.

Finally, you need to go back on the server and check and fix the file permissions. The .ssh directory should be readable and listable only by you, and the files inside should be readable by you alone. In most cases, ssh *will not work at all* if the file permissions aren't restricted. It's for your own good.

You can set the file permissions using the chmod command:

```
$ ssh yourname@example.com
Password:
Welcome to My Awesome Minecraft Server
Last login: Mon Feb 16 12:26:13 from xyzzy-plugh
Server$ cd .ssh
Server ~/.ssh$ chmod 700 .
Server ~/.ssh$ chmod 600 authorized_keys
```

Now from your computer, you should be able to ssh or scp without having to specify a password:

```
$ ssh yourname@example.com
Welcome to My Awesome Minecraft Server
Last login: Mon Feb 16 12:32:07 from xyzzy-plugh
Server$
```

And we're in!

Your next question may be, "Swell, but how do I get OUT?" Fair enough.

You can log out by pressing `Ctrl`-`d` or by typing exit. And now you're back to your local shell.

Admin with Root

On any modern system, an ordinary user doesn't usually have full permissions to do everything on the system. You usually have to type a password to get the authority of an administrator on the system. On Windows machines this account is called Administrator, and on Linux and Mac systems it's called *root*.

While you can log in directly as root with the appropriate password, that's usually frowned upon. It's too easy to make a typo and suddenly blow away half your system. Root is ultimately powerful, and with great power comes great responsibility.

But you still need to be able to execute certain commands as root without logging on as root. You can do that using the sudo command, which lets you *do* as the *super user* root would do. You preface the command you want to run with sudo, and it will prompt you for *your* normal user account password. Get it right, and then the rest of the command will be executed as root. For example, here I'm using sudo to run an adduser command to add the user "fred."

```
Remote $ sudo adduser fred
Password:
User 'fred' added.
```

This way it allows you to have the full power of root, but only in limited, controlled, well-known circumstances, and not just logged in as root.

In fact, if your SSH is set up so that it *does* allow root to log in directly, you should look up how to disable that feature. That way you have to log in using your user account and SSH key, and then provide your password via sudo. That's the safest way to allow root access for yourself, and not for the millions of hostile attackers who are eyeing your system at this very moment.

Securing Root Access

You might already be set up to use sudo. Log in to your server and try running some simple command (like id, which just reports who you are) using sudo:

```
Remote $ sudo id
[sudo] password for andy:
uid=0(root) gid=0(root)
groups=0(root),1(bin),2(daemon),3(sys),
4(adm),6(disk),10(wheel)
```

It worked! This machine is already set up so that I can sudo. But on a machine that isn't set up, you'll get this scary warning:

```
andy is not in the sudoers file. This incident will be reported.
```

Yikes! Sounds like the cops will come after us. Have no fear: it's only logging the attempt to a log file. All it means is that you have to add your name to the permissions file for sudo.

To do that, log in as root and add the following line to the bottom of the file /etc/sudoers (nano is a convenient editor to use over SSH; we'll cover how to install that and more in the next section):

```
andy    ALL=(ALL)       ALL
```

But use your name, not "andy"—unless your name actually is Andy.

Save the file and try to use sudo again.

Once you can successfully ssh in without a password, and you can use sudo to do things as root, then you can turn off the use of passwords and not allow root to ssh in directly.

Now obviously that sounds a little dangerous, as you could accidentally lock yourself out of the computer. To help prevent that, open one window and log in to your server as root. Leave that window open and leave it alone, then open a second window to start changing settings. In case you mess up and can't log in or sudo for some reason, you have this window still open—as root, the Great and Powerful—as a backup.

In your new window, log in as root and edit the file /etc/ssh/sshd_config. You want to find these two lines and uncomment them, or change them to read no:

```
PasswordAuthentication no
PermitRootLogin no
```

Then you need to restart the SSH daemon. On many systems you can do that by using this:

```
Server $ sudo service sshd restart
```

You might also want to change the default port from 22 to some other number. Since everyone knows that port 22 is SSH, attackers will bombard your server with attacks on that port. You should be safe by turning off root login and passwords, so that you *have* to have a public key to log on, but if you want to move to a different port to avoid any attacks, here's what you do.

In that same config file (/etc/ssh/sshd_config), add or change this line:

```
Port 2345
```

But pick a number other than 2345. You want a number greater than 1024, and preferably a number that does not appear in the file /etc/services. Those are numbers that other services might already be using (including 80 for web traffic).

When using ssh to connect to the server, you'll have to specify the new port number, which you can do with the -p option:

```
$ ssh -p 2345 andy@myexample.com
```

Installing Packages

Your Linux distribution may come with everything you need. Or it might be missing a few parts. To help keep things manageable, Linux breaks up all the utilities and programs into different software *packages*. For example, if you're not doing any work with publishing, you won't need TeX or Ghostscript. If you're not programming in C or C++, you won't need GCC. If you're not on a desktop machine, you probably don't need a window manager like Gnome or KDE.

All of these packages of software can be installed, removed, updated, and listed using a package manager. Every major Linux distribution uses a different package manager. In fact, you could almost say the package manager is what distinguishes one distribution from another, although there is some sharing going on.

These are some popular package manager commands:

- yum
- rpm
- apt-get
- deb

The details for each of these commands are different, but they all basically do the same thing: download and install a software package for you.

In particular, if you don't have SSH installed yet, you'll need the open-ssh package installed so you can log on to your server in a secure way. On Ubuntu, you'd run a command like this:

```
$ sudo apt-get install openssh-server
```

sudo runs the command as root; apt-get is the package-manager command under Ubuntu, and you're giving it the option to install the package named openssh-server.

On CentOS, you'd run a very similar command, but using yum instead of apt-get.

```
$ sudo yum install openssh-server
```

Similarly, you'll probably need a text editor on the server. You can't really run a full visual editor on the remote server over the Internet,[4] so you'll probably want a simple screen editor like nano:

```
$ sudo apt-get install nano
```

Installing Java

No matter what optional packages you may need or want, at a minimum you'll need Java to run your server. You can install it just like we did earlier in the book, but bear in mind one important detail: you need the official Oracle (formerly Sun) version of Java. The OpenJDK version of Java, which may be available or already installed on your system, is known to cause problems with Minecraft.

You may need to uninstall OpenJDK using your system's package manager. For instance, to remove the 1.6 version on a system that uses the Red Hat Package Manager (RPM), you'd run this:

```
$ rpm -e java-1.6.0-openjdk
```

Now go get the good Java. You'll have to download the installation program on your local computer, then scp it up to your server.

On your local machine, point your browser to http://www.java.com/en/download/manual.jsp and scroll down to the Linux section. Download the regular or 64-bit version (depending on your server) and follow the instructions for your flavor of Linux.

You'll need to set up your start_minescraft script and JARs on the server just as we did locally back in Chapter 2, *Add an Editor and Java*, on page 15.

Running Remotely

There's slight hitch with running a script like start_minecraft when you're logged in via ssh. As soon as you log out, the script will be killed. That's not very helpful in a server environment.

---

4. Actually you can, using the X Window System (XWindows), but it's fussy to set up and not a very satisfying experience.

Fortunately, you can use a command named screen to keep Java running even though you've logged out.[5] It takes an argument string of -d -m -S followed by a name for your server session. We'll use mcserver to name the session, so the new server-style startup script will look like this:

```
#!/bin/bash
cd "$( dirname "$0" )"
screen -d -m -S mcserver java -Xms1024M -Xmx1024M -jar craftbukkit.jar nogui
```

(Remember, start_minecraft needs to be executable; be sure to do a chmod +x start_minecraft if you get a "permission denied" error.)

That will start the server off in its own little world, which won't be affected by you logging off. If you want to "attach" to the server so you can issue commands and such, use screen with the -r option and the session name:

```
$ screen -r mcserver
```

And you'll be attached to the server with the usual spew and prompt:

```
16:47:49 [INFO] Done (1.163s)! For help, type "help" or "?"
>
```

To detach from your server session, press Ctrl-a then d. You'll be returned to your original shell, and your server will still be running in the background.

To see what processes you have running, use the ps command:

```
Server ~$ ps
  PID TTY           TIME CMD
  337 ttys000    0:00.09 -bash
  842 ttys020    0:13.78 /usr/bin/java -jar craftbukkit.jar
```

And to see all the processes on a machine, try ps ax. ps -? will list off the options. There are a lot.

In a pinch, if you need to kill off all Java processes, you can use

```
Server ~$ killall java
```

That asks Java nicely to exit now. It will try to do some cleanup and exit in a safe and reliable manner. However, if it's stubborn and won't behave, you can use the brutal

```
Server ~$ killall -9 java
```

which will kill all Java processes dead, right now—period.

---

5. There's a slightly simpler way to do this using the command nohup (named for "No Hangup"); however, you lose the ability to enter commands to the server easily.

Domain Name

When you first set up your VPS, your VPS provider will tell you the IP address for your server. That's the number anyone in the world can use to connect to your server. An IP address is usually four sets of numbers with periods in between, like 93.184.216.119 (example.com) or 127.0.0.1 (your local machine, localhost).

You can set up a domain name so that folks can find you by a name like pragprog.com or example.com instead of a number like 93.184.216.119. Your VPS provider may even be able to arrange this for you as an optional service, or you can use one of many providers on the Internet.

Typical costs are around $10–20 a year for *domain name registration*. That gives you the right to use your name. You also need someone to run a *DNS hosting* server that says your name corresponds to your IP address. Many registrars offer this service in addition to the name registration itself, or you can use a separate vendor.

To find out if the domain name you want is available, you can use the command-line tool whois. Be careful using any other tools to check for a domain name: squatters and other unsavory sorts have been known to watch for domain name searches on the Web and grab the name before you can, then try and sell it to you for a lot of money.

As with any service on the Internet, check around for reviews and comments. Some big-name DNS providers that advertise heavily during major sporting events have a very bad reputation.

What's Next

These few pages scratch the surface of what can be very deep topics.

There's a lot you can do as a Linux system administrator that we haven't covered, including running tasks at particular times, backing up data, applying system security and update patches, preventing griefers, tuning performance, and setting up your own email server; all kinds of fun.

Whole books are written on these topics, and this isn't one of them. But hopefully this is enough to get you started.

Cheat Sheets

Enthused by reading a chapter, you're sitting down to write some code only to get stuck: how do you do that thing in Java, again? It happens to all of us when learning a new language. One of the first things I do when trying to work in a new language is to find or write a "cheat sheet" to help me remember the details.

Java Language

This is not a complete list of every Java feature—it's just the important bits you might need, shown as examples in most cases.

Literal Data Types

Whole numbers

```
int i = 7; i = -5;
```

Numbers with fractional parts

```
double num = 3.14; num = 0.01; num = -3e15
```
(means -3 times 10 to the 15th power)

True or false

```
boolean shouldGetUp=true; shouldGetUp=false
```
(or any Boolean expression that resolves to true *or* false*)*

String of text characters

```
String s="Hello";
```

Array

```
String[] grades = {"A", "B", "C", "D", "F", "Inc"};
```

Math Operators

Add

    a + b

Subtract

    a - b

Multiply

    a * b

Divide

    a / b

Remainder

    a % b *(for whole numbers—integers—only)*

Specify order of terms

    ((a + b) * z) *(a + b will be added first, then multiplied by z)*

True-or-False Comparison Operators

Use any of these comparison operators between two values:

Equal to

    a == b

Not equal to

    a != b

Less than

    a < b

Greater than

    a > b

Less than or equal to

    a <= b

Greater than or equal to

    a >= b

And

    a && b *(must be something that's true or false)*

Or

    a || b *(must be something that's true or false)*

Not

!a *(must be something that's true or false)*

Java Language

Declare the package

package name.name.name;, usually using the inverse of your domain name, so a project Wonderful from the guys at pragprog.com would be in the package com.pragprog.wonderful.

Import a class

import org.bukkit.World tells the Java compiler you want to use this class. You can use a wildcard of "*"—as in import org.bukkit.*;—but you may get more uninvited classes than you wanted.

Declare a class

public class *name* { }.

Declare a function

public return-type name (argument types and names), as in public int myFunction().

Declare a block of code

Use braces, { and }.

Declare variables

type name; as in int i; or Stack<Location> myLocations; generics need the specific type(s) added within the angle brackets < and >.

Assign values to variables

a = 10; s = "Bob"; x=3.1415;.

Make decisions

Decide which code to run using an if (the else {} part is optional):

```
if (true or false comparison) { // is true
    doThis();
} else { // if false
    doOtherThing();
}
```

Loops

There are three ways to make a loop around a block of code:

- for-each construct: for(*type variable : collection*) Example: for (Player player : playerList) { *block* }
- for loop: for (int i=0; i< *limit*; i++) { *block* }
- while loop: while (*somethingIsTrue*) { *block* }

Create a new object

Foo thing = new Foo();, where Foo is the name of the class and thing is the variable to be assigned to the new object.

Call a function

Use parentheses, as in getServer(), which returns a Server object for a plugin.

Java Visibility Modifiers

final

Don't let me—or anyone else—change this value once I set it.

static

Keep this data or function around outside any given object.

You can mix and match final and static as needed.

public

Anyone else can see and use this function or data.

protected

This class and other classes in this package can see and use this function or data.

private

Only this class can see and use this function or data, not subclasses or other classes in the same package.

You use either public or private per declaration, so this code would create a publicly visible, unchangeable constant outside of any object:

```
public static final int pi = 3.1415;
```

Java Data-Type Conversions

int to double

Assign it: int now = 72; double temperature = now;.

double to int

Cast it; the fractional part is discarded: double when = 15.375; int day = (int)when;.

String to int

Use parseInt: int foo = Integer.parseInt("365");.

String to double

Use parseDouble: double foo = Double.parseDouble("3.1415");.

double to String

> Use valueOf: String.valueOf(3.1415);.

int to String

> Use valueOf: String.valueOf(72);.

Double to String

> (the class Double, not the primitive) Double.toString(3.1415);.

Integer to String

> (the class Integer, not the primitive) Integer.toString(72);.

String concatenation will convert automatically, so

```
String s = "Temperature is " + 72 + " degrees."
```

will result in the string

```
"Temperature is 72 degrees."
```

YAML Files

YAML (rhymes with "camel") files are used for plugin installation and configuration options. Here are some quick tips:

1. Indention counts: each indentation level counts as a child node.
2. Don't use tabs for indention; they are illegal.
3. Quote strings that include spaces, colons, or other special characters.

Here's a simple example of some common data types. It's an array of hashes, and each hash is a set of named properties. The top-level array is named songs. The first hash in songs contains the keys title, path, track_number, and bpm. title and path have string values, and track_number and bpm are integers.

```
songs:
  - title: "Greensleeves (Progressive Rock Version)"
    path: /iTunes/media/new/GodRestProg.mp3
    track_number: 3
    bpm: 120
  - title: "Silent Night"
    path: /iTunes/media/new/SilentNight.mp3
    track_number: 4
    bpm: 65
  - track: "God Rest Ye Merry Gentlemen"
    path: /iTunes/media/new/GodRestBlues.mp3
    track_number: 0
    bpm: 80
```

See http://www.yaml.org for the exhausting details.

Glossary

annotation

An added command to Java source code that modifies or adds information (such as tagging a function as an event handler).

argument

A value you pass to a function for it to use.

array

A sequential list of values, indexed with an integer offset.

Array

Java class that implements an array.

binary file

A file that contains binary numbers and is not human-readable.

block

A list of code statements within a pair of braces, { and }.

Boolean

A logical value that can be equal to only true or false.

cast

To change the interpretation of a value, usually from one object to a particular parent's type.

class

A recipe that tells the compiler how to make an object: what data and functions it should contain.

client

A piece of software that you run, usually with a graphical interface. It connects to a server.

command line

The terminal window where you can type in commands.

compile

To take a text file of human-readable language instructions and convert it into something the computer can run (usually a binary format). javac is the Java compiler.

constructor

A function in a class definition that is called when creating a new object. You can use this to set the object's variables and such.

current directory

In a shell, the directory that's current (*ha*, a tautology!)

deploy

To install a resource into a server environment.

DNS

Domain Name Service, the global system that translates a domain name like example.com to an IP address like 93.184.216.119.

double

A big floating-point number.

environment variable

Settings used by the shell and application programs.

event

An object that represents some real-world action, such as a mouse click.

exception

An error that interrupts the current function and starts running the top-most enclosing catch, or aborts the program if there isn't one.

executable

A file that the computer can run, usually a binary file with low-level machine instructions, but sometimes a text script run by a shell.

file system

The collection and organization of files and folders (directories) on the computer.

final

A Java keyword indicating that this variable can't be changed.

float

A not-so-big floating-point number.

floating point
> A number with a decimal point and fractional part, like 1.25.

function
> A list of Java instructions, declared with a return type, a name, parameters it takes, and a block of code between { and }.

global variable
> A variable that can be used by multiple functions and/or multiple classes.

hash
> A list of objects indexed by any kind of object (but usually by a string).

HashMap
> Java class that implements a hash.

import
> A Java keyword that lets you use a class from another package, such as java.util.HashMap (which is the HashMap class in the java.util package).

inherit
> To use something from a parent.

integer
> A whole number with no decimal point and no fractions, like 7.

I/O
> Input/output: sending and receiving data from somewhere else, such as a file or over the network.

iterator
> An object that lets you retrieve one value at a time from some kind of collection (like an ArrayList or HashMap).

JAR
> A Java Archive file that contains .class and configuration files.

keyword
> A word defined by Java as part of the language. You can't change keywords or use their names as variables.

listener
> A function that will be called when something interesting happens.

literal
> A value you type in directly, like 123, true, or "Notch".

localhost
> The computer's network name for itself.

local variable
> A variable declared with a block of { and }; can be used only within that block.

map
> See *HashMap.*

null
> A variable that would normally point to an object but isn't pointing to anything is set to the special value null.

object
> A collection of live variables and functions, built from a class recipe.

object-oriented
> Software based on the theory of objects that combine variables and functions into one pile of stuff.

package
> A collection of Java classes that belong together.

parameter
> A value in a function that has been passed in for it to use.

path
> A list of directories that the computer will search to find a command or other resource.

plugin
> A compiled piece of code that's added to an already-compiled piece of code.

port
> An agreed-upon number that lets computers communicate over a network. For example, the Web uses port 80, and Minecraft uses port 25565.

private
> A Java keyword that restricts visibility to the current class.

public
> A Java keyword that opens up visibility to all classes.

script
> A text file containing shell commands (or another text language, like Ruby or Python).

server

A piece of software that runs in the background, usually on another machine, that can serve multiple client connections. Can also refer to the remote machine.

shadow

A variable with the same name as another variable in its scope is said to *shadow* it. Chaos may ensue.

shell

See *command line.*

source code

Java language statements that you've typed into a file.

static

A variable or function that is not in any particular object.

string

A bunch of human-readable characters held in a variable.

symbol

A bunch of human-readable characters that has special meaning to the Java compiler as part of your program's language.

task

A piece of code running in a thread, with a well-defined purpose.

text file

A file that contains human-readable text characters.

thread

One list of functions, executed in order by the computer. Threads can be interrupted by other threads.

tick

An arbitrary unit of time. A Minecraft server tick is about 1/20 of a second.

variable

A named holder of data. Can be an immediate value, like 15, or can point to an object, like a Player or a Cow.

void

Nothing. A function that is declared to return void won't return any values, and doesn't need a return statement.

VPS

Virtual Private Server, a remote computer you can rent by the month or by the amount of CPU and network traffic you use.

YAML

A plain-text configuration file; uses a .yml suffix.

Common Imports

Here is a listing of all of the imported package and class names used in our plugins. If you get an error that a symbol can't be found, you may need to import the full class name. For instance, to use a HashMap you'd need to import java.util.HashMap, and to use a Block you'd need to import org.bukkit.block.Block.

You can always look up the full class name in the Java or Bukkit docs, but here are the most common ones for your convenience.

```
import java.util.ArrayList;
import java.util.Collection;
import java.util.HashMap;
import java.util.Iterator;
import java.util.List;
import java.util.Map;
import java.util.Set;
import java.util.Stack;
import java.util.logging.Logger;
import org.bukkit.Bukkit;
import org.bukkit.ChatColor;
import org.bukkit.Chunk;
import org.bukkit.Location;
import org.bukkit.Material;
import org.bukkit.Server;
import org.bukkit.WeatherType;
import org.bukkit.World;
import org.bukkit.block.Block;
import org.bukkit.block.Sign;
import org.bukkit.command.Command;
import org.bukkit.command.CommandSender;
import org.bukkit.configuration.file.FileConfiguration;
import org.bukkit.entity.Bat;
import org.bukkit.entity.Cow;
import org.bukkit.entity.Creeper;
import org.bukkit.entity.Entity;
import org.bukkit.entity.LivingEntity;
```

```java
import org.bukkit.entity.Player;
import org.bukkit.entity.Squid;
import org.bukkit.entity.TNTPrimed;
import org.bukkit.event.EventHandler;
import org.bukkit.event.Listener;
import org.bukkit.event.block.Action;
import org.bukkit.event.entity.EntityDamageEvent;
import org.bukkit.event.entity.EntityDamageEvent.DamageCause;
import org.bukkit.event.entity.EntityShootBowEvent;
import org.bukkit.event.player.PlayerInteractEvent;
import org.bukkit.event.player.PlayerTeleportEvent;
import org.bukkit.event.world.ChunkLoadEvent;
import org.bukkit.event.world.ChunkUnloadEvent;
import org.bukkit.plugin.Plugin;
import org.bukkit.plugin.java.JavaPlugin;
import org.bukkit.potion.PotionEffect;
import org.bukkit.potion.PotionEffectType;
import org.bukkit.scheduler.BukkitRunnable;
import org.bukkit.scheduler.BukkitTask;
import org.bukkit.util.Vector;
```

Bibliography

[Swi08]   Travis Swicegood. *Pragmatic Version Control Using Git*. The Pragmatic
            Bookshelf, Raleigh, NC and Dallas, TX, 2008.

[Swi10]   Travis Swicegood. *Pragmatic Guide to Git*. The Pragmatic Bookshelf, Raleigh,
            NC and Dallas, TX, 2010.

Index

SYMBOLS

&& (ampersands, two), *and* operator, 61, 242

< > (angle brackets), enclosing types in declarations, 97, 243

* (asterisk)
    multiplication operator, 48, 242
    wildcard character, 25

\ (backslash), in paths, 18

{ } (braces)
    enclosing array or hash values, 93
    enclosing code blocks, 42, 56, 213, 243

[ ] (brackets), 42, 93

$ (dollar sign), command prompt, 4

. (dot)
    current directory, 8, 13
    separating item parts, 42, 71–72

.. (dots, two), parent directory, 8, 11, 13

== (equal signs, two), *equal to* operator, 61, 242

! (exclamation point), *not* operator, 61, 243

!= (exclamation point, equal sign), *not equal to* operator, 61, 242

< (left angle bracket), *less than* operator, 61, 242

<= (left angle bracket, equal sign), *less than or equal to* operator, 61, 242

- (minus sign), subtraction operator, 48, 242

– (minus signs, two), *subtract one* operator, 48

( ) (parentheses)
    enclosing function arguments, 42
    grouping operations, 242

% (percent sign)
    command prompt, 4
    remainder operator, 242

+ (plus sign)
    addition operator, 48, 242
    concatenating strings, 49

++ (plus signs, two), *add one* operator, 48

" " (quotes)
    enclosing directories containing spaces, 11
    enclosing strings, 48

> (right angle bracket), *greater than* operator, 61, 242

>= (right angle bracket, equal sign), *greater than or equal to* operator, 61, 242

; (semicolon), terminating Java statement, 42, 213

/ (slash)
    division operator, 48, 242
    in paths, 18
    preceding Minecraft commands, 1, 39
    root directory, 8

/* */ (slash, asterisk), enclosing comments, 42

// (slashes, two), preceding comments, 42

~ (tilde), home directory, 10, 13

| | (vertical bars, two), *or* operator, 61, 242

A

abstraction, levels of, 69

add one operator (++), 48

addition operator (+), 48, 242

ampersands, two (&&), *and* operator, 61, 242

and operator (&&), 61, 242

angle brackets (< >), enclosing types in declarations, 97, 243

annotations, 247

apt-get command, 237

archiver utility, *see* jar command

arguments, 55–56, 247

Array class, 92–96, 247
    accessing elements of, 93–94
    assigning values to, 93–94
    declaring, 93–94
    iterating through, 94
    length of, 93

ArrayAddMoreBlocks plugin example, 99–100

ArrayList class, 97–100
    accessing elements of, 98
    assigning values to, 98
    clearing elements of, 99
    declaring, 97
    size of, 98

ArrayOfBlocks plugin example, 94–96

arrays, 92–93, 241, 247, *see also* specific array types

associative array, *see* HashMap class

asterisk (*)
  multiplication operator, 48, 242
  wildcard character, 25

author: item, configuration file, 36

authorized_keys file, 233–234

autocomplete, on command line, 8

B

BackCmd plugin example, 125–129, 157–162

backslash (\), in paths, 18

bash shell, *see* shell

.bash_profile file, 21

binary files, 31, 247

Bitbucket, 182, 184

block structured programming language, 87

BlockIterator object, 83–85

blocks (Minecraft), 65
  array of, 94
  breaking, 114
  finding nearby, 83–85
  items that would fall if destroyed, 114
  location of, 114
  material of, 114
  modifying, 114–119

blocks (code), *see* code blocks

Boolean conditions, *see* comparison operators

Boolean value, 241, 247

braces ({ })
  enclosing array or hash values, 93
  enclosing code blocks, 42, 56, 213, 243

brackets ([ ]), 42, 93

breakNaturally function, 114

build.sh file, 36–38, 148

BuildAHouse plugin example, 45–49

Bukkit project, *see also* Minecraft server
  classes, documentation for, 217–218
  wiki for, 219–220

bukkit.jar file, 24

BusyBox application, 3

C

CakeTower plugin example, 90–92

case sensitivity in Java, 41

cast, 79, 111, 244, 247

cat command, 12–13

catch keyword, 165

cd command, 4, 6–9, 12

characters, *see* strings

chmod command, 13, 25, 234

.class file-name suffix, 23

class files, 18, 20, 31

classes, 135, 247, *see also* objects; specific classes
  declaring, 35, 243
  defining, 69–73
  designing, 190–193
  documentation for, 217–219
  importing, 35, 71, 212, 243
  imports, common, 253
  multiple, in separate files, 135–137
  public, 35, 214, 243
  purpose of, 136

CLASSPATH environment variable, 23

client, 247, *see also* Minecraft graphical client

client-server application, xii–xiii

cloud server, 229–230
  domain name for, 240
  IP address for, 240
  Java for, installing, 238
  killing Java processes for, 239
  Linux distributions for, 230–232
  logging out of, 235
  packages for, installing, 237–238
  remote access to, 232–237
  root access for, 235–237
  running Minecraft remotely, 238–239
  services for, 230
  SSH keys for, 233–235
  VPS for, 230

cloud, backing up to, 181–183

cmd.exe application, 2–3

code, *see* source code

code blocks, 87–88, 213, 243, 247

code examples
  ArrayAddMoreBlocks plugin, 99–100
  ArrayOfBlocks plugin, 94–96
  BackCmd plugin, 125–129, 157–162
  BuildAHouse plugin, 45–49
  CakeTower plugin, 90–92
  code directory for, 5
  CowShooter plugin, 140–142
  FlyingCreeper plugin, 121–122
  font conventions for, xiv
  HelloWorld plugin, 5–7, 32–38
  LavaVision plugin, 84–85
  LocationSnapshot plugin, 154–157
  NameCow plugin, 66–67
  NamedSigns plugin, 106–111
  PlayerStuff plugin, 73–75
  Simple plugin, 49–52
  SkyCmd plugin, 78–83
  SquidBombConfig plugin, 150–151
  Stuck plugin, 114–119
  website for, xiv

command line, 1–4, 248
  autocomplete on, 8
  for cloud server, 232
  command prompt for, 4, 234
  copy and paste on, 9

commands (Git), 185

commands (Java), *see* java command; javac command

commands (Minecraft), 1, 39
  in configuration file, 36, 82
  creating, 79–83, 194–195
  not found, 216

commands (shell), 12, *see also* specific commands

commands: section, configuration file, 36, 82

comments, 42

comparison operators, 60–62, 242

compile, 248

compiler, *see* javac command

compiler warnings, hiding, 166–167

config.yml file, 147–150

configuration data, storing, 146–150

configuration files, 36, 245
config.yml file, 147–150
plugin.yml file, 35–36, 78, 82

constructors, 138, 248

conventions used in this book, xiv

coordinates, *see* Location object

copy and paste, on command line, 9

CowShooter plugin example, 140–142

cp command, 10, 13, 25

craftBukkit.jar file, 24, *see also* Minecraft server

current directory, 5, 248

D

damage function, 120

data types, 241
conversions between, 44–45, 244–245
numbers, 46–48
strings, 48–49
for variables, 43–44

data, storing
configuration data, 146–150
game data, 146, 151–167

decision statements, 59, 243

default directory, *see* home directory

deploy, 248

Desktop directory, 4, 11–12

desktop server, 221
LogMeIn tool for, 222–223
manual setup for, 223–227
Minecraft port for, 221

DHCP reservation, 227

dictionary, *see* HashMap class

directories, *see also* paths
changing, 4
creating, 9–10
current directory, 5, 248

Desktop directory, 4, 11–12
home directory, 4–5, 10
listing, 4
listing files in, 7
moving between, 5–9
parent directory, 8, 11, 13
for plugins, 32
root directory, 8
spaces in, 10

division operator (/), 48, 242

DNS (Domain Name Service), 224, 248

dollar sign ($), command prompt, 4

domain name, for cloud server, 240

dot (.)
current directory, 8, 13
separating item parts, 42, 71–72

dots, two (..), parent directory, 8, 11, 13

doubles, 47, 248

dynamic DNS registration, 224

dynamic IP address, 224

E

echo command, 13

editor, 15–18
creating files, 17–18
Sublime Text editor, 16
syntax highlighting in, 17

entities, 65
damage to, 119
finding nearby, 83–85
health of, 120
hurling lightning bolts, 121
inflicting damage, 120
launching projectiles, 119
location of, 119
modifying, 119–120
potion effects for, 121
spawning, 120–122
teleporting, 119
velocity of, 119

entry points, for functions, 54

environment variables, 248
CLASSPATH environment variable, 23

PATH environment variable, 20–22
PS1 environment variable, 234

equal signs, two (==), *equal to* operator, 61, 242

equal to operator (==), 61, 242

errors, 211
building plugins, 38
compiler warnings, hiding, 166–167
exceptions, catching, 165–166
java command, 23
Java commands not found, 20–22
javac command, 22, 211–215
line numbers of, 22, 211
Minecraft command not found, 216
permission denied for running server, 25
plugin not loading, 215
server, 215–216
unquoted directories containing spaces, 11
version mismatch, 28

@EventHandler keyword, 123, 127

events, 122–124, 202–207, 248
enabling listening of, 123
implementing, 123, 127
importing, 123
list of, 123
listener for, 123–124, 127–129, 136–137

examples, *see* code examples

exceptions, 165–166, 248

exclamation point (!), *not* operator, 61, 243

exclamation point, equal sign (!=), *not equal to* operator, 61, 242

executables, 248

environment variables, 248

extends keyword, 77

F

file system, 5, 248

files
binary files, 31, 247
class files, 20, 31
configuration files, 35–36, 78, 82, 147–150, 245

copying, 10, 13, 25
  creating, 17–18
  executables, 248
  JAR files, 31, 249
  listing, 4, 7
  text files, 12, 251
  YAML files, 252
  zip files, xiv
final keyword, 248
final modifier, 244
firewall, opening ports on, 224–226
floating points, 47, 249
floats, 47, 248
FlyingCreeper plugin example, 121–122
folders, *see* directories
for statement, 58, 94, 243
for-each statement, 99–100, 243
functions, 249
  arguments for, 55–56, 247
  calling, 55, 57, 244
  constructors, 138
  creating, 52–56, 195–202
  declaring, 243
  designing, 190–193
  entry points for, 54
  listeners, 249
  name of, 56
  parameters for, 55, 250
  public, 55, 243
  scope of parameters in, 88
  static, 55, 251
  tasks, 138–139
  void, 56, 251

G

game data, storing, 146, 151–167
  in database, 152
  in HashMap, 152–154, 162–167
  in local files, 151–153
garbage collection, 105
getConfig function, 148
getDataFolder function, 152
getDrops function, 114
getHealth function, 120
getLastDamage function, 119
getLocation function, 114, 119
getNearbyEntities function, 80
getPlayer function, 71

getServer function, 71
getType function, 114
Git, 169–177
  adding files to remember, 170
  backing up to the cloud, 181–183
  Bash shell for, 170
  branches in, 177–181
  commands, list of, 185
  committing changes, 171
  configuring, 170
  ignoring files, 173
  installing, 170
  log for, 171
  repository for, 170
  status of, 172
  undoing changes, 174–177
.git directory, 170
GitHub
  backing up to the cloud, 182–183
  sharing code, 183–185
.gitignore file, 173
global variables, 88–90, 249
graphical client, *see* Minecraft graphical client
greater than operator (>), 61, 242
greater than or equal to operator (>=), 61, 242

H

hasPermission function, 129
hash, 249
HashMap class, 101–104, 249
  accessing elements of, 102
  assigning values to, 102
  creating, 103, 108
  storing game data in, 152–154, 162–167
heap, 105
HelloWorld plugin example
  building, 36–38
  configuration file, 35–36
  directory structure, 5–7, 32–34
  source code, 34–35
home directory, 4–5, 10

I

I/O (input/output), 249
id_rsa.pub file, 233

if statement, 59, 243
ifconfig command, 227
import statement, 35, 71, 212, 243, 249, 253
inherit, 249
input/output, *see* I/O
instanceof keyword, 79, 164
integers, 46, 249
IP address
  for cloud server, 240
  external, 224
  internal, 227
ipconfig command, 227
items, 65
iterators, 249

J

JAR (Java Archive) files, 31, 249
jar command, 18
java command, 12, 18–23, 32
Java Development Kit, *see* JDK
.java file-name suffix, 7, 23
Java language, xi, 243–244
  as block structured, 87
  case sensitivity of, 41
  comments, 42
  comparison operators, 242
  data type conversions, 244–245
  data types, 241
  math operators, 242
  visibility modifiers, 244
javac command, 12, 18–22, 31, 211–215
JavaPlugin class, 77
JDK (Java Development Kit)
  commands not found for, 20–22
  installing, 18–19, 238
  version of, 19

K

keywords, 249, *see also* specific keywords

L

launchProjectile function, 119
LavaVision plugin example, 84–85
Leather material, 141

left angle bracket (<), *less than* operator, 61, 242

left angle bracket, equal sign (<=), *less than or equal to* operator, 61, 242

less than operator (<), 61, 242

less than or equal to operator (<=), 61, 242

levels of abstraction, 69

Linux
    command line, using, 2
    command prompt, 4
    opening firewall, 226
    remote, for cloud server, 230–232

listeners, 249
    as separate classes, 136–137
    creating, 123–124, 127–129

literals, 48, 241, 249

local variables, 88, 250

localhost, 250

Location object, 80–81, 153

LocationSnapshot plugin example, 154–157

LogMeIn tool, 222–223

loop statements, 58, 62, 99–100, 243

ls command, 4, 7, 12

M

Mac OS X
    command line, using, 2
    command prompt, 4
    internal IP address, checking, 227
    opening firewall, 225

main: item, configuration file, 36

map, *see* HashMap class

math operators, 47–48, 242

Minecraft
    commands, 1, 39, 79–83
    modes in, changing, 39
    playing, 39
    versions of, 28

Minecraft graphical client
    connecting to server, 26–29
    installing, 23–24

Minecraft plugins, *see also* code examples
    building, 31–34, 36–38, 193–208

configuration file, 35–36
    designing, 187–193
    directory structure, 32–34, 193
    not loading, 215
    recognition of, in Minecraft, 77–78
    running, 38–39
    source code, 34–35

Minecraft server
    errors from, 215–216
    installing, 24–25
    reloading, 38
    running, 25–26
    stopping, 26
    stopping and restarting, 38

minus sign (-), subtraction operator, 48, 242

minus signs, two (--), *subtract one* operator, 48

mkdir command, 9–10, 13

mkplugin.sh file, 49, 193

multiple threads, 134–135

multiplication operator (*), 48, 242

mv command, 13, 25

N

name: item, configuration file, 36

NameCow plugin example, 66–67

NamedSigns plugin example, 106–111

new keyword, 73, 103, 105

not equal to operator (!=), 61, 242

not operator (!), 61, 243

null value, 250

numbers, 46–48, 241
    floating points, 47, 249
    integers, 46, 249
    math operators for, 47–48, 242

O

object-oriented programming, 65, 250

objects, 65–69, 250, *see also* classes; specific objects
    creating, 73, 244
    parts of, 71–72

onCommand function, 54, 79–80, 109–110

onDisable function, 54, 146

onEnable function, 54, 123, 146, 148

onLoad function, 54, 146

online resources, xiv
    Bukkit classes documentation, 217–218
    Bukkit project, 24
    Bukkit wiki, 219–220
    BusyBox application, 3
    dynamic DNS registration, 224
    Git, 170
    IP address, checking, 224
    Minecraft installer, 23
    Oracle Java classes documentation, 219
    port accessibility, checking, 226
    for this book, 220
    YAML format, 36

open-ssh package, 237

operators
    comparison, 60–62, 242
    math, 47–48, 242

or operator (||), 61, 242

Oracle Java classes, documentation for, 219

P

package statement, 35, 243

packages, 250
    declaring, 243
    deploying plugins from, 156
    importing, 71
    imports, common, 253
    installing on cloud server, 237–238

parameters, 55, 88, 250

parent directory, 8, 11, 13

parentheses (( ))
    enclosing function arguments, 42
    grouping operations, 242

PATH environment variable, 20–22

paths, 20–22, 250

percent sign (%)
    command prompt, 4
    remainder operator, 242

PermaMap class, 152–157, 161–167

permissions
  checking, 129–130
  setting, 130
permissions.yml file, 130
PermissionsBukkit plugin, 130
playSound function, 51
Player object, 70–75, 153
  checking validity of, 79
PlayerStuff plugin example, 73–75
Plugin object, 77
plugin.yml file, 35–36, 78, 82
plugins, 31, 250, see also Minecraft plugins
plus sign (+)
  addition operator, 48, 242
  concatenating strings, 49
plus signs, two (++), add one operator, 48
ports, 221, 250
  checking accessibility to, 226
  forwarding, 226–227
  Minecraft, 221
  setting priority of, 227
private keyword, 104–106, 244, 250
.profile file, 21
programming languages, xi, see also Java language
prompt for command line, 4, 234
protected modifier, 244
PS1 environment variable, 234
public keyword, 104, 244, 250
  classes, 35, 214, 243
  functions, 55, 243
pwd command, 5, 11–12

Q

QoS (Quality of Service), 227
quotes (" ")
  enclosing directories containing spaces, 11
  enclosing strings, 48

R

reload command, 38
remainder operator (%), 242
remote access to cloud server, 232–237
resources, see online resources

right angle bracket (>), greater than operator, 61, 242
right angle bracket, equal sign (>=), greater than or equal to operator, 61, 242
rm command, 13
root access, 235–237
root directory, 8
runTaskLater function, 139
runTaskTimer function, 139
runtime application, see java command

S

saveDefaultConfig function, 148
scheduling tasks, 139
scp command, 232
screen command, 239
scripts, 250
  build.sh file, 36–38, 148
  mkplugin.sh file, 49, 193
search path, see PATH environment variable
secure shell (SSH), 232
security
  backing up to the cloud, 181–183
  permissions, 129–130
  sharing code, 183–185
  tracking code changes, 169–177
semicolon (;), terminating Java statement, 42, 213
sendMessage function, 51
server, xii–xiii, 251, see also client-server application; cloud server; desktop server; Minecraft server
Server object, 71
server.log file, 215
setHealth function, 120
setLastDamage function, 120
setPassenger function, 121
setType function, 114
setVelocity function, 119
.sh file-name suffix, 7
shadowing, 91–92, 251
shell, 2, 232, 251, see also command line
  with Git, 170
shell scripts, see scripts
Sign object, 111

Simple plugin example, 49–52
SkyCmd plugin example, 78–83
slash (/)
  division operator, 48, 242
  in paths, 18
  preceding Minecraft commands, 1, 39
  root directory, 8
slash, asterisk (/* */), enclosing comments, 42
slashes, two (//), preceding comments, 42
source code, xiv, 31, 251, see also code examples; Java language
  sharing, 183–185
  style practices for, 184
  tracking changes to, 169–177
spaces, in directory names, 10
spawn function, 120
spawnArrow function, 120
spawnCreature function, 120
spawnEntity function, 120
spawnFallingBlock function, 121
SquidBombConfig plugin example, 150–151
SSH (secure shell), 232
ssh command, 232
.ssh directory, 233
SSH keys, 233–235
ssh-keygen command, 233
sshd command, 232
stack, 105, 127
start_minecraft script, 25, 238
static IP address, 224
static keyword, 55, 89, 244, 251
strikeLightning function, 121
strings, 48–49, 241, 251
  concatenating, 49, 245
Stuck plugin example, 114–119
Sublime Text editor, 16
subtract one operator (–), 48
subtraction operator (-), 48, 242
sudo command, 235–237
@SuppressWarnings keyword, 166
symbols, 251
synchronous tasks, 135
syntax highlighting, 17

T

tasks, 251
  creating, 138
  scheduling to continue running, 139
  scheduling to run later, 139
  synchronous, 135
teleport function, 119
text, *see* strings
text commands, *see* commands
text editor, *see* editor
text files, 251
  configuration files as, 147
  Java files as, 18, 31, 41
  scripts as, 250
  viewing contents of, 12
threads, 134–135, 251
ticks, 251
tilde (~), home directory, 10, 13
time, units of, *see* ticks
try keyword, 165
.txt file-name suffix, 12
types, incompatible, 214

U

unzip command, xiv

V

variables, 42–45, 87–88, 251
  assigning, 43–44, 243
  creating, 43
  declaring, 212, 243
  environment variables, 248
  global, 88–90, 249
  local, 88, 250
  scope of, 88
  shadows of, 91–92, 251
  static, 89, 251
version: item, configuration file, 36
vertical bars, two (| |), *or* operator, 61, 242
Virtual Private Server, *see* VPS
visibility modifiers, 244
void keyword, 56, 251
VPS (Virtual Private Server), 230, 252

W

website resources, *see* online resources
while statement, 62, 243
whois command, 240
Windows
  BusyBox application, 3
  command line, using, 2–3
  command prompt, 4
  internal IP address, checking, 227
  opening firewall, 224
  paths, syntax for, 18
working directory, *see* current directory
writeObject function, 163

Y

YAML files, 147, 245, 252,
  see also configuration files
.yml file-name suffix, 7, 252
yum command, 238

Z

zip files, xiv

Other books by Andy Hunt

Time to rewire your brain for better thinking and learning, and then see what it takes to be a modern software developer.

Pragmatic Thinking and Learning

Software development happens in your head. Not in an editor, IDE, or design tool. You're well educated on how to work with software and hardware, but what about *wetware*—our own brains? Learning new skills and new technology is critical to your career, and it's all in your head.

In this book by Andy Hunt, you'll learn how our brains are wired, and how to take advantage of your brain's architecture. You'll learn new tricks and tips to learn more, faster, and retain more of what you learn.

You need a pragmatic approach to thinking and learning. You need to *Refactor Your Wetware*.

Printed in full color.

Andy Hunt
(290 pages) ISBN: 9781934356050. $34.95
http://pragprog.com/book/ahptl

Practices of an Agile Developer

Want to be a better developer? This book collects the personal habits, ideas, and approaches of successful agile software developers and presents them in a series of short, easy-to-digest tips.

You'll learn how to improve your software development process, see what real agile practices feel like, avoid the common temptations that kill projects, and keep agile practices in balance.

Venkat Subramaniam and Andy Hunt
(208 pages) ISBN: 9780974514086. $29.95
http://pragprog.com/book/pad

Mobile Games and Sound

Build mobile games for Android and iOS devices, and see how to add live sound to your apps.

Create Mobile Games with Corona

Develop cross-platform mobile games with Corona using the Lua programming language! Corona is experiencing explosive growth among mobile game developers, and this book gets you up to speed on how to use this versatile platform. You'll use the Corona SDK to simplify game programming and take a fun, no-nonsense approach to write and add must-have gameplay features. You'll find out how to create all the gaming necessities: menus, sprites, movement, perspective and sound effects, levels, loading and saving, and game physics. Along the way, you'll learn about Corona's API functions and build three common kinds of mobile games from scratch that can run on the iPhone, iPad, Kindle Fire, Nook Color, and all other Android smartphones and tablets.

Printed in full color.

Silvia Domenech
(220 pages) ISBN: 9781937785574. $36
http://pragprog.com/book/sdcorona

Programming Sound with Pure Data

Sound gives your native, web, or mobile apps that extra dimension, and it's essential for games. Rather than using canned samples from a sample library, learn how to build sounds from the ground up and produce them for web projects using the Pure Data programming language. Even better, you'll be able to integrate dynamic sound environments into your native apps or games—sound that reacts to the app, instead of sounding the same every time. Start your journey as a sound designer, and get the power to craft the sound you put into your digital experiences.

Tony Hillerson
(196 pages) ISBN: 9781937785666. $36
http://pragprog.com/book/thsound

The Joy of Math and 3D Programming

Rediscover the joy and fascinating weirdness of pure mathematics, or get started programming 3D games in JavaScript.

Good Math

Mathematics is beautiful—and it can be fun and exciting as well as practical. *Good Math* is your guide to some of the most intriguing topics from two thousand years of mathematics: from Egyptian fractions to Turing machines; from the real meaning of numbers to proof trees, group symmetry, and mechanical computation. If you've ever wondered what lay beyond the proofs you struggled to complete in high school geometry, or what limits the capabilities of the computer on your desk, this is the book for you.

Mark C. Chu-Carroll
(282 pages) ISBN: 9781937785338. $34
http://pragprog.com/book/mcmath

3D Game Programming for Kids

You know what's even better than playing games? Creating your own. Even if you're an absolute beginner, this book will teach you how to make your own online games with interactive examples. You'll learn programming using nothing more than a browser, and see cool, 3D results as you type. You'll learn real-world programming skills in a real programming language: JavaScript, the language of the web. You'll be amazed at what you can do as you build interactive worlds and fun games. Appropriate for ages 10-99!

Printed in full color.

Chris Strom
(250 pages) ISBN: 9781937785444. $36
http://pragprog.com/book/csjava

Learn Hardware, Learn Ruby!

Get into the DIY hardware spirit with the Raspberry Pi, or learn to program using Ruby, the language of Ruby on Rails web applications.

Raspberry Pi: A Quick-Start Guide (2nd edition)

The Raspberry Pi is one of the most successful open source hardware projects ever. For less than $40, you get a full-blown PC, a multimedia center, and a web server—and this book gives you everything you need to get started. You'll learn the basics, progress to controlling the Pi, and then build your own electronics projects. This new edition is revised and updated with two new chapters on adding digital and analog sensors, and creating videos and a burglar alarm with the Pi camera. *Printed in full color.*

Maik Schmidt
(176 pages) ISBN: 9781937785802. $22
http://pragprog.com/book/msraspi2

Learn to Program (2nd edition)

For this new edition of the best-selling *Learn to Program*, Chris Pine has taken a good thing and made it even better. First, he used the feedback from hundreds of reader e-mails to update the content and make it even clearer. Second, he updated the examples in the book to use the latest stable version of Ruby, and also to use code that looks more like real-world Ruby code, so that people who have just learned to program will be more familiar with common Ruby techniques.

Not only does the Second Edition now include answers to all of the exercises, it includes them twice. First you'll find the "how you could do it" answers, using the techniques you've learned up to that point in the book. Next you'll see "how Chris Pine would do it": answers using more advanced Ruby techniques, to whet your appetite as well as providing sort of a "Rosetta Stone" for more elegant solutions.

This fourth printing of Learn to Program, 2nd edition has been updated for Ruby 2.0. *Printed in full color.*

Chris Pine
(194 pages) ISBN: 9781934356364. $24.95
http://pragprog.com/book/ltp2

The Pragmatic Bookshelf

The Pragmatic Bookshelf features books written by developers for developers. The titles continue the well-known Pragmatic Programmer style and continue to garner awards and rave reviews. As development gets more and more difficult, the Pragmatic Programmers will be there with more titles and products to help you stay on top of your game.

Visit Us Online

This Book's Home Page
http://pragprog.com/book/ahmine
Source code from this book, errata, and other resources. Come give us feedback, too!

Register for Updates
http://pragprog.com/updates
Be notified when updates and new books become available.

Join the Community
http://pragprog.com/community
Read our weblogs, join our online discussions, participate in our mailing list, interact with our wiki, and benefit from the experience of other Pragmatic Programmers.

New and Noteworthy
http://pragprog.com/news
Check out the latest pragmatic developments, new titles and other offerings.

Save on the eBook

Save on the eBook versions of this title. Owning the paper version of this book entitles you to purchase the electronic versions at a terrific discount.

PDFs are great for carrying around on your laptop—they are hyperlinked, have color, and are fully searchable. Most titles are also available for the iPhone and iPod touch, Amazon Kindle, and other popular e-book readers.

Buy now at *http://pragprog.com/coupon*

Contact Us

Online Orders:	*http://pragprog.com/catalog*
Customer Service:	*support@pragprog.com*
International Rights:	*translations@pragprog.com*
Academic Use:	*academic@pragprog.com*
Write for Us:	*http://pragprog.com/write-for-us*
Or Call:	+1 800-699-7764

CPSIA information can be obtained at www.ICGtesting.com
Printed in the USA
LVOW02s1611080614

389118LV00003B/9/P

31901055541702